T0397337

Sponsored Editorial Content in Digital Journalism

For advertisers and news publishers, brand sponsored content has offered attractive solutions to problems of ad-avoidance and financing journalism. This book is an investigation into the practices, possibilities and problems of sponsored editorial content across various national and regional contexts.

Sponsored editorial content is material with similar qualities and format to content that is typically published on a platform or by a content provider, but which is paid for by a third party. Brand sponsored content may not be the remedy for ad-dependent media some advocates predicted but its expansion has impacted on the organisation, practices and identities of journalism in profound and far-reaching ways. This book explores the features and implications of content that blends, merges and disguises material that is sponsored with material that is or appears to be independent editorial.

The chapters range across countries and regions from China and Israel to Europe and North America. Following a general introduction, authors address political and commercial sponsorship across production, content and audience research, developing and combining these in innovative ways to advance the study of paid-for content in contemporary digital journalism. This book was originally published as a special issue of the journal *Digital Journalism*.

Jonathan Hardy is Professor of Communications and Media at the University of the Arts London. His books include *Branded Content: The Fateful Merging of Media and Marketing* (2022) and *Critical Political Economy of the Media* (2014). He co-edited *The Advertising Handbook* (2018/2009) and edits the book series *Routledge Critical Advertising Studies*.

Sponsored Editorial Content in Digital Journalism

Edited by
Jonathan Hardy

LONDON AND NEW YORK

First published 2023
by Routledge
4 Park Square, Milton Park, Abingdon, Oxon OX14 4RN

and by Routledge
605 Third Avenue, New York, NY 10158

Routledge is an imprint of the Taylor & Francis Group, an informa business

Chapters 1–3 and 5–8 © 2023 Taylor & Francis
Chapter 4 © 2020 Raul Ferrer-Conill, Erik Knudsen, Corinna Lauerer, and Aviv Barnoy. Originally published as Open Access.

With the exception of Chapter 4, no part of this book may be reprinted or reproduced or utilised in any form or by any electronic, mechanical, or other means, now known or hereafter invented, including photocopying and recording, or in any information storage or retrieval system, without permission in writing from the publishers. For details on the rights for Chapter 4, please see the chapter's Open Access footnote.

Trademark notice: Product or corporate names may be trademarks or registered trademarks, and are used only for identification and explanation without intent to infringe.

British Library Cataloguing in Publication Data
A catalogue record for this book is available from the British Library

ISBN13: 978-1-032-45354-5 (hbk)
ISBN13: 978-1-032-45355-2 (pbk)
ISBN13: 978-1-003-37657-6 (ebk)

DOI: 10.4324/9781003376576

Typeset in Myriad Pro
by Newgen Publishing UK

Publisher's Note
The publisher accepts responsibility for any inconsistencies that may have arisen during the conversion of this book from journal articles to book chapters, namely the inclusion of journal terminology.

Disclaimer
Every effort has been made to contact copyright holders for their permission to reprint material in this book. The publishers would be grateful to hear from any copyright holder who is not here acknowledged and will undertake to rectify any errors or omissions in future editions of this book.

Contents

	Citation Information	vi
	Notes on Contributors	viii

1 Introduction—Sponsored Editorial Content in Digital Journalism: Mapping the Merging of Media and Marketing 1
Jonathan Hardy

2 The Creation of Branded Content Teams in Spanish News Organizations and Their Implications for Structures, Professional Roles and Ethics 23
Miguel Carvajal and Iker Barinagarrementeria

3 Sponsored Content in Spanish Media: Strategies, Transparency, and Ethical Concerns 44
Dolors Palau-Sampio

4 The Visual Boundaries of Journalism: Native Advertising and the Convergence of Editorial and Commercial Content 65
Raul Ferrer-Conill, Erik Knudsen, Corinna Lauerer, and Aviv Barnoy

5 "It's in the Air"—Sponsored Editorial Content as a Path for Stealth Government Propaganda: The Case of Israeli Media 88
Anat Balint

6 Native Advertising in the Chinese Press: Implications of State Subsidies for Journalist Professional Self-Identification 110
Dan Wang and Steve Zhongshi Guo

7 Sponsored Content in 2020: Back to the Future? 127
Lisa Lynch

8 Journalism and the Voice Intelligence Industry 136
Joseph Turow

Index 143

Citation Information

The chapters in this book were originally published in the journal *Digital Journalism*, volume 9, issue 7 (2021). When citing this material, please use the original page numbering for each article, as follows:

Chapter 1
Sponsored Editorial Content in Digital Journalism: Mapping the Merging of Media and Marketing
Jonathan Hardy
Digital Journalism, volume 9, issue 7 (2021), pp. 865–886

Chapter 2
The Creation of Branded Content Teams in Spanish News Organizations and Their Implications for Structures, Professional Roles and Ethics
Miguel Carvajal and Iker Barinagarrementeria
Digital Journalism, volume 9, issue 7 (2021), pp. 887–907

Chapter 3
Sponsored Content in Spanish Media: Strategies, Transparency, and Ethical Concerns
Dolors Palau-Sampio
Digital Journalism, volume 9, issue 7 (2021), pp. 908–928

Chapter 4
The Visual Boundaries of Journalism: Native Advertising and the Convergence of Editorial and Commercial Content
Raul Ferrer-Conill, Erik Knudsen, Corinna Lauerer, and Aviv Barnoy
Digital Journalism, volume 9, issue 7 (2021), pp. 929–951

Chapter 5
"It's in the Air"—Sponsored Editorial Content as a Path for Stealth Government Propaganda: The Case of Israeli Media
Anat Balint
Digital Journalism, volume 9, issue 7 (2021), pp. 952–973

Chapter 6

Native Advertising in the Chinese Press: Implications of State Subsidies for Journalist Professional Self-Identification
Dan Wang and Steve Zhongshi Guo
Digital Journalism, volume 9, issue 7 (2021), pp. 974–990

Chapter 7

Sponsored Content in 2020: Back to the Future?
Lisa Lynch
Digital Journalism, volume 9, issue 7 (2021), pp. 991–999

Chapter 8

Journalism and the Voice Intelligence Industry
Joseph Turow
Digital Journalism, volume 9, issue 7 (2021), pp. 1000–1006

For any permission-related enquiries please visit:
www.tandfonline.com/page/help/permissions

Notes on Contributors

Anat Balint, School of Journalism and Mass Communications, San José State University, San José, CA, USA.

Iker Barinagarrementeria, Social Sciences Department, Miguel Hernández University, Elche, Spain.

Aviv Barnoy, Department of Information Systems, Zefat Academic College, Zefat, Israel; Department of Philosophy, University of Haifa, Haifa, Israel.

Miguel Carvajal, Social Sciences Department, Miguel Hernández University, Elche, Spain.

Raul Ferrer-Conill, Department of Media and Social Sciences, University of Stavanger, Stavanger, Norway.

Steve Zhongshi Guo, School of Communication, Hong Kong Baptist University, Kowloon Tong, Hong Kong SAR.

Jonathan Hardy, Media School, London College of Communication, University of the Arts London, London, UK.

Erik Knudsen, Department of Information Science and Media Studies, University of Bergen, Bergen, Norway.

Corinna Lauerer, Department of Media and Communication, LMU Munich, Munich, Germany.

Lisa Lynch, Program in Media and Communications, Drew University, Madison, Wisconsin, USA.

Dolors Palau-Sampio, Facultat de Filologia, Traducció i Comunicació, Departament de Teoria dels Llenguatges i Ciències de la Comunicació, Universitat de València, València, Spain.

Joseph Turow, The Annenberg School for Communication, University of Pennsylvania, Philadelphia, PA, USA.

Dan Wang, School of Communication, Hong Kong Baptist University, Kowloon Tong, Hong Kong SAR.

Introduction—Sponsored Editorial Content in Digital Journalism: Mapping the Merging of Media and Marketing

Jonathan Hardy

ABSTRACT
Sponsored editorial content is material with similar qualities and format to content that is typically published on a platform or by a content provider, but which is paid for by a third party. The growth of sponsored content in digital journalism over the last two decades has attracted wide-ranging research into developing practices, arrangements and their industrial, cultural and societal consequences. This introduction to a special issue on sponsored editorial content discusses the phenomena and how it has been understood and addressed by academic researchers, industry practitioners, regulatory agencies and civil society stakeholders. The article discusses definitions and definitional debates, provides a mapping of research approaches and findings, and identifies paths for future research, including those developed by authors for this special issue.

This introduction to a special issue on sponsored editorial content describes the evolving phenomena, considers definitional issues, provides an overview of the main research approaches, topics and findings, discusses the contribution of the researchers for this issue, and indicates some topics and issues for future research. *Sponsored editorial content is material with similar qualities and format to content that is typically published on a platform or by a content provider, but which is paid for by a third party.* This sponsored content covers two main, converging, forms. The first is advertising, where brand-controlled content and storytelling extends into formats that resemble editorial and where so-called native advertising builds on earlier integrations of advertising and editorial, such as advertorials. The second is sponsorship, where a sponsor pays for but does not control the journalistic output, formally at least: underwriting but not writing the content. Under institutionally sedimented arrangements, practices and expectations, advertisers have controlled advertising content and publishers have controlled editorial, including sponsored editorial. Those arrangements have been disrupted by the growth and proliferation of forms of content that are financed by brands or other sponsors but published, and variously "produced" and co-created, by news and other content publishers.

Amid falling display advertising and subscription revenues, brand sponsored editorial content has offered publishers the potential for increased earnings, and marketers a means to tackle ad-avoidance and boost engagement (Harms, Bijmolt, and Hoekstra 2017). Sponsored content was the second most important revenue generator (44%), after advertising (70%) and ahead of subscription (31%), according to a worldwide newsroom survey (ICFJ 2017). Since then, the continuing structural decline in advertising revenue, has intensified efforts to diversity revenue streams and develop readers' share of revenue. These trends were exacerbated by, but pre-date, precipitate falls in advertising, and other, revenues in 2020–2021 arising from the Covid pandemic. A survey of 200 "digital leaders" in 29 countries in December 2018, found that native advertising (75%) was among the top three most important revenue sources for news publishers, with subscription (78%) behind display advertising (81%), yet native fell to 8% as the main revenue priority for the year ahead (Newman 2019: 5, 23). In the following year's survey, covering 43 countries, reader subscription was considered the most important revenue source (76%) followed by display advertising (66%) and native advertising (61%); yet, opinion was split, with 44% considering that subscription models could only work for a minority of publishers (Newman 2021: 13–14). So, editorial-like content funded by brands has not assuredly advanced as the saviour of journalism, yet most news publishers continue rely on advertising as their main funding source. As that funding diminishes, the struggle to attract marketers increases the drive to offer embedded "native" forms of advertising, including sponsored editorial content. This is occurring the context of a broader shift to "native" formats within advertising overall, with eMarker, for instance, estimating that native would represent nearly 65% of total US digital display advertising spending in 2020 (Benes 2019).

Over the last decade, news publishers have restructured newsrooms and established teams to produce content, funded by brands or others, that blur traditional demarcations between editorial and advertising. Advertising that resembles editorial long predates the digital age, but brands are increasingly involved in the production of publisher-hosted branded content, including a range of practices and artefacts described as paid content, sponsored content, native advertising, programmatic native, brand journalism, content recommendation and clickbait. While commercial publishers leverage the business opportunities of sponsored content, these activities are transforming journalistic practices and generating critical debates on their implications for the purposes and performance of journalisms and on the extension of marketers' voice and ventriloquism across communications spaces.

Overview

Content paid for by brands and produced in association with brands expanded in news publishing and wider journalistic output from the 2000s, increased in scale and scope from the 2010s, and is the focus of the research discussed in this article. However, the phenomena need to be situated in the longer histories of media and marketing communication interrelationships, including the governance of their separation and integration. The integration of advertising in news publishing includes reading notices in the nineteenth century (Baldasty 1992), advertorials from the early twentieth century (Lynch 2018) and the expansion of brand publishing and custom publishing from the 1980s (Turow 1997). *Forbes'* Brand Voice started in November 2010 when it was originally named AdVoice. The *New York Times* (NYT) began its "Paid Posts" service in late 2013. In January 2014 when it ran its first native advertisement (for Dell) the NYT attracted over 40 advertisers, with native advertising, paid content integrated into the form and format of surrounding content, making up nearly 10% of its total annual digital advertising revenue, $128 million (Sebastian 2015).

The period from 2012–2019 was one of rapid revenue growth, market action and debate in the US and other advanced economies. Native advertising was a key topic at the Cannes marketing festival in 2013 (Dvorkin 2013). BI Intelligence forecast spending on native advertising rising from $4 billion in 2013 to $7.9 billion in 2015 (Rosin 2015). An American Press Institute Report (Sonderman and Tran 2013) described how many commercial publishers placed "growing hopes for a new revenue stream … sponsored content," as they grappled with the prospect of declining revenue streams from display advertising and subscription. A survey of 4,000 US marketers by Salesforce found that native advertising was the third most popular publishing strategy, along with video ads, becoming "an important component of most major brands" marketing repertoire with a growth in the number of native advertising platforms (Richter 2017). With marketers able to reach consumers more directly and effectively online and becoming less reliant on doing so via publishers, commercial news brands moved to offer more integrated advertising opportunities (Marshall and Alpert 2016). Ad tracker MediaRadar found more than 1,000 US publisher sites selling native advertising in 2017, up from 218 in 2015 (Moses 2017).

Branded content has become an increasingly important revenue stream for news publishers. According to a WAN-IFRA global study, news providers secured on average 20% of their ad revenues from native content in 2017; the news executives surveyed expected that revenue share to increase to 36% by 2021 (Carroll 2019). For some digital native publishers, branded content was the biggest source of advertising revenue. Buzzfeed, eschewed digital display ads until 2017 and instead depended for all its revenue on branded content, notably its listicles (Sonderman and Tran 2013). It had estimated revenue from native advertising of $120 million in 2014, with an average fee of $92,300 for each campaign (Agius 2015). The following year Buzzfeed had an estimated income of $250 m, mostly from branded content (Marshall and Alpert 2016). According to Chittum (2014) the economically successful adoption of native advertising by digital news outlets such as *The Huffington Post* and *Buzzfeed* influenced and encouraged adoption by established legacy publishers such as *The New York Times* and *The Guardian*. Publishers adopted a variety of models, with some larger publishers establishing content studios that integrated ad selling with content creation. Publishers moved into activities traditionally undertaken by advertising agencies, carrying out research for brands, creating ads and promoting branded content across their own outlets and social media (Marshall and Alpert 2016; Feng and Ots 2018). The New York Times' T Brand Studio in 2015 employed 110 people and generated some $35 million revenue, approximately 18% of total digital advertising revenue (Marshall and Alpert 2016). In Spain, the major news publishers launched branded content units between 2014–2016 (Palau-Sampio 2021). In the UK, the *Guardian* launched its content marketing agency, Guardian Labs in 2014, and remodelled it in 2017 to make it more integrated with the newsroom. The restructured 62-person Labs team increased revenue by 66% in the first half of 2018 (Davies 2018).

Multiple factors shape these ongoing changes, yet underlying the growth of branded content are the opportunities and challenges arising from transformations in digital communications. The migration of users from legacy media to new digital sites and activities has continued to disrupt all marketing communications. In digital media, so-called banner blindness and the notoriously low click-through rates for banner ads prompted efforts to develop more attractive and effective ad formats. Native advertising formats can evade the increasingly mainstream use of Adblocking software. Brands have sought to produce or sponsor content to meet a wide range of informational or entertainment purposes. Embedded advertising is also integral to the business models of the major social media platforms, whose growing share of advertising revenue increases pressures on ad-dependent publishers (Couldry and Turow 2014; Couldry and Mejias 2019; Hardy 2021). Formatting "native" ads to match the surrounding content, or reassembling programmatic native ads based on response data, is increasingly easy, inexpensive and automated for marketers. The regulatory conditions that have enabled, or failed to constrain, integrated advertising are also important factors (Casale 2015; Lynch 2018; Hardy 2021).

Sponsored content needs to be understood in the context of evolving political economies affecting relations between advertisers, marketing agencies, media publishers and platforms (Sinclair 2020). A core triad of actor types remain: marketers, marketing agencies and media, around which an expanding range of intermediary actors provide specialized services, and where activities associated with the triad are combined. Further, the core actors themselves incorporate hybridity, by offering services historically associated with other institutionally constituted actors: publishers becoming advertising agencies, while marketers and agencies become media content providers. Finally, all processes are affected by automation and the rise of ad tech firms involved in programmatic advertising buying, selling, creation, distribution and promotion (IAB 2019).

Definitions and Debates

Some accounts suggest that definitions are clear and that terms such as native advertising are "not contested" (Bachmann, Hunziker and Rüedy 2019: 96), others that overlapping terms are used interchangeable. Neither is wholly accurate. Instead, definitional clarity exists but it is circumscribed, applicable only across specific contexts of usage by industry practitioners, regulators, academics and others. A broad term that encompasses brand sponsored editorial, is branded content, the practice of marketing by the creation of content that is funded or produced by marketers. This refers to all forms of brand involvement in the production and reception of communications content and experience. Other general terms include content marketing, or consumer content marketing (CCM), the latter described as "[p]aid marketing messages developed to simulate a news story or entertainment program that is cohesive with the media's content structure, including assimilated design that is consistent with the media platform. Also known as native advertising and custom publishing" (PQ Media 2018).

Advertising company Sharethrough (n.d.) defines native advertising as "a form of paid media where the ad experience follows the natural form and function of the user experience in which it is placed." The term is used is used to refer to "paid advertising content that is designed to look like, and published alongside, nonpaid editorial content" (Wojdynski, 2019) and as "any paid advertising that takes the specific form and appearance of editorial content from the publisher itself" (Wojdynski and Evans 2016: 157). Reviewing US practice in the mid 2010s, Wojdynski (2016) identifies sponsored content, partner content, advertorials, and branded journalism, as among the key terms used, but argues native advertising became the most widely adopted. He suggests this is because the two words convey its inclusion criteria: messages that are "native" to non-paid content, while at the same time being paid advertising. However, the core claim of being "native" is itself promotional, and so definitions that represent it as a putatively neutral description are problematic, at least as a foundation for research. Some definitions are too particular, combining or excluding elements that need to be differentiated. For instance, Ferrer-Conill (2016: 905) defines native advertising as "a form of paid content marketing, where the commercial content is delivered adopting the form and function of editorial content with the attempt to recreate the user experience of reading news instead of advertising content." However, only some native advertising seeks to recreate "reading news," as the continuities with advertorials and "reason why" advertising copy demonstrate.

There are then a range of terms used, and definitional inexactitude. The problems are compounded for comparative research, as discussed below. I suggest that the best approach is to identify and differentiate the components in practices and to engage reflexively and critically with the terms used in relevant practice and governance discourses, in specific media system contexts. Key differential features include advertising placement type, content type, content location and publisher type. All these are subject to formal, informal and increasingly part-automated transactional arrangements between parties and so the other key differentiators can be summarized as actors, payment, disclosure and control.

The Interactive Advertising Bureau Playbook, first produced in 2013 and since updated (IAB 2019), provided a useful, operational guide to terms that are influential in English language usage. The IAB (2019: 7) defines branded content (and native content) as "paid content from a brand that is published in the same format as full editorial on a publisher's site, generally in conjunction with the publisher's content teams themselves." Such content requires disclosure that it is paid for, and "should be considered as a native ad type" (IAB 2019:7). This substantive content (the text, images and graphic elements that make up an article, "story" or other item of branded content) is distinct from two other categories of "native advertising," which are both vehicles for the promotion of the branded content. These are in-feed and content recommendation ads. In-feed is a form of native advertising that appears in publishers' content feed, with the advertising unit usually surrounded by the publisher's editorial content. The native ad link takes users to a third-party website, but may link to a section of the publisher's own site carrying brand sponsored content. By contrast, content recommendation ads usually appear *below* articles, carried in a designated section with other content recommendation ads, and "does not mimic the appearance of the editorial content feed" (IAB 2019: 19). Content recommendation ads also always link to pages outside the publisher's site.

Returning to what has been referred to as branded content, the substantive content, there are important sets of distinctions which will help to clarify but not resolve the use of another key term: sponsored. First, branded content/native advertising are forms of "paid media" that are distinct from the "earned media" achieved through traditional public relations. Of course, that division has been tested, crossed and blurred in practices that predate native advertising, including editorial secured alongside advertising spending or publishers' use of "colour separation charges" to create a market for paid editorial coverage. However, the distinction between advertising and non-advertising content continues to structure regulations and governance. For instance, the UK self-regulatory organization (SRO) the Advertising Standards Authority (ASA), under arrangements established in the 1960s, regulates marketing communications but not editorial, public relations or sponsorship.

The other key distinction is control over the communication content—editorial control—which may lie with the marketer, publisher or jointly (IAB UK 2018). Where marketers control paid communications, that content is generally recognized as advertising. When there is payment but editorial control lies with the publisher, a traditional description is sponsorship. Much branded content is a mixture of marketer and publisher control, so that the forms, practices, discourses, identifications, governance arrangements and user expectations are in flux. Paid advertising is associated with full control, as in display advertising where artwork is supplied by the marketer; by contrast, sponsorship is associated with payment without control. These distinctions can be illustrated by UK governance. As an EU member state until January 2021, the UK was subject to the Unfair Commercial Practices Directive (European Parliament and Council 2005/29/EC) which prohibits "[u]sing editorial content in the media to promote a product where a trader has paid for the promotion without making that clear in the content or by images or sounds clearly identifiable by the consumer (advertorial)" (Annex 1, Item 11). The Directive is incorporated into UK law in the Consumer Protection from Unfair Trading Regulations 2008, enforced by the Competition and Markets Authority. However, the ASA enforces codes on marketing communications written by the marketing and media industries, the Committee of Advertising Practice (CAP), and applies a dual test of whether the brand pays for *and* exercises control over content. As CAP (2019) explains "The broad principles of this exemption [for sponsorship] have also been applied to editorial content where there has been payment by a marketer (in money or 'in kind') but they have no editorial control … Such content is, however, still likely to fall within the scope of The Consumer Protection from Unfair Trading Regulations 2008 …."

In the United States, a key structuring component in the legal-regulatory system is persuasive content. Advertising refers to paid persuasive communications, "where the communication features or advocates for a sponsor's products or services," "whereas the term 'sponsorship' typically refers to communications that are not persuasive in nature" (Campbell and Grimm 2019: 117). However, increasing "[u]se of the terms 'sponsored content', 'sponsored post', and 'sponsored' in conjunction with native advertising has likely eroded the traditional distinction between the meanings of 'advertising' and 'sponsorship'" in both industry and regulatory discourse (Campbell and Grimm 2019: 115). Likewise, in academic discourse, sponsored content has been defined as "the integration of brands or branded persuasive messages in editorial media content in exchange for compensation by a sponsor" (Eisend et al. 2020: 344; van Reijmersdal, Neijens, and Smit 2009). Yet, this conflates differences in sponsor control. There would be benefit in greater rigour and consistency in delineating between varieties of payment and control, yet their complex comingling in practices undermines definitional separation. It seems preferable, therefore, to remain attendant to all relevant terms and delineations across practices and legal-regulatory discourses while retaining broader terms. Serazio (2021b) has suggested using brand journalism, as this incorporates the two key interacting elements of brand and journalism. Yet, that term is originally associated with the production and self-publishing of journalism on brands' own media (Bull 2013; Arrese and Pérez-Latre 2017) and there is value in the breadth of "sponsored editorial content" as encompassing: addressing content beyond journalism, and sponsorship beyond brands.

The definition I advance is: *sponsored editorial content is material with similar qualities and format to content that is typically published on a platform or by a content provider, but which is paid for by a third party*. Sponsored editorial content encompasses both editorial-like material that is paid for and controlled by the marketer/source and brand "sponsored" but publisher-controlled editorial that falls outside those definitions. All such content involves payment or other economic consideration by a party other than the publisher. Control is not axiomatic, yet is precisely at issue in assessing the outcome of payment. Designated advertising, paid media, is controlled communication by marketers. Earned media is content supplied without payment, with control over usage lying with the publisher. Such demarcations are blurred and hybridized by many factors beyond branded content, including the transactional relationships and interdependencies between sources and content publishers. There are multiple, intersecting spectrums across source interest, source influence, source disclosure; journalist/self-publisher/publisher self- and cross-promotion, interests, influence and disclosure. Yet while the economic beneficiaries of content, and the interrelationships of promotional exchanges, cover a wide expanse that must be incorporated in analysis and policy advocacy, this holism must not deflect from assessing the conjuncture of third-party payment with the presentation of content *"with similar qualities and format to content that is typically published."*

Definitions are integral to the exercising of regulatory authority, making formal legal-regulatory documentation arguably the most authoritative source, followed by the codes and statements of self-regulatory agencies, professional associations and trade bodies that are components of broader governance arrangements. Definitions are also a fascinating site of discursive struggles to persuade various stakeholder interests, and to shape and order the way practices are understood, valued and governed. For marketing professionals, the drive to establish positive associations with novel practices, disassociated from the old, discredited ones, is evident in the rearticulation of advertorial. Advertorial is a portmanteau term describing advertisements that appear as publisher's editorial content (Cameron and Ju-Pak 2000). In common use since the 1950s, the term is associated with advertising-as-article in magazines, and to a lesser extent, news publications. While contexts vary, the term is still used by publishers to label content, including to meet legal requirements to identify advertising material, yet has been superseded by the term native advertising within industry discourses, with the latter encompasses digital production and evolving formats. Yet, the term native advertising is used to enact a set of claims for a transition from old to new, that need to be interrogated by scholars, not merely endorsed. Sonderman and Tran (2013) state:

> Advertorials seek to present advertising as editorial content to convey claims and messages the reader wouldn't otherwise find credible. By contrast, sponsored content (done well) is properly labelled and clearly associates the brand with the content—the goal is to have the reader know and appreciate the brand's involvement, not to hide it.

Such differences are rhetorically constructed, but inaccurate and misleading as descriptions of either past or present practices. Fulgoni, Pettit and Lipsman (2017: 362) adopt a similar schema, describing advertorials as "interruptive to the print experience and [which] can be seen as misleading readers by offering funded content that masquerades as editorial." A more persuasive argument is that advertorials are associated with marketer supplied material rather than content produced by the publisher (Sirrah 2019; Apostol 2020). However, that demarcation is approximate, at best, and does not account for the continued use of "advertorial" by publishers to cover diverse kinds of publisher-hosted sponsored content, from advertiser-supplied to publisher co-created. As the research outlined below indicates, it is vital to recognize, and analyse, the discursive efforts to detoxify "branded content" across industry and academic discourses, including how definitional inexactitude serves processes of camouflage that make up the phenomena of "native" advertising itself (Serazio 2021b).

Finally, we need clarity about the objects of analysis to enable cross-national comparability. We now have an emerging body of single country and comparative research, as discussed below. Yet, differences in the terms used, their meanings and values and how they map to practices across linguistic and geo-cultural divisions remains a surprisingly neglected component. Building a foundation for cross-national comparative research will require not only suitable standardization but also greater reflexivity on the significance and implications of language-in-use across diverse and differentiated contexts.

Research Review

Up to the mid-2010s, researchers commented on the paucity of studies of branded content in news publishing. Ferrer-Conill (2016: 905) found "very few studies focus on the actual introduction of native advertising in journalistic contexts." Since then, published research output has increased significantly, notably on topics such as the effects of disclosure of sponsored content (Eisend, van Reijmersdal, Boerman, and Tarrahi 2020), but remains underdeveloped in some core areas for digital journalism research.

My research has identified 150 academic journal articles on sponsored content in journalism up to the end of 2019. Nine journal articles deal with advertorials and

Table 1. English language Academic Journal articles.

Year	No. of Publications	Year	No. of publications
2000	1	2010	0
2001	1	2011	0
2002	0	2012	3
2003	3	2013	4
2004	2	2014	6
2005	4	2015	15
2006	3	2016	21
2007	2	2017	16
2008	1	2018	22
2009	3	2019	34

hybrid journalism advertising formats and were published before 2000. Twenty were published between 2000–2009, with the remaining 121 published between 2010–2019. A journal article search (updated June 2021) was conducted using Ebsco for the search terms branded content ($n = 162$) and sponsored content ($n = 87$). A second search strategy included searching academic publisher databases for related journal outputs. A third strategy was to examine the reference lists of the articles identified through the database searches. The literature review also includes the results of searches of publications and reference lists to include books, book chapters and other academic outputs. The criteria for selection were substantive discussion of brand sponsored content (and all variant terms) in relation to the production and publication of print-based journalism.

Table 1 presents journal outputs only per year from 2000. This indicates the patterns of growth and topic selection in research. It is not a robust quantitative measure as search methods, inclusion criteria and English language publication bias make selection imprecise. Yet, it does show a pattern of increased scholarly attention and provides the basis for the qualitative mapping of research work and approaches discussed below.

There have been at least 21 journal articles published in 2020. Here I draw on this literature for a short review of key topics, approaches and selected findings.

Criticality

The research literature can be mapped on an axis of criticality, from affirmative scholarship guided by industry concerns for marketing effectiveness, business opportunities or revenue growth, through to research informed by, or explicating, critical perspectives. The practices of "embedding commercial messages into traditionally non-commercial content" (Boerman and van Reijmersdal 2016: 116) are subject to critiques that branded content camouflages marketing communications, risks "confusing and alienating some readers" (Marshall and Alpert 2016) and blurs the boundaries between advertising and editorial in ways that undermine independent journalism. The inclusion of paid content designed to be "native" to its editorial environment has generated most concerns, ranging from deception and reader awareness (Wojdynski and Evans 2016) to the impact on editorial integrity, credibility and trust in publishing (Levi 2015; Piety 2016; Einstein 2016).

Hardy (2017b, 2018, 2021) identifies three main problem areas: consumer welfare, media integrity, and marketers' power. Policy-oriented discussion, and a significant share of scholarship, has focussed on consumer welfare and addressed the labelling of native advertising, identification challenges for users (Amazeen and Wojdynski 2020; Li and Wang 2019), and their implications for governance. Critically oriented researchers evaluate industry practices as deceptive and as instrumental efforts to overcome users' knowledge and capabilities. The implications of branded content for the quality, integrity and purposes of journalism are the focus of work by legal, political science, marketing and media scholars. The creation of content on behalf of marketers that looks very similar to editorial content has the potential to undermine the editorial integrity of the publication, critics argue (Levi 2015; Serazio 2019a). This highlights concerns to safeguard qualities of the communication channel, not just protect consumers from deception (Goodman 2006). One version argues that native advertising is parasitic, destroying what it feeds on; advertisers wants to harness reader trust but in doing so undermine it. For Piety (2016: 101), "native advertising threatens to spread advertising's low credibility to all content, thereby destroying the reason advertisers wanted to mimic editorial content in the first place." This is extended in critiques that argue that branded content undermines the capacity to provide the trusted information and commercially disinterested opinion needed for democratic governance: "although native advertising serves as a temporary (and partial) solution to the crisis in the news industry, it might also—paradoxically—disrupt the core functions of journalism in order to ensure the news industry's survival" (Lynch 2018: 5).

The separation norm, of which church and state is an American institutionalized formulation, is linked to a broader norm, whereby "maintaining a certain degree of independence from those who are covered in the press … is in place to give citizens a sense of autonomy while establishing the legitimacy of journalism's democratic professional values" (Ferrer-Conill 2016: 906). Criticism focuses on the potential impact on editorial decision-making and output arising from pressures from, or dependency on, brand sponsorship (Atal 2018; Ferrer-Conill 2016). As an Advertising Age article puts it, "[w]hen you are a publisher that peddles native advertising, you're more vulnerable to advertising pressure" (Goefron 2015). Native advertising violates principles of editorial independence, or artistic integrity, because it creates the risk that "non-advertising" content will be shaped in accordance with advertisers' wishes. Radical political economic critiques go further in their concern about the system-wide consequences for communication provision of privileging marketers' voices (Hardy 2017b, 2021). The extension of brand voice into non-commercial spaces increases inequality in communication power. Such critique of branded content connects with those of market-driven journalism (McManus 1994) and hypercommercialism (McChesney 2013) and more recent ones concerning commercial personalization, clickbait, adtech, dataveillance, digital platforms and capitalism (Couldry and Mejias 2019).

Affirmative-tending research is characterized by its alignment with goals of improving marketing effectiveness for sponsored content and profitability for dominant commercial media and marketers (Wang and Huang 2017; Campbell and Evans 2018; Wang, Xiong, and Yang 2019). Becker-Olsen (2003) found sponsored content improved consumer purchase intentions and disposition towards brands compared to banner ads. Fulgoni et al. (2017) discuss industry research showing higher reader engagement with sponsored stories over display ads and call for time-spent metrics to be included in evaluating branded-content impressions. Another strand of media economics and business research assesses branded content as a necessary response to challenges for news publishers. Some of this literature acknowledges disbenefits but argue for the economic necessity of sponsored content to fund directly, or cross-subsidize, journalistic purposes, and to aid news publishers in challenging market conditions including their relationship with platforms (Watson et al. 2018; Nielsen and Ganter 2018). A third strand draws variously on organizational sociology, management and culturalist scholarship to align with managerially defined discourses of innovation against traditional resistance. Here, separation norms are recast as defensive moves by incumbent, professional elites and the embrace of marketing as unavoidable, innovative and responsive to market demand and users (Deuze 2005; see Hardy 2017a). Scholarly alignment with the perspective of selected actors or stakeholder interests may be perfectly justifiable, but should reflexively acknowledged, with research seeking to explicate not merely replicate the framings advanced by selected participants. Such reflexivity necessarily involves and requires greater dialogue and engagement across critical and affirmative research.

Approaches

We can apply a division in the literature at the point that studies begin to address native advertising in journalism and to a lesser extent branded content, content recommendation and other terms used from the 2000s. Before that there is a longer history of relevant research into media, advertising and public relations interrelationships in journalism. That includes research on advertorials discussed in a literature review by Kim, Pasadeos and Barban (2001). Drawing on that mapping Bachmann, Hunziker and Rüedy (2019) distinguish three main strands of empirical work concerning the blurring of editorial and advertising in a journalistic context: (a) content analysis of practices (b) interviews and surveys with practitioners ("media managers or advertisers") (c) experimental studies to examine persuasion and perception of recipients. While illuminating, their mapping conflates topics and methods and is selective. In this special issue Ferrer-Conill et al. (2020) identify three main foci for native advertising in journalisms: normative implications, practices, and effects on readers. This is apposite but normativity issues, for journalisms, users and societies, arguably run through each topic and interconnect. So, I propose instead this mapping of four topic areas:

a. Industry practices—including political economy, institutional arrangements, production processes and practices, professional identities and attitudes
b. content
c. users—consumption and use, awareness, attitudes
d. governance

Industry Practices
Analysis ranges from macro-level studies of the changing political economy of journalism to studies of the organization of practices at sectoral and organizational levels,

with many also addressing attitudes and self-reflections of practitioners. Studies identify a range of configurations for branded content production and para-journalistic labour. Sonderman and Tran (2013) identify four main business models in US media: an underwriting model (brand sponsors publisher-controlled editorial), an agency model (publisher employs workers to create custom content in partnership with brands); a platform model (publisher provides space for publisher-owned content, e.g., Forbes' BrandVoice) and an aggregated/repurposed model where a publisher allows its content to be repurposed for brand communications. They identify the agency model as the most commonly adopted arrangement comprising "a separate stable of writers/editors," removed from the newsroom although "newsroom people may have some say in final approval" (Sonderman and Tran 2013). Subsequent studies identify greater hybridization of news and branded content production. Chadha (2016) found that journalists at hyperlocal news start-ups composited their business and editorial duties. Boyles (2016) examines "intrapreneurial" units whereby legacy publishers adopted innovative features from digital natives. Boundaries between journalism and commercial interests are relatively more fluid at digital natives than legacy news organizations and more differentiated across sectors, such as lifestyle and business-to-business. Common findings are overlapping roles for staff (Drew and Thomas 2018: 199; Porlezza and Splendore 2016). Researchers draw variously on organizational sociology, social psychology cultural anthropology and transdisciplinary media industries studies. Analysis of branded content as a liminal space between editorial and advertising sales connects to wider analysis of practices, cultures and identities of those engaged in and around journalisms, with many drawing Bourdieu's field theory and boundary object analysis.

Research on the perspectives of news organization staff includes Artemas, Vos, and Duffy 2018; Coddington 2015, Drew and Thomas 2018. Interviews with various actor types involved in production include Harms, Bijmolt, and Hoekstra 2017; Poutanen, Luoma-Aho, and Suhanko 2016; Schauster et al., 2016; Atal 2018. Serazio (2020, 2021a) conducted 28 in-depth interviews with brand journalism professionals who operate in the United States. Drew and Thomas (2018) interview individuals in editorial and business departments. The general findings are that pre-existing church-state walls have become progressively porous (Artemas, Vos, and Duffy 2018; Carlson 2015; Coddington 2015; Ferrer-Conill 2016). Church and State has served as an influential "boundary marker" differentiating journalistic values from market-driven influences (Ferrer-Conill 2016), yet has been progressively eroded, critics argue, with the wall become variously a "curtain," permeated, collapsing (Coddington 2015), and, for some publishers at least, an archaeological curiosity (Hardy 2018). The adoption of sponsored content has been accompanied by the creation of "hybrid" editors (Poutanen, Luoma-Aho, and Suhanko 2016). Drew and Thomas (2018: 197) examine how "once-sedimented institutional and organizational logics are being negotiated and, potentially, reshaped." They cite the New York Times's Innovation Report (Mashable 2014) which advocated a shift in attitudes and practices at the news organization and stated that "[t]he very first step should be a deliberate push to abandon our current metaphors of choice—'The Wall' and 'Church and State'—which project an enduring need for division" (Drew and Thomas 2018: 196–7). Almar Latour (2015), executive editor of

The Wall Street Journal, proposed replacing the metaphor of walls with canals, "purpose-built and with a clear narrow focus" whereby "news organizations that align with business colleagues on relevant issues will be better positioned to respond to competitive threats." Artemas, Vos, and Duffy (2018) identify a shift away from "building" metaphors to "ecological" metaphors that endorse closer business and editorial collaboration and which serve to frame more integrated practices "in natural, and hence amoral, terms," rendering them beyond "the realm of normative consideration" (Artemas et al. 2018: 1015). Whereas for Artemas et al. these are framing strategies, Cornia, Sehl and Nielsen (2020: 186, 182) suggest that a new norm of integration has emerged, based on concepts of "collaboration, adaptability and business thinking," that "supplement the traditional value of editorial autonomy and norms of accuracy, fact-based discourse and a commitment to the practice of reporting, but seek to ensure it through integration rather than separation." Processes of normalization are identified by Ferrer-Conill (2016: 912) whereby "the long-standing divide between editorial and commercial content has started to be questioned by powerful actors within the industry." Carlson (2015: 861) advances the concept of norm entrepreneurship, identifying a new normative accommodation with sponsored content: a "curational norm of providing a coherent mix of both editorial and advertising content" based around "an imperative of providing content that audiences would find attractive."

The boundaries between editorial and advertising are established and negotiated in normativities and practices worldwide, but take context-specific forms, values and meanings of vital importance for analysis, as the contributions to this special issue attest and advance. This special issue confirms and enriches analyses of normalization by examining specific configurations of news publishing, notably in Spanish media. Carvajal and Barinagarrementeria (2021) identify three organizational models (integrated, autonomous and emerging), each involving hybrid professionals, linking commercial, editorial and design practices. Carvajal and Barinagarrementeria (2021) find that "those in more senior roles seek to normalize advertising–editorial hybrid forms through a set of arguments regarding the editorial quality, ethical standards and sustainability of their news organizations." Palau-Sampio (2021) examines newsroom journalists involvement in branded content production in Spain, while Wang and Guo (2021) examine hybridization in Chinese state news media, through their study of TeKan, governmental, paid content occurring in the context of "a business model imposed by the central government to enforce the political directive of media convergence."

Content

Content research ranges across studies examining sponsors, authors, article types, how articles are written, analysis of text content, visual, layout and positioning, and studies assessing user engagement with selected content. The main sponsors of paid-for editorial have been commercial brand owners, but overtly political actors have also adopted sponsored content. Ferrer-Conill (2016: 911) describes how El País and El Periódico published articles sponsored by Area Metropolitana de Barcelona (AMB) "in a contract worth over half a million euros that was disclosed in the governmental official journal, but not on the newspaper's website." The Irish government strategic communications unit arranged for sponsored content to appear in local, regional and national newspapers, including the *Irish Independent* and *The Irish Times* in 2014. The unit was disbanded following a review and majority vote in the Irish Parliament, the Dáil (Hennessy 2018). The UK government was criticized by the advertising self-regulator, the ASA, for advertorials carried in Metro regional papers, Metro online and Mail Online, on welfare benefit that were deemed to have "the potential to create some ambiguity as to whether or not they were ads or editorial" (ASA 2019) and where all the complaints made against article claims were upheld, a damning verdict on a government "information" campaign. Scholars have examined the phenomena of corporations taking out sponsored content in publications that have carried critical editorial, providing opportunities for confusion over information or editorial stance, or as a platform for rebuttal. Supran and Oreskes (2017) found that Exxon provided misleading information on climate change over a 40-year period, including in advertisements and advertorials in the *New York Times*. The phenomena includes state actors paying for presence in publications that carried critical journalism, as the Thai government did with sponsored content carried by Reuters (Carroll 2019). In this issue, Balint (2021) examines the Israeli government's use of sponsored content within multimedia campaigns. Wang and Guo (2021) examine the relations of journalists at state news media with Chinese state paid content. As these studies indicate researchers need to integrate studies of information management, strategic communications and commercial speech to track their deployment by sources across journalisms.

The majority of systematic content studies have examined formats, positioning, labelling and other identification markers. There has been an emphasis on textual over other visual objects, but that is being redressed, including by studies in this special issue. Zamith, Mañas-Viniegra and Núñez-Gómez (2021) use neuromarketing analysis of eye tracking to assess how users read combinations of headline, text and image. Ferrer-Conill et al. (2020) compare the visual features by which native advertising is distinguished from news items. This innovative study examines the contradictions between "coinciding" visual objects which help to mimic news articles such as "lead paragraph, text size, text font, text colour, background colour, authorship bylines, banners," and "disclosing" objects that identify and distinguish native advertising "use of borders, number and explanation of disclosures, stating the advertiser and their logos." In a five-nation comparative study, the authors find that "both national and organizational characteristics matter when shaping the visual boundaries of journalism"; disclosure and transparency levels tend to be lower in commercial publications than legacy and up-market outlets, while "online-only and mass-market publications tend to employ visual objects that facilitate mimicking content."

In this issue Palau-Sampio (2021) examines the range of brand sponsors found across Spanish publications. Such systematic content analysis of sponsors or stories remains rare, by contrast there are numerous studies of labelling and disclosure. Wojdynski and Evans (2014) examine disclosure practices in 28 US publications and find significant variation in the language used and positioning of disclosures, with some form of the word "sponsored" the most commonly used. Studies show variation in practices that may be attributed to different regulatory obligations, regulatory adherence and customary practices in media systems (Ferrer-Conill 2016).

Users—Consumption and Use, Awareness, Attitudes

Labelling can be the sole means by which users can distinguish paid content from editorial, and so is a key determinant of awareness of advertising content (Wojdynski 2016; Boerman, van Reijmersdal, and Neijens 2012). This is the principal focus of user research, dominated by experimental research methods, that examine attention, comprehension and recall and assess or infer influence and persuasion. Boerman and van Reijmersdal (2016) review 21 studies and conclude that the literature is inconclusive about several effects of disclosures of sponsored content, including whether disclosures encourage readers to ignore sponsored content or activate critical processing. Apostol (2020) examines thirty-seven research articles examining attitudinal responses to native advertising in editorial, published between 2003 and early 2020. The majority used experimental methods, some with qualitative research components, including interviews with survey respondents (Becker-Olsen 2003) usability testing and semi-structured interviews (Krouwer, Poels, and Paulussen 2017). Eisend et al.'s (2020) meta-data review of 61 papers that examine the effects of disclosure of sponsored content, across journalism and other media, finds that readers often fail to identify native advertising content and fail to recognize or comprehend disclose labelling (Amazeen and Muddiman 2018; Amazeen and Wojdynski 2020; Boerman and Van Reijmersdal 2016; Hyman, Franklyn, Yee, and Rahmati 2017). Across experimental research, Howe and Teufel (2014) find that user recognition of native advertising had no effect on their estimation of a news website's credibility. However, Amazeen and Wojdynski (2020) find that readers who recognize an online article as native advertising have less favourable opinions of the host news publisher, while Amazeen and Muddiman (2018) argue that both legacy and online news publishers damage their brand reputation through native advertising. For marketers and media "disclosure increases the likelihood of criticism of the brand, message, and source" (Eisend et al. 2020: 364), . Yet, if there are incentives to disguise NA, the findings provide a contrary pressure on regulators to strengthen the disclosure of NA in ways that go beyond the more discretionary approaches some regulators have so far adopted.

Governance

The interface between branded content and national regulation has been examined (Campbell and Grimm 2019) and specific rules and practices, such as labelling, have been reviewed in cross-national contexts, with recommendations from many scholars for better labelling and disclosure (Iversen and Knudsen 2019). Governance analysis can integrate examination of all forms of rule-making with studies of media production, political economy, social action and discourse (Hardy 2021). Ferrer-Conill (2016: 912–3) advocates the development of "analytical tools for studying native advertising in journalistic context" and longitudinal approaches that study the evolution of implementation of native advertising. Such longitudinal and comparative research is required across the study of sponsored content practices and governance . In the special issue Ferrer-Conill et al. (2020) examine native advertisements in 21 news brands published across five countries: Germany, Norway, Sweden, Spain, and Israel. While governance is not the main focus, each of the special issue papers engages with governance and contributes to this developing research agenda. Several papers examine

Spain showing how this mature market for sponsored content also illustrates complexities across rule-formation and adherence. Formal rules lack specificity in addressing native advertising, industry codes are developing but are not embedded across institutional practices contributing to inconsistencies, idiosyncrasies and confusion across those involved in content production, as well as for users (see also Hardy 2018, 2021).

Summary: Special Issue Contributions and Future Research. The papers in this special issue make a significant contribution to research, developing new frameworks, making theoretical and empirical advances and providing fresh perspectives on established topics. The main methods for research to date have been content analysis, interviews and experimental audience research. The special issue includes ethnographic field work (Wang and Guo); surveys, interviews, archival study, quantitative content analysis incorporating visual analysis (Ferrer-Conill, Knudsen, Lauerer and Barnoy). The authors engage a wider range of theories including social identity (Wang and Guo), material object (Ferrer-Conill et al) and Habermas' theory of strategic and communicative action (Balint).

In commentaries, Joseph Turow (2021) assesses the implications of the frontiers of the voice intelligence industry for digital journalism, including serving personalised sponsored content based on combining voice profiling with other information collected on an individual. Lisa Lynch (2021) updates her review of possible trajectories for native advertising (Lynch 2018) to consider the faltering of some prestige publishers' branded content studio strategies amid advertising market contraction and competition from the Google-Facebook duopoly and other opportunities for advertisers. Both articles indicate that news publishers' routes to advertising revenue growth, whether through podcasting or voice profiling, are likely to involve further accommodation with brand sponsored content.

The wide-ranging research of the last 15 years has occurred in a period of claims, hype, hope and experimentation. There are ever-attendant risks that the findings of excellent research into specific configurations of practices in time and space may be cited as if it was sufficient to describe general and enduring features. Instead, the ephemeral qualities of sponsored content must be incorporated reflexively. Sponsored content has grown significantly but been an unreliable resource for media and marketers. Several of the digital natives who relied on sponsored content have stumbled, contracted or closed (Hardy 2021; Lynch 2021). Key issues for marketers including scale and measurement. For media, sponsored content has involved costs, including paid promotion of client-sponsored content, generating low profit margins. Revenue from all forms of advertising was in steep decline for many legacy publishers before the 2020 Covid pandemic, but then collapsed as the virus outbreak led to worldwide restrictions on public life. In the UK, the *Telegraph* cut the branded content activities of its agency Spark in 2020, although Chief Executive Nick Hugh promised to continue "editorially integrated partnerships tied to our reader-first approach" (cited in Spanier 2020). Sponsored content is also ephemeral in challenging ways for researchers. Publishers' branded content, like other advertising material, is ignored, or inconsistently captured in news databases and publishers' digital archives, and is especially ephemeral online, with problems including inconsistent tagging, the removal or alteration of labelling, and, in some instances, the removal of sponsor identification after paid promotions, so that the presence of brand sponsored content is entirely erased, at least without web archive recovery tools.

As well as mapping evolution in branded content practices, there are still large research gaps across the intersection of journalism and branded content. More research is needed on the liminal "spaces," institutional and ideational, of branded content production. How do workplace organizational arrangements and social relations differ? What are the labour practices and divisions between staff journalists/content studio creatives, freelancers and subcontracted labour? How do younger or early career journalists assess and navigate tensions between normativities and exigencies? There are tendencies in research to conflate branded content producers and (all) journalists, whereas we need more careful assessment of stratification and demarcations in workplaces, more attention to tensions, accommodations, and antimonies. As Carvajal and Barinagarrementeria (2021) ask in this special issue "why is the lack of consensus about the use of native advertising in the newsrooms important, and what does this debate reveal about how scholars and industry stakeholders perceive branded content and native advertising?" Above all, we need to examine the factors that influence differential, and changing, responses to branded content across journalistic networks and across positions and identities within specific institutional configurations.

Within digital journalism studies, the research addressing sponsored content has tended to replicate general biases. The majority of studies have examined news journalism over other journalisms, and print-based/online text-based publishers over primarily audio or audiovisual journalisms. There is an extensive literature on branded content audiovisual but the interface of journalism and brands across all converging media forms is underexamined, although studies of online and mobile native advertising are increasing. The neglect of other journalisms is also being addressed, for instance, Hanusch et al. (2020) examine lifestyle journalisms' particular susceptibility to commercial pressures. However, studies of sponsored content are needed across a range of publishing sectors including the Black press, social enterprise, radical and alternative media (Medeiros 2019). Historic studies of *Ms* show how the tensions of serving advertisers within feminist publishing were negotiated (Steinem 1990) yet many more contemporary studies are needed.

Some sponsored content phenomena may indeed be short-lived. Formats and arrangements will change, yet the shifts from media and advertising separation to integration are far-reaching. Sponsored content illustrates a deepening convergence between marketing communications and journalism, between those with the resources for pay for presence in third party communication and those involved in the production of communications activities that carry the weight of expectations, assumptions and responsibilities of journalism. A profound reorganization of digital journalism is underway affecting financing, resourcing and content decisions, across circuits of production and consumption. Digital journalism studies must contribute to analysis of the social as well as industrial implications, as marketers voice extends further into channels where multivocality and disinterested speech are so vital for political democracy and for our decision-making as consumers and citizens.

Acknowledgements

I wish to thank Joseph Turow and Lisa Lynch for their insightful commentaries, all the authors who have shared compelling research for this special issue, the reviewers for their intellectual and temporal generosity and the editor for his tremendous support and guidance throughout.

Disclosure Statement

The author declared no potential conflicts of interest with respect to the research, authorship and/or publication of this article.

ORCID

Jonathan Hardy (iD) http://orcid.org/0000-0003-0150-4799

References

Agius, Aaron. 2015. "Native Advertising, a Boon for the Media, Can Help You Cut Through the Noise." *The Entrepreneur*, January 14. https://www.entrepreneur.com/article/239952.

Amazeen, Michelle A., and Ashley R. Muddiman. 2018. "Saving Media or Trading on Trust? The Effects of Native Advertising on Audience Perceptions of Legacy and Online News Publishers." *Digital Journalism* 6 (2): 176–195.

Amazeen, Michelle A., and Bartosz W. Wojdynski. 2020. "The Effects of Disclosure Format on Native Advertising Recognition and Audience Perceptions of Legacy and Online News Publishers." *Journalism* 21 (12): 1965–1984.

Apostol, Nicoleta-Elena. 2020. "What is Known about Native Advertising in Editorial Contexts? A Descriptive Literature Review." *Journal of Media Research* 13 (2(37)): 59–81.

Arrese, Ángel, and Francisco J. Pérez-Latre. 2017. "The Rise of Brand Journalism." In *Commercial Communication in the Digital Age: Information or Disinformation?*, edited by Gabriele Siegert, M. Bjørn von Rimscha, and Stephanie Grubenmann, 121–139. Berlin: De Gruyter.

Artemas, Katie, Tim P. Vos, and Margaret Duffy. 2018. "Journalism Hits a Wall: Rhetorical Construction of Newspapers' Editorial and Advertising Relationship." *Journalism Studies* 19 (7): 1004–1020.

ASA. 2019. "ASA Ruling on Department for Work and Pensions in association with Associated Newspapers." *ASA*, November 6. https://www.asa.org.uk/rulings/department-for-work-and-pensions-G19-1021769.html.

Atal, Maha Rafi. 2018. "The Cultural and Economic Power of Advertisers in the Business Press." *Journalism* 19 (8): 1078–1095.

Bachmann, Philipp, Séverine Hunziker, and Tanja Rüedy. 2019. "Selling Their Souls to the Advertisers? How Native Advertising Degrades the Quality of Prestige Media Outlets." *Journal of Media Business Studies* 16 (2): 95–109.

Baldasty, Gerald J. 1992. *The Commercialization of News in the Nineteenth Century*. Winsconsin: University of Winsconsin Press.

Balint, Anat. 2021. "It's in the Air'—Sponsored Editorial Content as a Path for Stealth Government Propaganda: The Case of Israeli Media." *Digital Journalism*: 1–22. doi:10.1080/21670811.2021.1899010

Becker-Olsen, Karen L. 2003. "And Now, a Word from Our sponsor - A Look at the Effects of Sponsored Content and Banner Advertising." *Journal of Advertising* 32 (2): 17–32.

Benes, Ross. 2019. "Driven by Social, Native Accounts for Nearly Two-Thirds of Display Ad Spend." *eMarketer*, April 16. https://www.emarketer.com/content/driven-by-social-native-accounts-for-nearly-two-thirds-of-display-ad-spend.

Boerman, Sophie C., and Eva A. van Reijmersdal. 2016. "Informing Consumers about 'Hidden' Advertising. A Literature Review of the Effects of Disclosing Sponsored Content." In

Advertising in New Formats and Media: Current Research and Implications for Marketers, edited by Patrick de Pelsmacker, 115–146. Bingley: Emerald.

Boerman, Sophie C., Eva A. van Reijmersdal, and Peter Neijens. 2012. "Sponsorship Disclosure: Effects of Duration on Persuasion Knowledge and Brand Responses." *Journal of Communication* 62 (6): 1047–1064.

Boyles, Jan L. 2016. "The Isolation of Innovation: Restructuring the Digital Newsroom through Intrapreneurship." *Digital Journalism* 4 (2): 229–246.

Bull, Andy. 2013. *Brand Journalism*. Abingdon: Routledge.

Cameron, Glen T., and Kuen-Hee Ju-Pak. 2000. "Information Pollution? Labeling and Format of Advertorials." *Newspaper Research Journal* 21 (1): 65–76.

Campbell, Colin, and Pamela E. Grimm. 2019. "The Challenges Native Advertising Poses: Exploring Potential FTC Responses and Identifying Research Needs." *Journal of Public Policy & Marketing* 38 (1): 110–123.

Campbell, Colin, and Nathaniel J. Evans. 2018. "The role of a companion banner and sponsorship transparency in recognizing and evaluating article-style native advertising." *Journal of Interactive Marketing* 43: 17–32.

CAP [Committee of Advertising Practice]. 2019. "Remit: Sponsorship." *CAP*, September 4. https://www.asa.org.uk/advice-online/remit-sponsorship.html.

Carlson, Matt. 2015. "When News Sites Go Native: Redefining the Advertising–Editorial Divide in Response to Native Advertising." *Journalism* 16 (7): 849–865.

Carroll, Joshua. 2019. "Reuters Article Highlights Ethical Issues with Native Advertising." *Columbia Journalism Review*, January 24. https://www.cjr.org/watchdog/reuters-article-thai-fishing-sponsored-content.php.

Carvajal, Miguel, and Iker Barinagarrementeria. 2021. "The Creation of Branded Content Teams in Spanish News Organizations and Their Implications for Structures, Professional Roles and Ethics." *Digital Journalism*: 1–21. doi:10.1080/21670811.2021.1919535

Casale, A. J. 2015. "Going Native: The Rise of Online Native Advertising and a Recommended Regulatory Approach." *Catholic University Law Review* 65 (1): 129–154.

Chadha, Monica. 2016. "What I Am versus What I Do: Work and Identity Negotiation in Hyperlocal News Startups." *Journalism Practice* 10 (6): 697–714.

Chittum, Ryan. 2014. "Native Ads Grow Up." *Columbia Journalism Review*, January 10. https://archives.cjr.org/the_audit/native_ads_grow_up.php.

Coddington, Mark. 2015. "The Wall Becomes a Curtain: Revisiting Journalism's News-Business Boundary." In *Boundaries of Journalism: Professionalism, Practices, and Participation*, edited by Matt Carlson and Seth C. Lewis, 67–82. New York, NY: Routledge.

Cornia, Alessio, Annika Sehl, and Rasmus Kleis Nielsen. 2020. "'We No Longer Live in a Time of Separation': A Comparative Analysis of How Editorial and Commercial Integration Became a Norm." *Journalism* 21 (2): 172–190.

Couldry, Nick, and Ulises A. Mejias. 2019. *The Costs of Connection: How Data Is Colonizing Human Life and Appropriating It for Capitalism*. Stanford: Stanford University Press.

Couldry, Nick, and Joseph Turow. 2014. "Advertising, Big Data, and the Clearance of the Public Realm: Marketers' New Approaches to the Content Subsidy." *International Journal of Communication* 8 (2014): 1710–1726.

Davies, Jessica. 2018. "How The Guardian Overhauled Its Content Studio to Make It More Efficient." *Digiday*, September 5. https://digiday.com/media/guardian-overhauled-content-studio-make-efficient/

Deuze, M. 2005. "What Is Journalism? Professional Identity and Ideology of Journalists Reconsidered." *Journalism* 6 (4): 442–464.

Drew, Kevin, and Ryan J. Thomas. 2018. "From Separation to Collaboration." *Digital Journalism* 6 (2): 196–215.

Dvorkin, Lewis. 2013. "Inside Forbes: What's next for native ads? Controversy gives way to market realities." Forbes, 8 July. https://www.forbes.com/sites/lewisdvorkin/2013/07/08/inside-forbes-whats-next-fornative-ads-controversy-gives-way-to-market-realities/#439a316874b9

Einstein, Mara. 2016. *Black Ops Advertising Native Ads, Content Marking, and the Covert World of the Digital Sell*. New York: OR Books

Eisend, Martin, Eva A. van Reijmersdal, Sophie Boerman, and Farid Tarrahi. 2020. "A Meta-Analysis of the Effects of Disclosing Sponsored Content." *Journal of Advertising* 49 (3): 344–366.

European Parliament and Council. 2005. *DIRECTIVE 2005/29/EC of 11May 2005 concerning the Unfair Business-to-Consumer Commercial Practice, "Unfair Commercial Practices Directive.* Brussels: European Parliament and Council.

Feng, Songming, and Mart Ots. 2018. "Seeing Native Advertising Production via the Business Model Lens: The Case of Forbes"s BrandVoice Unit." *Journal of Interactive Advertising* 18 (2): 148–161.

Ferrer-Conill, Raul. 2016. "Camouflaging Church as State: An Exploratory Study of Journalism's Native Advertising." *Journalism Studies* 17 (7): 904–914.

Ferrer-Conill, Raul, Erik Knudsen, Corinna Lauerer, and Aviv Barnoy. 2020. "The Visual Boundaries of Journalism: Native Advertising and the Convergence of Editorial and Commercial Content." *Digital Journalism*: 1–23. doi:10.1080/21670811.2020.1836980

Fulgoni, Gian, Raymond Pettit, and Andrew Lipsman. 2017. "Measuring the Effectiveness of Branded Content across Television and Digital Platforms." *Journal of Advertising Research* 57 (4): 362–367.

Goefron, Martin. 2015. "BuzzFeed's editorial fumble doesn't have to be a buzzkill for native advertising." *Advertising Age*, May 7. http://adage.com/article/digitalnext/buzzfeed-s-editorial-fumble-a-buzzkill/298386/.

Goodman, Ellen. 2006. "Stealth Marketing and Editorial Integrity." *Texas Law Review* 85: 83–152.

Hanusch, Folker, Sandra Banjac, and Phoebe Maares. 2020. "The Power of Commercial Influences: How Lifestyle Journalists Experience Pressure from Advertising and Public Relations." *Journalism Practice* 14 (9): 1029–1046.

Hardy, Jonathan. 2017a. "Money, (Co)Production and Power." *Digital Journalism* 5 (1): 1–25.

Hardy, Jonathan. 2017b. "Commentary: Branded Content and Media-Marketing Convergence." *The Political Economy of Communication* 5 (1): 81–87. http://www.polecom.org/index.php/polecom/article/view/79.

Hardy, Jonathan. 2018. "Branded Content: Media and Marketing Integration." In *The Advertising Handbook*, edited by Jonathan Hardy, Helen Powell, and Iain MacRury, 4th ed., 102–122. Abingdon, Oxon: Routledge.

Hardy, Jonathan. 2021. *Branded Content: The Fateful Merging of Media and Marketing*. Abingdon: Routledge.

Harms, Bianca, Tammo H. A. Bijmolt, and Janny C. Hoekstra. 2017. "Digital Native Advertising: Practitioner Perspectives and a Research Agenda." *Journal of Interactive Advertising* 17 (2): 80–91.

Hennessy, Michelle. 2018. "What Happens Next? Report Finds No Evidence of Wrongdoing by Strategic Communications Unit." *Thejournal.ie*, March 27. https://www.thejournal.ie/strategic-communications-unit-2-3927435-Mar2018/.

Howe, Patrick, and Brady Teufel. 2014. "Native Advertising and Digital Natives: The Effects of age and Advertisement Format on News Website Credibility Judgments." *International Symposium on Online Journalism #ISOJ* 4 (1): 78–90.

Hyman, David A., David Franklyn, Calla Yee, and Mohammad Rahmati. 2017. "Going Native: Can Consumers Recognize Native Advertising: Does It Matter." *The Yale Journal of Law and Technology* 19: S.77.

IAB [Interactive Advertising Bureau]. 2019. *Native Advertising Playbook 2.0*, May. New York: IAB. http://www.iab.com/guidelines/native-advertising/.

IAB UK. 2018. "IAB UK Advocates for Greater Transparency with Latest Release of Content and Native Guidelines." https://www.iabuk.com/press-release/iab-uk-advocates-greater-transparency-latest-release-content-and-native-guidelines.

ICFJ. 2017. *ICFJ Survey: The State of Technology in Global Newsrooms*. https://www.icfj.org/our-work/state-technology-global-newsrooms.

Iversen, Magnus H., and Erik Knudsen. 2019. "When Politicians Go Native: The Consequences of Political Native Advertising for Citizens' Trust in News." *Journalism* 20 (7): 961–978.

Kim, Bong-Hyun, Yorgo Pasadeos, and Arnold Barban. 2001. "On the Deceptive Effectiveness of Labeled and Unlabeled Advertorial Formats." *Mass Communication and Society* 4 (3): 265–281.

Krouwer, Simone, Karolien Poels, and Steve Paulussen. 2017. "To Disguise or to Disclose? The Influence of Disclosure Recognition and Brand Presence on Readers" Responses toward Native Advertisements in Online News Media." *Journal of Interactive Advertising* 17 (2): 124–137.

Latour, Almar. 2015. "From Walls to Canals." *NiemanLab*. https://www.niemanlab.org/2014/12/from-walls-to-canals/.

Levi, Lili. 2015. "A 'Faustian Pact'? Native Advertising and the Future of the Press." *Arizona Law Review* 57: 647–711.

Li, You, and Ye Wang. 2019. "Brand Disclosure and Source Partiality Affect Native Advertising Recognition and Media Credibility." *Newspaper Research Journal Summer Journal* 40 (3): 299–316.

Lynch, Lisa. 2018. *Native Advertising: Advertorial Disruption in the 21-st Century News Feed.* Abingdon: Routledge.

Lynch, Lisa. 2021. "Sponsored Content in 2020: Back to the Future?" *Digital Journalism*: 1–9. doi: 10.1080/21670811.2021.1901059

Marshall, Jack, and Lukas I. Alpert. 2016. "Publishers Take On Ad-Agency Roles With Branded Content." *Wall Street Journal*, December 11. https://www.wsj.com/articles/publishers-take-on-ad-agency-roles-with-branded-content-1481457605

Mashable. 2014. "The New York Times Innovation Report." May 16. https://mashable.com/2014/05/16/full-new-york-times-innovation-report/?europe=true.

McChesney, Robert. 2013. *Digital Disconnect.* New York: The New Press.

McManus, John H. 1994. *Market-Driven Journalism: Let the Citizen Beware?* London: Sage

Medeiros, Vince. 2019. "Youth Media and the Business of Content: Conflict, Agency and Counter-Hegemony in a Branded Age." Unpublished thesis, Goldsmiths College, London.

Moses, Lucia. 2017. "'The Model Can't Hold': Publishers Face Content Studio Growing Pains." *Digiday*, March 9. https://digiday.com/media/model-cant-hold-publishers-face-content-studio-growing-pains/.

Newman, Nic. 2019. *Journalism, Media, and Technology Trends and Predictions 2019.* Oxford: Reuters Institute for the Study of Journalism.

Newman, Nic. 2021. *Journalism, Media, and Technology Trends and Predictions 2021.* Oxford: Reuters Institute for the Study of Journalism.

Nielsen, Rasmus K., and Sarah A. Ganter. 2018. "Dealing with Digital Intermediaries: A Case Study of the Relations between Publishers and Platforms." *New Media & Society* 20 (4): 1600–1617.

Palau-Sampio, Dolors. 2021. "Sponsored Content in Spanish Media: Strategies, Transparency, and Ethical Concerns." *Digital Journalism* 1–21. doi 10.1080/21670811.2021.1966314

Piety, Tamara. 2016. "Killing the Golden Goose. Will Blending Advertising and Editorial Content Diminish the Value of Both?" In *Blurring the Lines: Market-Driven and Democracy-Driven Freedom of Expression*, edited by M. Edstrom, A. T. Kenyon, and E. M. Svensson, 101–108. Goteborg: Nordicom.

Porlezza, Colin, and Sergio Splendore. 2016. "Accountability and Transparency of Entrepreneurial Journalism: Unresolved Ethical Issues in Crowdfunded Journalism Projects." *Journalism Practice* 10 (2): 196–216.

Poutanen, Petro, Vilma Luoma-Aho, and Elina Suhanko. 2016. "Ethical Challenges of Hybrid Editors." *International Journal on Media Management* 18 (2): 99–116.

PQ Media. 2018. *Global Branded Entertainment Marketing Forecast 2018.* https://www.pqmedia.com/product/global-branded-entertainment-marketing-forecast-2018/.

Richter, Scott. 2017. "The Future of Native Advertising for Brands and Publishers." *The Entrepreneur*, March 9. https://www.entrepreneur.com/article/290186.

Rosin, Brett. 2015. "Why Native Advertising Is a No-Brainer for Publishers and Marketers." *Publisher Insider*, March 5. http://www.mediapost.com/publications/article/245070/why-native-advertising-is-a-no-brainer-for-publish.html

Schauster, Erin E., Patrick Ferrucci, and Marlene S. Neill. 2016. "Native Advertising is the New Journalism: How Deception Affects Social Responsibility." *American Behavioral Scientist* 60 (12): 1408–1424.

Sebastian, Michael. 2015. "Native Ads Were 'Inside' 10% of Digital at The New York Times Last Year." *Advertising Age*, February 3. https://adage.com/article/media/york-times-sold-18-2-million-worth-native-ads/296966.

Serazio, Michael. 2020. "Making (Branded) News: The Corporate Co-optation of Online Journalism Production." *Journalism Practice* 14 (6): 679–696.

Serazio, Michael. 2021a. "The Other 'Fake' News: Professional Ideals and Objectivity Ambitions in Brand Journalism." *Journalism* 22 (6) 1340–1356.

Serazio, Michael. 2021b. "How News Went Guerrilla Marketing: A History, Logic, and Critique of Brand Journalism." *Media, Culture & Society* 43 (1): 117–132.

Sharethrough. n.d. "Native Advertising Insights." https://www.sharethrough.com/nativeadvertising.

Sinclair, John. 2020. "Cracking under Pressure: Current Trends in the Global Advertising Industry." *Media International Australia* 174 (1): 3–16.

Sirrah, Ava. 2019. "Guide to Native Advertising." *Tow Center for Digital Journalism*, September 6. https://www.cjr.org/tow_center_reports/native-ads.php#_edn1.

Sonderman, Jeff, and Millie Tran. 2013. "Understanding the rise of sponsored content." American Press Institute, November 13. https://www.americanpressinstitute.org/publications/reports/white-papers/understanding-rise-sponsored-content.

Spanier, Gideon. 2020. "Telegraph to "Significantly Downsize" Branded Content Arm Spark." *Campaign*, June 17. https://www.campaignlive.co.uk/article/telegraph-significantly-downsize-branded-content-arm-spark/1686858.

Steinem, Gloria. 1990. "Sex, Lies and Advertising." *Ms*, July/August: 18–28.

Supran, Geoffrey, and Naomi Oreskes. 2017. "Assessing ExxonMobil's Climate Change Communications (1977–2014)." *Environmental Research Letters* 12 (8): 084019.

Turow, Joseph. 2021. "Journalism and the Voice Intelligence Industry." *Digital Journalism* 1–7. doi:10.1080/21670811.2020.1829979.

Turow, Joseph. 1997. *Breaking up America, Advertisers and the New Media World*. Chicago: University of Chicago Press.

Van Reijmersdal, Eva A., Peter Neijens, and Edith Smit. 2009. "A New Branch of Advertising: Reviewing Factors That Influence Reactions to Product Placement." *Journal of Advertising Research* 49 (4): 429–450.

Wang, Dan, and Steve Guo. 2021. "Native Advertising in the Chinese Press: Implications of State Subsidies for Journalist Professional Self-identification." *Digital Journalism* 1–17. doi: 10.1080/21670811.2021.1968919.

Wang, Ruoxu, and Yan Huang. 2017. "Going Native on Social Media: The Effects of Social Media Characteristics on Native Ad Effectiveness." *Journal of Interactive Advertising* 17 (1): 41–50.

Wang, Pengyuan, Guiang Xiong, and Jian Yang. 2019. "Serial Position Effects on Native Advertising Effectiveness: Differential Results across Publisher and Advertiser Metrics." *Journal of Marketing* 83 (2): 82–97.

Watson, Sara M., Emily Bell, Nushin Rashidian, and Abigail Hartstone. 2018. *The Future of Advertising and Publishing*. New York: Columbia University Academic Commons.

Wojdynski, Bartosz W. 2019. "Advertorials and Native Advertising." In *The International Encyclopedia of Journalism Studies*, edited by T. Vos and F. Hanusch. Massachusetts: Wiley-Blackwell.

Wojdynski, Bartosz W., and Nathaniel J. Evans. 2016. "Going Native: Effects of Disclosure Position and Language on the Recognition and Evaluation of Online Native Advertising." *Journal of Advertising* 45 (2): 157–168.

Wojdynski, Bartosz W. 2016. "Native advertising: Engagement, deception, and implications for theory." In *The New Advertising: Branding, Content and Consumer Relationships in a Data-Driven Social Media Era* edited by R. Brown, V. K. Jones, and B. M. Wang. Santa Barbara, CA: Praeger/ABC Clio. pp. 203–236.

Wojdynski, Bartosz, and Nathaniel J. Evans. 2014. "Deception by design: Analyzing native advertising practices on news Web sites." Paper presented at the Association for Education in Journalism and Mass Communication Annual Conference, Montreal, QC, Canada.

Zamith, Fernando, Luis Mañas-Viniegra, and Patricia Núñez-Gómez. 2021. "Cognitive Perception of Native Advertising in the Spanish and Portuguese Digital Press." *Digital Journalism*. doi:10.1080/21670811.2021.1919536

The Creation of Branded Content Teams in Spanish News Organizations and Their Implications for Structures, Professional Roles and Ethics

Miguel Carvajal 🆔 and Iker Barinagarrementeria

ABSTRACT
Over the last decade, top media organizations have restructured their newsrooms and created branded content teams, or studios, devoted entirely to the production of new native advertising formats in order to leverage this business opportunity. The goal of this exploratory study is to analyse how news organizations in Spain implement this strategy and create branded content teams, changing the structure of their newsrooms and shaping the practices and roles of the editors and journalists involved. Semi-structured interviews with professionals ($n = 11$) who work at news outlets ($n = 8$) were carried out in order to explain their structural, professional and ethical challenges. The results show that branded content teams can be classified into three organizational models (integrated, autonomous and emerging) and they are usually formed by hybrid professionals, linking commercial, editorial and design practices. The study participants justify the new practice adopting the role of norm entrepreneurs. Despite the warnings and risks, the interviewees asserted that by inserting an appropriate disclaimer in these new formats, credibility and transparency are not endangered. They also believe that sponsored content will become a fundamental pillar for the business models of their news organizations.

Introduction

Native advertising and branded content are increasingly important revenue streams for news outlets (Carvajal and Pastor 2018). Over the last decade, top media organizations have restructured their newsrooms and created branded content teams, or studios, devoted entirely to the production of new native advertising formats in order to leverage this business opportunity. At the same time, the ethos of editors and journalists within and beyond these teams is being transformed by activities that involve creating and distributing branded content in conjunction with advertisers.

This response has drawn considerable attention from academia. On the one hand, the introduction of branded content teams and native advertising formats is viewed as an innovation of the media business model aimed at improving the value proposition for brands and mitigating the overwhelming power of social media platforms in capturing advertising expenditure (Carvajal et al. 2015; García-Avilés et al. 2018; Watson et al. 2018; Nielsen and Ganter 2018; Lynch 2018). On the other hand, the proliferation of these units in newsrooms weakens the traditional separation of editorial and marketing departments, and also jeopardizes the credibility of journalistic brands (Carlson 2015; Ferrer-Conill 2016).

Criticism centres around potential pressure from advertisers regarding news content (Atal 2018), the challenge faced by users in identifying native advertising (Amazeen and Wojdynski 2020; Li and Wang 2019), and the risks of "alienating readers once they do figure out that some of the publication's content is sponsored by advertisers" (Amazeen and Wojdynski 2020: 16). This sponsored content trend is seen as an extension of McChesney's idea of "hyper-commercialism" that erodes the fundamental values of journalism (Carlson 2015) and endangers its perceived quality (Bachmann, Hunziker, and Rüedy 2019).

In the meantime, news organizations continue to introduce this new revenue stream as a way to diversify their business model, and the professionals who comprise these teams assume and justify their role in the sustainability of their media outlets (Cornia, Sehl, and Nielsen 2020; Lynch 2018; Duffy and Rui Jun 2020). This trend appears in leading markets, including Spain, where prominent news organizations, such as *El País*, *El Mundo*, *El Confidencial*, *El Español*, and regional press groups along the lines of Henneo, Godó, Vocento and Prensa Ibérica, which are among the top 10 media outlets with the most users in Spain (comScore 2019).

In 2019, Spain had a population of 47 million people and an internet penetration of 91% (Instituto Nacional de Estadística 2020), where two out of every three people used their smartphones to access online news. According to the Digital News Report (Reuters 2019), 10% of Spain's population was willing to pay for online news and overall trust in news was 43% (-1), with the nation ranked 19th out of 38 countries.

This article examines how news organizations in Spain implement this strategy and create branded content teams, shaping the roles and practices of professionals. We follow the same path as Cornia, Sehl, and Nielsen (2020) when focussing on the rhetorical and normative discourses of editors to understand how they legitimise new working practices that are inconsistent with traditional norms. We also see how the interviewees justify their work by overcoming the problems of editorial-advertising integration and stretching the meanings of their ethical and professional standards (Carlson 2015).

The goal of this exploratory study is to gain a better understanding of how these teams are organized after identifying the presence of three organizational models. Branded content teams follow a similar pattern and, in general, offer the same services, and their organization varies according to the size of the corresponding media outlet. Semi-structured interviews with the editors ($n = 11$) of news outlets regarding this new advertising alternative were carried out in order to address their ethical and professional challenges.

Theoretical Background

We theoretically frame the emergence of branded content teams as a phenomenon related to the transformation of news organizations in the context of media innovation. However, native advertising and branded content are changing the practices and norms of the editors and journalists involved, and could undermine their professional role and the fundamental values of journalism within their organizations.

The challenges for sustaining the business model provide the context for internally restructuring and reconfiguring media outlets, and redefining editorial practices (García-Avilés et al. 2018). The resulting changes lead to hiring professionals for various roles, ranging from marketing to data backgrounds, to help develop new practices and values (Valero-Pastor and Carvajal 2017; García-Avilés 2018). These teams emerge in response to the communication industry's adaptation and survival because media outlets transform how their editorial departments are organized in order to help create value (Küng 2017).

Branded content, innovation and data teams make it possible for professionals specialized in techniques and subject matters to create greater economic value for their organizations (Salaverría 2015; Valero-Pastor and Carvajal 2017; García-Avilés 2018). This type of structure favours specialization, innovation, adaptation to market fluctuations and employee creativity (Cornia, Sehl, and Nielsen 2020; Küng 2017: 172). They are made up of multidisciplinary roles, depending on the nature of the projects they offer (Lynch 2018).

Recent research based on interviews with lifestyle magazine editors and news editors showed the emergence of "hybrid editors" in newsrooms, serving as a link between sales and editorial departments (Poutanen, Luoma-Aho, and Suhanko 2016). The changing nature of journalistic work and organizations is affecting the professional status, roles and practices of journalists, eliminating the professional control that previously existed because the division of labour in media production has become much less clear (Witschge and Nygren 2009).

Business objectives have been integrated more intensely into the editorial agenda of commercial news media outlets within the ongoing transformation of news organizations (Baumann 2013; Waldenström, Wiik, and Andersson 2019). Dominant digital intermediaries are restructuring the environment in which news outlets operate, and even larger media organizations are struggling to adapt to their growing dependence on players such as Google and Facebook (Nielsen and Ganter 2018). These platforms have decimated the digital advertising market for online news operations, resulting in desperate attempts to find alternative revenue streams such as sponsored content and native advertising (Lynch 2018). Following this trend, news start-ups with various organizational formulas coexist in the digital marketplace, offering branded content and other marketing services (Deuze and Witschge 2017; Valero-Pastor and González-Alba 2018: 561; García-Avilés et al., 2018).

The integration of editorial and advertising departments poses a threat to the tenets of social responsibility of the press (Schauster, Ferrucci, and Neill 2016). Native advertising and branded content generate obvious concerns about the deterioration of the traditional separation between advertising and editorial departments (Carlson 2015; Coddington 2015; Ferrer-Conill 2016). News outlets that stand for high quality could undermine their quality by engaging in native advertising (Bachmann, Hunziker, and Rüedy 2019). The widespread use of these formats that endanger journalistic autonomy is criticized as part of a global process that is not limited to branded content but rather to an industry crisis (Carlson 2015; Ferrer-Conill 2016; Goyanes and Rodríguez-Castro 2019).

According to Lynch (2018), native advertising has a number of competing genealogies and manifestations, leading to disagreements about what it actually refers to. For the purpose of this study, native advertising is a paid media strategy that enables brands to control the content that is published. Sponsored editorial content can be used to describe various kinds of brand involvement, including native advertising. However, it also includes content that is sponsored/supported by brands (paid) but where editorial control rests with the publisher or is shared.[1] Native advertising is labelled with different types of disclaimers such as sponsored content, branded content, or promoted content (Amazeen and Muddiman 2018).

In Spain, overall, professionals involved in branded content teams—such as the interviewees of this study—use the term "branded content" when referring to content features that are paid for by the advertiser but created by the publisher, and the process is supervised by the brand at the beginning (briefing) and at the end of the process.[2]

Branded content (or sponsored editorial content) and native advertising are part of a new marketing strategy used by companies to connect with audiences (Hardy, MacRury, and Powell 2018; Feng and Ots 2018). Both strive to emulate editorial content in order to enhance the advertiser's brand and its message's appeal (Harms, Bijmolt, and Hoekstra 2017). These formats sometimes fail to provide basic information as to the existence of commercial interests (Perales Albert 2018; Ferrer-Conill et al. 2020).

Amazeen and Muddiman conclude that by blurring content in this manner, the credibility of online publishers is diminished (2018). However, effectively designed disclosure labels facilitate the recognition of native advertising (Amazeen and Wojdynski 2020; Wojdynski and Evans 2016). Indeed, Li and Wang (2019) found that any effort to increase advertising recognition with an intent to be transparent would not hinder the perceived credibility of news outlets.

Nevertheless, in a recent study, editors and journalists state the need to move away from traditional normative models so as to integrate these new solutions (Cornia, Sehl, and Nielsen 2020). Some journalists do not view branded content as a threat to professional autonomy but rather as a way to work together to ensure commercial sustainability. However, this new form of cooperative interdependence between advertisers and journalists alters news practices profoundly (Carlson 2015), as has been shown in existing studies focussed predominantly on US media outlets. The discourse on journalistic independence and autonomy is being questioned by the growing trend of adopting native advertising in the digital editions of traditional news media outlets (Ferrer-Conill 2016).

Our work is based on the premise that the challenges of integrating editorial-advertising content are well known, as outlined in the theoretical framework, but similar studies on Spanish news outlets have not been carried out to date. Therefore, it is essential to understand how commercial and journalistic discourses are assimilated by editors in order to confirm the existence, in other markets, of trends that have already been studied in English-speaking countries.

To understand how news organizations in Spain implement branded content and create dedicated teams, the study addresses the following research questions:

- RQ1: How are branded content teams structured in their news organizations?
- RQ2: How do these new practices affect their professional routines and roles, and how do they face the ethical challenge?
- RQ3: In what way do these professionals believe that this new revenue source will impact the sustainability of their organizations?

Methodology

To answer our research questions, we relied on a qualitative methodology of a descriptive nature that addresses the phenomenon in order to understand it within its practical context. Studying the inclusion of branded content teams requires a more holistic approach because they combine market principles and technologist-driven cultures, norms and practices (Westlund and Lewis, 2014).

The Interviews

The interviews consisted of in-person meetings and phone calls that took place between March and September 2019 and lasted an average of 40-60 min. A recording and transcription of each conversation is available in a digital repository for private queries. The material was used by the team to filter the research results.

In the interviews, we collected general data about these departments, such as their origin, structure and the roles involved, but we also focussed on the ethical and normative approach of professionals. The data set provided a glimpse into these branded content teams and helped us to define the rhetoric of editors and journalists, delving into the troublesome aspects noted in literature.

The first section (organization and workflows) includes descriptive questions about how the organization operates (What steps are involved in creating a piece, from start to finish? Which is more common: projects that are proposed by brands or by the media outlet?). The second section (ethical and professional challenges) contains questions aimed at evaluation (Do you believe that branded content is labelled accordingly? Is the editorial department involved in any of the creation phases? What type of support or resistance have you encountered from your editorial department? Do they fail to defend this format because it is their job? Could it negatively affect the media outlet's reputation?). In the case of the latter (importance for the business model), the goal is to understand how they view their role within the organization (How important is this revenue stream for your media outlet? In what direction is this type of content headed?).

However, the conversations did not follow this order. At the beginning of each interview, the participants were informed that their answers would be anonymous. Questions were first asked to profile the interviewee and introduce them into the conversation. Once a level of trust had been established, the more challenging questions were asked in order to obtain more elaborate responses than by asking directly.

Finally, the full answers were transcribed by two researchers and then read independently to summarize and highlight the most relevant aspects using the six-step process proposed by Braun and Clarke (2006).

The Sample

The current media system in Spain emerged from of a profound economic crisis that resulted in the elimination of more than 12,000 jobs between 2008 and 2015, but also incentivized media innovations and the creation of more than 500 news start-ups (Asociación de la Prensa de Madrid (APM) 2015). Legacy newspapers such as *El País* and *El Mundo*, along with regional groups like Vocento, Prensa Ibérica and Godó, now have counterparts in the form of thriving digital outlets that include *El Confidencial*, *Eldiario.es* and *El Español*. These leading digital publications have uncovered top news stories and proven their appeal to new demands of the public (Mancinas Chávez, Moreno-Cabezudo, and Ruiz-Alba 2019).

For the purpose of our study, eight Spanish news organizations were selected: newspapers with print and digital outlets (*El País*, *El Mundo*), two digital native publications (*El Confidencial*, *El Español*), and several media publishing groups (Henneo, Godó, Prensa Ibérica and Vocento). The selected sample is intentional and represents digital native media (2) and newspapers with traditional print versions (6). Additionally, the sample is also representative of local and regional publishers (4), and national news media (4). It is worth noting that these selections represent industry trends exclusively from commercial enterprises. Additionally, eight of the media outlets selected are ranked in the top 10 in terms of monthly unique visitors according to comScore indexes (September 2019). On a nationwide level, the sample is not representative of the vast media industry. However, it is useful for the purpose of this research because it makes it possible to explore the arguments of editors at top news outlets.

Two of the interviewees work for media groups that operate a combined total of more than 27 local newspapers. Both chains have implemented corporate strategies that impact all of their regional dailies (Carvajal and García Avilés 2008). The remaining respondents—who help produce and plan this type of sponsored content—offer a more comprehensive vision of each phase and of how these departments are organized. As far as the personal profile for the sample, the interviewees were selected within each organization among professionals involved only in producing branded content as opposed to regular editorial tasks (Table 1). They work exclusively in their branded content positions and all are former journalists (most previously formed part of news departments). It is worth noting that all the interviewees have degrees and experience in journalism. Of the total, seven are managing editors with key responsibilities in the tasks at hand, three are professionals who write and edit content, and the eleventh is a product manager. The tasks for several managing editors include coordinating production efforts, creative direction, negotiations and sales. In Spain, "editors" are also known as "directors" (with managerial duties), as opposed to regular "editors" who produce content (writing and editing). In our sample, we interviewed both types of editors. It should be noted that they frequently refer to themselves

Table 1. List of interviewees, roles and main tasks in their branded content (BC) team.

News outlet	Role	Main tasks
El Español	BC Managing Editor	Managing
Prisa (El País)	BC Managing Editor	Managing
El Confidencial	BC Editor	Managing, producing and designing
Prensa Ibérica	BC Editor	Producing, writing and editing
Henneo (20 Minutos)	BC Editor	Producing, writing and editing
Vocento (Abc)	BC Managing Editor	Managing
El Confidencial	BC Project Manager	Account planning, writing and editing
Prisa (El País)	BC Managing Editor	Managing
Godó (La Vanguardia)	BC Managing Editor	Managing
Unidad Editorial (El Mundo)	BC Managing Editor	Managing
Henneo (20 Minutos)	BC Managing Editor	Managing

* The interviewees' roles are only linked to branded content teams.

"journalists", although they were not producing journalism (gathering and reporting news, etc.) at the time of the interview.

Results

The branded content team that serves *El País* (Prisa Content) was founded in 2014. This unit serves the entire group and is made up of more than 100 people. Most of the editors were brought over from *El País*. The Godó's Brands Lab was created in early 2016, initially with two people, although it now has 15 team members who create branded content projects and special actions for the group's media outlets. They include SEO specialists, analytics experts and designers, in addition to seven content editors. Unidad Editorial developed the first branded content projects in 2012, but their team dates back to 2014, when UEStudio was founded. The group consists of nine editors who write branded content, two camera operators/editors, three production staff members, six designers and two analytics experts, in addition to accounting and project managers.

In 2015, Henneo created a specific brand content unit, made up of 11 editors and two designers, at its Zaragoza headquarters. In 2018, the unit was expanded to Madrid in the form of a team with two editors and a designer who offered their services from the capital following the acquisition of *20 Minutos*. The *El Confidencial* branded content team was founded in 2014, although it focussed on other production tasks. In 2016, it was renamed EC Brands and established as a creative agency that offers services for brands. The team has grown significantly, reaching a total of 16 professionals, of which eight are former journalists. The *El Español* branded content team emerged with the creation of the news outlet in 2016. The unit grew progressively and by 2019 was comprised by three journalists editing branded content who receive assistance from other editorial staff members, particularly in the area of photography/video and design.

The branded content team at Prensa Ibérica was founded in 2017 with two professionals. The unit is now made up of four people: the managing editor, a designer and two editors. The team's work is very horizontal and collaborative because it is organized as a creative team that serves the group's regional newspapers. Similarly, the branded content unit at Vocento (Content Factory) is made up of five professionals:

two editors, two designers and a project manager. Created in 2016, it works centrally for the group's news outlets and forms part of the group's advertising marketer.

RQ1. Structure, Processes and Roles

The size of news outlets is the first conditioning factor for the organizational structure of these departments. In small-sized native media outlets, the average team consists of a managing editor, two editors, a product manager (who coordinates the dates and times for posting content on the website), a designer and a person who handles technological development. All of the departments analysed, regardless of their size, work with external partners specialized in various areas, such as audiovisual production and user analytics.

In the news outlets researched, three organizational models were identified in relation to the rest of the entity. Medium or large-sized national media outlets tended to have an *autonomous model*. In other words, the team is self-sufficient and has all the professionals needed to create this type of content, from the beginning to the final results assessment report for the advertiser (performance metrics). This organizational model does not depend on the editorial department for any key phases of the production process.

There is a second organizational structure we refer to as the *integrated model*. This formula shares the branded content team's design and audiovisual production resources with the rest of the editorial department. Due to its limited size, the branded content team must rely on developers and tech specialists from corporate departments.

Finally, the *emerging model* has been identified in print-centered publishers with less experience in formats, new narratives and other innovative journalism elements. These small departments only include journalists and are sometimes one-person teams. Based on the needs that arise (design, technology and web optimization), the branded content team must rely on the resources of cross-company departments.

In all of these models, the analytics service is centralized within the organization. However, the interviewees state that their branded content departments prepare reports containing consumption data for clients. This task is usually done by product managers, a hybrid professional that sometimes does not write or create content, but remains in contact with the brand, focuses the idea, advises production and ensures the narrative goal of the piece is attained (Poutanen, Luoma-Aho, and Suhanko 2016). These professionals are usually former journalists from the newsroom who have taken on responsibilities in the area of design or new formats, or who have special training in corporate communication.

In addition to the aforementioned product manager, these teams are comprised by other multidisciplinary professionals with journalism training. For example, one of the members of a branded content team holds a degree in Journalism but specializes in this field thanks to a master's degree in Corporate Communication and prior experience in advertising. Another respondent explained that they try to recruit creative profiles with a background in business or public relations. According to this participant, the ultimate goal of this mix is to achieve that complicated balance between the brand's needs and creating useful and interesting information for readers.

However, the highest authority is always an editor with experience in news departments. In fact, an interviewee acknowledges that they prefer professionals who have a journalism background in the branded content team. According to a product manager at a digital news outlet, "It is better if they have never worked in corporate because their journalism profile is perfect for identifying interesting angles for readers."

Although the idea of a project originates from a brand, it is increasingly common for product managers to submit proposals to a media outlet's sales department. This flow of proposals emanating from the branded content team and passed on to prospective clients through sales teams relates to other models discussed in the literature (Lynch 2018), where the unit liaises with the client without the sales department's involvement. The business opportunity in selling a variety of storytelling services opens the door for clients who seek new marketing opportunities, forcing news organizations to turn their studios into ad agencies and selling the narratives that journalists produce (Lynch 2018, p. 97-100). According to a product manager at a digital news outlet, "The sales team catches the prey, and we prepare and serve it". However, the interviewees explain that brands (or agencies) are the ones who take the first step when it comes to launches, campaigns or reputation crises.

Based on what was mentioned in interviews, the workflow for branded content follows a similar pattern as that of an advertising agency: first the strategy is devised alongside the brand, delving into its communication goals, and then a proposal is prepared. If the client approves the proposal, the editors produce the content. The terms of the agreement determine the frequency, location and date when the piece will be published in the news outlet's portals.

As far as the separation of sales and editorial departments, the interviewees note that their media outlets keep the branded content team separate from the editorial department, with clearly differentiated tasks. The only exception occurs with designers and programmers, who in some of their organizations tend to be shared with other editorial teams, such as at *El Español*, *El Mundo* and Henneo.

Do they encounter resistance in the editorial department of their newsrooms? It depends on the case. Participants confirm this reality, but they generally do not address any specific complaints. The clearest answer is from an editor who notes that resistance emerges when the branded content fails to add value or is not aligned with the media outlet's philosophy. Another participant from a legacy media admits that the news outlet's traditional departments know very little about branded content, leading to reluctance: "On a positive note, departments with an eye on the future (developments, new narratives, formats and leadership) are familiar with branded content, and they support us."

Branded content teams are more aligned with the organization's business goals and values (Poutanen, Luoma-Aho, and Suhanko 2016; Cornia, Sehl, and Nielsen 2020). The need to innovate the business model leads to the creation of these departments, which have a strong business acumen. A respondent asserted that there is no friction between their department and the editorial team. To confirm whether or not that tension exists between professionals on both sides, responses should be obtained from the other journalists. Another branded content editor admits that the supervisor must have authority and a journalistic background to gain such credit from the rest of the newsroom:

> Branded content is a solution and a response to prevent conflict with editorial departments because the content is created according to the editorial style and interests of readers (branded content managing editor at a news group).

There are no issues or reservations, explained a respondent, because "it deals with information of interest that the newspaper could publish without the involvement of a brand. Brands and agencies must be evangelized because many still struggle to accept that this format is advantageous over traditional advertising."

With regard to the location and the editorial calendar, a participant admits that the same criteria is used as for traditional advertising. In other words, the space, frequency and location are determined by the media outlet (explicitly or implicitly). In this sense, a respondent states, news content takes precedence over branded content:

> If a colleague from the editorial department has an exclusive, this piece has priority over branded content, which is in turn postponed. These concepts are not timeless. They usually have an angle, or at least that is the goal, and we publish them on the dates that make the most sense.

A managing editor acknowledges that they primarily look after the top section of the front page and position ad-oriented articles along the sides: "We pay attention to the content and make sure it does not sound too much like an advertisement, particularly if it will appear in a prime location on the front page." These decisions are aligned with the news outlet's management, and according to interviewees, editorial guidelines are strictly followed. When asked about the specifics of these guidelines, it seems that a specific document containing branded content parameters does not exist, and they instead refer to an abstract set of rules and norms.

In Spain, there is no specific mention of native advertising or branded content in government regulations. According to article nine of the country's General Advertising Law, all advertising activities should be easily identifiable as such and the media must clearly differentiate informative statements from those that merely serve advertising purposes. However, native advertising is specifically regulated by the independent advertising self-regulatory organization (SRO), which specifies that any "commercial communications must be identifiable as such, regardless of the means, format, or media used" (Autocontrol 1996, 2019):

> When commercial communications, including "native advertising," appear in a medium that contains news or editorial content, they must be presented in a way that they are easily recognizable as ads and, when necessary, labelled as such. It must be obvious that the real intent is advertising [...] (article13).

The results show that these branded content teams were created using the same formulas at all of the media outlets analysed, with the organization's size as the fundamental difference in terms of the number of newsroom staff members. Therefore, the emergence of three organizational models shows that the most evolved model is quite similar to how an advertising agency operates. The data reveal that the primary focus of these teams is to serve advertisers and to bring in revenue for the media outlet, but their discourse is based on journalistic values, such as the creation of quality content. The results reveal that keeping these teams separated from the rest of the editorial staff is perceived as a protective barrier against potential pressure from brands regarding news content, although the ramifications and guidelines of these activities remain unclear. Lastly, the representatives of these teams handle discourses that are more aligned with managerial practices, probably because some of them hold leadership roles in these units.

RQ2. Ethical and Professional Challenges

Publishers involved in the study also have their own codes of conduct, but they do not specifically mention any limits on native advertising or rules on disclaimers, labels and warnings when using branded content. Five media outlets involved in the sample are affiliated with the Trust Project, an international consortium in which dozens of news organizations work towards transparency and accountability in global news, but there is no specific mention of this practice.

On a professional level, the only ethical reference belongs to FAPE, the leading professional journalist organization in Spain, with more than 49 federated and 17 linked associations that together represent about 19,000 members. The organization promulgates a code of principles and deontological standards for the journalistic profession. Article six states that "so as to not mislead or confuse users, journalists are required to make a formal and rigorous distinction between information and advertising," and warns that "its simultaneous exercise with advertising goes against the ethics of the journalistic profession", among other institutional or private activities that could affect the principles and deontological standards of journalism (FAPE, Code of Ethics 1993 and updated in 2017).

Respondents in the study believe that branded content pieces are undertaken with the same professional and ethical standards as news content. Among the terms used by interviewees when referring to producing this format, the words "quality," "rigor," "interest" and "editorial coherence" stand out.

> The content must be socially relevant or interesting for our readers in order to publish it. Since the team is made up of former journalists, we follow journalistic criteria. We do not publish anything that has not been verified. If an advertiser includes false information, we won't publish it (branded content managing editor of a digital-only news organization).

They believe that this new concept is a hybrid alternative that balances the brand's message with the newspaper's values and philosophy in order to provide useful and interesting content for readers. Unlike native advertising, which has a stronger commercial and persuasive nature, branded content reflects the advertiser's brand values through a story that goes beyond the product, in which making an impact is not the goal:

> This content is not shared by a company and does not consist of advertising messages with a journalistic touch. Fundamentally, branded content is content. It is content that creates value in several directions: for readers, for brands and for the newspaper (branded content editor of a digital-only news outlet).

Previous studies have shown that sponsored content represents commercial advocacy that must be kept completely separate from journalistic values, which respondents believe they protect and secure. In this age of hybrid editors, there is a need to develop such a journalistic code of ethics on sponsored content, which would make the blurred boundaries as distinct as possible (Poutanen, Luoma-Aho, and Suhanko 2016).

An editor from a digital news outlet explains that the journalistic approach is constantly being debated. "We take great pains to ensure the team is equally comprised by people with corporate and journalism backgrounds in order to find that middle ground," explains the participant. "95% of the headlines we publish have been agreed upon by everyone."

However, a respondent from a regional press group points out that branded content is published because "there is an investment, a payment, a collaboration or a brand sponsorship." This participant notes that it is essential to find a balance between news and business because "if branded content is merely viewed as a revenue stream, it will have a very short lifespan."

Do they include an appropriate disclaimer? Participants responded affirmatively to the question. "Our brand and reputation are on the line, so we rigorously follow the recommendation and label absolutely everything," explains a managing editor. Interviewees mention the importance of transparency with readers to ensure credibility. "We cannot take the risk of readers feeling deceived; they must always be perfectly aware of sponsored content," notes another respondent. In fact, they continue, it is essential for the content to be labelled accordingly because this is what brands want: "Sometimes they want a bigger logo, but we have to dissuade them".

In any case, editors understand that unless a disclaimer is used, branded content could be perceived as intrusive, just like traditional advertising. A branded content editor at a regional group believes that this could "undermine readers' trust" and affect the newspaper's reputation. Another participant argues that they try to avoid the confusion by adding a formal disclaimer:

> Confusion is avoided if a disclaimer appears at the top. We always include a disclaimer near the top, and on social media, clients are tagged as partners and a disclaimer is added.

Another respondent from a national news outlet also states,

> We believe that a disclaimer is essential. Just like opinion pieces are labeled accordingly, the same applies to branded content.

Interviewees distance themselves from advertorials and defend the journalistic value of branded content, which uses stories to connect with the brand's values, but above all, it does so "with the audience's interests in mind since this is what clients want." However, a former branded content editor warns that some of the local editorial departments within the group at which they worked are unfamiliar with the format, resulting in "content more along the lines of an advertorial rather than branded content, and leading to lower quality." In a comparative study on audience perceptions and expectations of content creators and journalists, Banjac and Hanusch (2020) find that a shift towards commercial and market-driven imperatives among both actors leads audiences to disconnect because they feel like consumers sought out primarily for financial gain.

Still, another editor acknowledges that they "work hard to ensure the quality of the topics covered so readers receive valuable information as opposed to an advertorial, regardless of whether a piece has been paid or sponsored by a brand":

> We do not create ads, banners or third-party content. Sometimes a piece may seem more like an advertorial than branded content because companies struggle to understand the formula and remain stuck on traditional paper formats. However, this is becoming less common.

They follow the entity's editorial criteria to ensure the branded content does not tarnish the media outlet's standards and editorial style. "We are aware of what can and cannot be done. Many topics are off limits, such as health content, which we believe should follow editorial criteria and requires a certain level of authority for our readers," explains another respondent. As a participant puts it,

> The aim of our branded content is to position leisure as a fundamental part of the project by creating editorial narratives focused on entertainment, and indirectly linking them to the brand's values.

As shown by Amazeen (2019), in soft-news contexts, consumers tend to be less likely to perceive the commercial intent in native advertising as commercial in nature, and this could indicate that consumers already perceive soft news as having some degree of commerciality.

When participants are asked whether it is possible that readers will be unable to identify a piece as a sponsored content, this depends on the efforts of the professionals involved and also on the format. Data from interviews revealed the complexity and editorial hybridization of this phenomenon. For example, as far as the design and integration in the feed (look and feel), an editor explains that the pieces they create are identical to the rest of the content: they use the same fonts, page layout and visual code as for the rest of the news in the website. The home page also has the same visual style, except for the addition of a logo and/or disclaimers such as "Sponsored by [the brand]" or "[The news outlet] for [the brand]". In fact, these pieces are usually created through the media outlet's CMS (content management system).

> Some of our branded content pieces are read just as much as any news article, despite having a "Powered by" banner (branded content editor).

On the other end of the spectrum, another respondent asserted that all branded content must have a different design and the writer's name is always omitted to keep the piece from being confused with a news article. In effect, editors use external CMS templates that are managed directly by the branded team. This decision not only covers the look and feel or editorial criteria, but it also addresses functionality: the piece must be replicated in more than a dozen of the group's outlets, each with its own design.

Could they possibly be undermining the credibility of their brands?

> Conventional advertising is decreasingly effective, so new revenue streams must be found. This is not a bad thing, and when handled accordingly, there is no reason for it to be viewed in a negative light (product manager at a digital-only news operation).

As another editor puts it answering the same question,

Past formulas were worse. If we criticize branded content, then what can be said about advertorials that could not be altered in any way? It is good that the messages brands want to share are filtered by the media and follow their criteria. Which is better? Publishing a piece created by the brand or making something with journalistic criteria? It is useful and interesting information about a popular topic that awakens interest, as proven by analytics. However, a brand happens to be behind it.

A respondent believes that branded content specialists serve as a firewall for business propaganda and public relations. This self-legitimizing perception reveals not only how editors are working together with managers to ensure commercial sustainability, but also how they are actually establishing new boundaries through the practices, discourses and values that set them apart from other fields, i.e. *branded content vs. propaganda* (Carlson and Lewis 2015). However, an editor warns that at precarious or smaller media outlets, there is a risk of producing this type of content with lower standards, thereby betraying the format's supposed positive aspects.

The findings show that there is a hidden contradiction between the participants' perceptions as editors and creators of content for readers and as marketing service providers for brands. The interviewees acknowledge the commercial origin of branded content, however, they do not view branded content as merely an advertising format. This finding is in line with Cornia, Sehl, and Nielsen (2020), in which senior editors and managers stress the need to abandon traditional norms and move towards more integrated organizational solutions, which they associate with positive values such as dialogue, openness, sensitivity and an understanding of other peoples' contributions to shared goals (Cornia, Sehl, and Nielsen 2020).

According to the participants, branded content would cease to be valuable and simply become an advertorial without the editorial insight of a journalist's mindset and storytelling techniques. In Spain, there is the general perception that certain native advertisements resemble advertorials, so the participants have distanced themselves from this traditional format because there is no editorial involvement. They do not view branded content as advertising, however, it is sold as such, arranged as such and negotiated as such. The use of the term "content" could disguise this conceptual weakness. In summary, there is a range of justifications appealing to different values (for brands, publishers, readers) that the participants suggest are mutually beneficial. The value for brands and publishers can be measured more easily in economic terms, but the value for readers requires a more comprehensive understanding of the benefits, beyond clicks and page views. Competing for a place in a site's most-viewed section is not an adequate way to measure quality for readers, although this perception reflects a deeper and wider issue with what constitutes public interest.

RQ3. Future Business Implications

The interviewees were asked as to the importance of this revenue stream for their news outlet, and the fairly unanimous response was "very important." Over the past year, their departments have grown and are likely to continue to do so based on the upward advertising spending forecasts for this category, as they confirmed.

The interviewees note that their sponsored editorial content studies produce more for an increasing number of clients. Among the portfolio of journalistic formats and genres, they provide news, the most basic and direct format, with the same style as the rest of the pieces in the website. Participants also agree on the growing importance of video content and multimedia features.

A managing editor believes that the number of branded content requests will increase. In the medium term, proposals will have to be turned down in favour of bigger projects involving long-term relationships between brands and news outlets. "Projects that are more solid and lasting will arise," asserted the respondent.

An editor notes that there is room for growth in persuading certain agencies and clients that cling to formats similar to advertorials. "They understand this upon seeing content of this type among the daily top reads, thanks to the quality of the texts and the connection with readers," suggests another.

Another respondent predicts greater success "with the smart use of data in an effort to adapt content to readers and segment those who are truly interested." To achieve this, the idea is to collect information through surveys, registration systems and cookies. Another editor agrees that data will facilitate personalization, making "branded content as important to readers as other information."

With regard to future trends, a product manager believes that interactivity works very well: when gamification, participation or audience engagement are integrated, there is a spike in consumption time and in positive feedback from readers. For the coming years, the interviewees are certain that, beyond formats and passing trends, content will be key: the bridge between informative and business elements is to create pieces that benefit news outlets and brands, without diminishing reader trust.

The findings show the general consensus that this activity will be a key element in the business model of their media outlets. This agreement is particularly evident in those who hold leadership roles, as opposed to editors and product managers who lack a global perspective of their unit and its impact on the company's numbers. It is important to highlight that branded content editors and other managing journalists are not representative of the broader journalistic professional culture (Carlson 2015). In any case, the discourse of those interviewed replaces journalistic categories such as public interest, editorial responsibility or reader trust, with concepts that are more aligned with the business side, such as innovation, the future, solutions or value creation. On the other hand, as Carlson (2015) notes, the move from the traditional norm of separation to the new norm of integration is not a wholesale rejection of established editorial values, but a shift towards a new set of practices that remain committed to accuracy, fact-based reporting and other journalistic principles.

A new norm of integration, based on combining established editorial values with the concepts of collaboration, adaptation and business thinking, has emerged and already plays a central role in our interviewees' rhetorical and normative discourses (Carlson 2015). The shift is made clear by the terminology used by employees in the interviews and justifies the existence of these teams. Tellingly, Artemas, Vos, and Duffy (2018) find the use of metaphors for introducing an amoral discourse that legitimated closer collaboration between editorial and advertising and presented evidence for how a rhetorical deconstruction or renegotiation of journalism's cultural capital might come about (Artemas, Vos, and Duffy 2018). This has been the case when dealing with the different titles and roles of the editors involved, who sometimes call themselves "journalists" even though they are not technically producing news of any kind. "We can observe a growing diversity in media content, reflecting a fragmentation of the audiences and a blurring of media genres such as journalism, entertainment and fiction, making journalism more difficult to define as a profession" (Witschge and Nygren 2009).

The adoption of native advertising is slowly showing signs that the discourse on journalistic independence and autonomy is changing from within (Ferrer-Conill 2016). Following Carlson's (2015) findings, if the norm of separation was supposed to enable professional autonomy in the past, our interviewees argue that the norm of integration (in-house branded content teams) is necessary to enable professional autonomy in the future. Editors describe positive consequences from this commercial orientation, such as newspaper content that is better and sharper, or news that is more relevant to the audience, but this has also led to drastic deteriorations from the perspective of others in journalism (Waldenström, Wiik, and Andersson 2019).

Conclusions

This article shows how news organizations in Spain introduce branded content teams to adapt their business model to a new advertising demand. The paper is a study of the people who form part of branded content teams and who do not work as regular journalists. Therefore, it is a study of the new practices and values adopted by those involved in producing branded content. The professionals who comprise these teams assume and justify their role in the sustainability of their media outlets (Cornia, Sehl, and Nielsen 2020; Lynch 2018). The study identifies three organizational models (autonomous, integrated, emerging) in the creation of branded content teams and each of them differ in size, scope and profiles. They are usually comprised by editors who previously worked in news departments and now have new roles as managers, editors and product managers.

We theoretically frame the emergence of branded content teams as a phenomenon related to the transformation of news organizations in the context of media innovation. However, native advertising and branded content are changing the practices and norms of the workers involved, and could undermine their professional role and the fundamental values of journalism. We follow the same path as Cornia, Sehl, and Nielsen (2020) when focussing on the rhetorical and normative discourses of editors to understand how they rationalize their role, how they take on risks and how they evaluate this organizational strategy at their media outlet. The interviews show how they react to ethical concerns and to potential threats affecting the media outlet's reputation.

The research focussed on editors from eight Spanish media outlets that offer branded content. Three organizational models were identified. Medium or large-sized national media outlets have an *autonomous model* that does not rely on the editorial department for any of the key phases within the production process. There is a second organizational structure we refer to as the *integrated model* that shares the branded content team's design and audiovisual production resources with the rest of the editorial department. Finally, the *emerging model* has been identified at laggard media outlets with less experience. These small departments are sometimes one-person teams.

The study reveals the emergence of a hybrid editor that sometimes does not write or create content, but remains in contact with the brand, focuses the idea, advises production and ensures the narrative goal of the piece is attained (Poutanen, Luoma-Aho, and Suhanko 2016). These professionals are usually former journalists from the editorial department who have taken on responsibilities in the area of design or new formats, or who have special training in corporate communication, linking commercial, editorial and visual practices.

We have verified that the professionals involved in branded content teams justify these practices. The respondents studied have seamlessly incorporated the "business" discourse that past studies predicted, and from their perspective, it does not pose an ethical risk. This rationalization of their work is in line with other conceptual research initiatives (Schauster, Ferrucci, and Neill 2016; Cornia, Sehl, and Nielsen 2020). In balancing the quality of their editorial content with their desire to justify their commercial tasks, branded content team members have found an interstice to embrace their work. The acceptance of their activity suggests that in Spain, branded content has become normalized in a wide range of newsrooms.

Following Carlson (2015), our work provides evidence of the emergence of "norm entrepreneurs," particularly among those in management roles. Our data show that those in more senior roles seek to normalize advertising–editorial hybrid forms through a set of arguments regarding the editorial quality, ethical standards and sustainability of their news organizations. The results show that the rhetorical and normative discourses of editors attempt to legitimise their new work practices to overcome the problems of editorial-advertising integration by stretching the meanings of their professional standards (Carlson 2015).

The existence of native advertising and branded content teams is as a threat to the traditional separation of church and state as has been warned by many authors (Carlson 2015; Coddington 2015; Ferrer-Conill 2016; Lynch 2018). However, the data we obtained reveal that five of these teams operate independently from the editorial department. Compared with other newsroom editors, they are more in contact with the sales department, which assigns projects to them. However, the study's ethnographic focus cannot determine the degree to which these teams have affected the editorial outcome of their organizations, which is one of the fundamental aspects of this separation.

The study provides a deeper understanding of the rationales that branded content defenders employ. It shows how they differentiate branded content from other advertising formats, emphasize its hybrid nature, and highlight its usefulness and interest for readers. In their eyes, this format provides interesting information and is markedly different from an advertorial, a term that has sometimes been used to play down the importance of branded content and criticize it as an old entity. There is a clear contradiction between this vision and the marketing strategy implemented by these teams to attract advertisers. If branded content is not advertising, then why is it sold as such, arranged as such and negotiated as such? The use of the term "content" disguises this conceptual weakness and opens new windows to justify this practice.

Specifically, the study finds that there is agreement as to the importance of transparency with readers in order to ensure the credibility and therefore the future of the business model. The analysis of interviews indicates that branded content editors do not want their readers to feel deceived. They want them to have a clear understanding of which content is sponsored, and believe that if readers are informed accordingly, these formats will not harm the journalistic brand's credibility. However, as other studies have found, in the balance between transparency and deception, news organizations do not boldly push for transparency and instead remain ambiguous (Ferrer-Conill et al. 2020).

Extending the conceptualization in previous contributions by Cornia, Sehl, and Nielsen (2020), the study demonstrates how editors from branded content view this new advertising format as a much-needed alternative to help ensure sustainable journalism. As a result, they believe that the branded content teams at media outlets are in the best position to offer these services to brands. In light of the ever-changing digital ecosystem, the interviewees' appreciation of branded content and their essential role in sustaining the business show how editorial and commercial integration became a norm. As Carlson (2015) argues, changes in professional norms are also presented as being necessary to survive in an increasingly challenging media environment.

In conclusion, our findings show a positive endorsement of branded content among those involved in these units, which include managing editors, editors and product managers. It should be clarified that our study examines only commercial enterprises where the integration of such practices is more common and reflects professionals' adaptation to comply with a news organization's goals and values (Goyanes and Rodríguez-Castro 2019).

While this work addresses the creation of branded content teams and the attitudes of the professionals within those units, it does have certain limitations and shortcomings. More data is needed, especially to gain a deeper understanding of how branded content teams impact the entire structure of the newsrooms. By selecting a sample that is more representative of journalists and reporters, we could better assess how their practices and routines may be affected by the existence of those units. Another limitation is linked to the absence of an extensive content analysis that makes it possible to measure the reality of published pieces, specifically in terms of labelling. It would also be convenient to set up field work research efforts that measure the degree to which these teams are isolated from the rest of the editorial staff, and whether these organizational models provide effective protection against internal or external commercial pressure. Future research should further expand on the three organizational models that have been identified for branded content teams and their evolution in Spain's media industry.

Notes

1. In Spain, "sponsored content" —as opposed to "branded content"— consists of pieces, formats or sections created entirely by the newsroom and then financed by a brand, and labeled accordingly (using formulas such as "sponsored by" ["patrocinado por"] or "supported by" ["con el apoyo de"]). The professionals involved in our study do not engage with this latter form of sponsorship.

2. The Spanish translation of "branded content" is "contenido de marca," but the interviewees regularly used the English version instead, sometimes shortened to simply "branded" and omitting "content." Spanish journalism professionals frequently use English terms for innovative phenomena, such as "product manager," "fact-checking," and "clickbait," as well as acronyms like "SEO" (search engine optimization) and "CMS" (content management system).

Disclosure Statement

No potential conflict of interest was reported by the author(s).

ORCID

Miguel Carvajal (iD) http://orcid.org/0000-0001-6547-6171

References

Amazeen, M. A. 2019. "News in an Era of Content Confusion: Effects of News Use Motivations and Context on Native Advertising and Digital News Perceptions." *Journalism & Mass Communication Quarterly* 97 (1): 161–187. doi:10.1177/1077699019886589.

Amazeen, M. A., and A. R. Muddiman. 2018. "Saving Media or Trading on Trust?" *Digital Journalism* 6 (2): 176–195.

Amazeen, M. A., and B. W. Wojdynski. 2020. "The Effects of Disclosure Format on Native Advertising Recognition and Audience Perceptions of Legacy and Online News Publishers." *Journalism* 21 (12): 1920–1965.

Artemas, K., T. P. Vos, and M. Duffy. 2018. "Journalism Hits a Wall." *Journalism Studies* 19 (7): 1004–1020.

Asociación de la Prensa de Madrid (APM). 2015. "Informe anual de la profesión periodística."

Atal, M. R. 2018. "The Cultural and Economic Power of Advertisers in the Business Press." *Journalism* 19 (8): 1078–1095.

Autocontrol. 1996, 2019. "Code of Advertising Practice."

Bachmann, P., S. Hunziker, and T. Rüedy. 2019. "Selling Their Souls to the Advertisers? How Native Advertising Degrades the Quality of Prestige Media Outlets." *Journal of Media Business Studies* 16 (2): 95–109.

Banjac, S., and F. Hanusch. 2020. "A Question of Perspective: Exploring Audiences' Views of Journalistic Boundaries." *New Media & Society* 1–19.

Baumann, S. 2013. "Adapting to the Brave New World: Innovative Organisational Strategies for Media Companies." In *Media Innovation. A Multidisciplinary Study of Change*, edited by T. Storsul and A. H. Krumsvik, 77–92. Göteborg: Nordicom.

Braun, V., and V. Clarke. 2006. "Using Thematic Analysis in Psychology." *Qualitative Research in Psychology* 3 (2): 77–101.

Carlson, M. 2015. "When News Sites Go Native: Redefining the Advertising–Editorial Divide in Response to Native Advertising." *Journalism: Theory, Practice & Criticism* 16 (7): 849–865.

Carlson, M., and S. C. Lewis. 2015. *Boundaries of Journalism: Professionalism, Practices and Participation*. London: Routledge.

Carvajal, M., F. Arias, S. Negredo, and A. Amoedo. 2015. "Aproximación Metodológica al Estudio de la Innovación en Periodismo." *Observatorio* 9 (3): 15–31.

Carvajal, M., and J. A. García Avilés. 2008. "From Newspapers to Multimedia Groups." *Journalism Practice* 2 (3): 453–462.

Carvajal, M., and J. M. V. Pastor. 2018. "Revenue Streams within Spain's Journalism Industry, According to Its Editors." *Hipertext.Net* 17: 83–94.

Coddington, M. 2015. "The Wall Becomes a Curtain: Revisiting Journalism's News–Business Boundary." In *Boundaries of Journalism: Professionalism, Practices, and Participation*, edited by Carlson, M., Lewis, S. C., 67–82. New York: Routledge.

comScore. 2019. "Data downloaded from comScore website in Spain."

Cornia, A., A. Sehl, and R. K. Nielsen. 2020. "We No Longer Live in a Time of Separation: A Comparative Analysis of How Editorial and Commercial Integration Became a Norm." *Journalism* 21 (2): 172–190.

Deuze, M., and T. Witschge. 2017. "Beyond Journalism: Theorizing the Transformation of Journalism." *Journalism* 19 (2): 1–17.

Duffy, A., and L. C. Rui Jun. 2020. "'It's Complicated': Cognitive Dissonance and the Evolving Relationship between Editorial and Advertising in US Newsrooms." *Journalism Practice*.

FAPE, Code of Ethics. 1993, 2017.

Feng, S., and M. Ots. 2018. "Seeing Native Advertising Production via the Business Model Lens: The Case of Forbes's BrandVoice Unit." *Journal of Interactive Advertising* 18 (2): 148–161.

Ferrer-Conill, R. 2016. "Camouflaging Church as State." *Journalism Studies* 17 (7): 904–914.

Ferrer-Conill, R., E. Knudsen, C. Lauerer, and A. Barnoy. 2020. "The Visual Boundaries of Journalism: Native Advertising and the Convergence of Editorial and Commercial Content." *Digital Journalism*

García-Avilés, J. A. 2018. "Resultados de la Innovación en Los Laboratorios de Medios: El Caso de El Confidencial.LAB." *El Profesional de la Información* 27 (2): 359–366.

García-Avilés, J. A., M. Carvajal, and F. Arias-Robles. 2018. "Implantación de la Innovación en Los Cibermedios Españoles: Análisis de Las Percepciones de Los Periodistas." *Revista Latina de Comunicación Social* 73 (3): 369–384.

García-Avilés, J. A., M. Carvajal, A. De Lara-González, and F. Arias-Robles. 2018. "Developing an Index of Media Innovation in a National Market. The Case of Spain." *Journalism Studies* 19 (1): 25–42.

Goyanes, M., and M. Rodríguez-Castro. 2019. "Commercial Pressures in Spanish Newsrooms: Between Love, Struggle and Resistance." *Journalism Studies* 20 (8): 1088–1109.

Hardy, J., I. MacRury, and H. Powell. 2018. *The Advertising Handbook*. London: Routledge.

Harms, B., T. Bijmolt, and J. C. Hoekstra. 2017. "Digital Native Advertising: Practitioner Perspectives and a Research Agenda." *Journal of Interactive Advertising* 17 (2): 80–91.

Instituto Nacional de Estadística. 2020. https://www.ine.es/

Küng, L. 2017. "Reflections on the Ascendancy of Technology in the Media and Its Implications for Organisations and Their Leaders." *The Journal of Media Innovations* 4 (1): 77–81.

Li, Y., and Y. Wang. 2019. "Brand Disclosure and Source Partiality Affect Native Advertising Recognition and Media Credibility." *Newspaper Research Journal* 40 (3): 299–316.

Lynch, L. 2018. *Native Advertising: Advertorial Disruption in the 21st-Century News*. New York: Routledge.

Mancinas Chávez, R., J. A. Moreno-Cabezudo, and N. Ruiz-Alba. 2019. "Liderazgo de la Prensa Nativa Digital Frente a la Prensa de Referencia en España. El Caso Cifuentes en Eldiario.es, El Confidencial, El País y El Mundo." *Revista Latina de Comunicación Social* 74 (12): 1434–1451.

Nielsen, R. K., and S. A. Ganter. 2018. "Dealing with Digital Intermediaries: A Case Study of the Relations between Publishers and Platforms." *New Media & Society* 20 (4): 1600–1617.

Perales Albert, A. 2018. "Reflexiones en Torno al Engan̄o en Las Comunicaciones Comerciales", *Methaodos*." *Revista de Ciencias Sociales* 6 (1): 52–63.

Poutanen, P.,. V. Luoma-Aho, and E. Suhanko. 2016. "Ethical Challenges of Hybrid Editors." *International Journal on Media Management* 18 (2): 99–116.

Reuters. 2019. "Digital News Report." Reuters Institute for the Study of Journalism.

Salaverría, R. 2015. "Los Labs Como Fórmula de Innovación en Los Medios." *El Profesional de la Información* 24 (4): 397–404.

Schauster, E. E., P. Ferrucci, and M. S. Neill. 2016. "Native Advertising is the New Journalism: How Deception Affects Social Responsibility." *American Behavioral Scientist* 60 (12): 1408–1424.

Valero-Pastor, J. M., and M. Carvajal. 2017. "Organización de Equipos Multidisciplinares: El Periodismo de Datos en El País." *Textual & Visual Media* 10: 247–262.

Valero-Pastor, J. M., and J. A. González-Alba. 2018. "Las Startups Periodísticas Como Ejemplos de Innovación en el Mercado Mediático Español. Estudio de Casos." *Revista Latina de Comunicación Social* 73 (4): 556–582.

Waldenström, A., J. Wiik, and U. Andersson. 2019. "Conditional Autonomy." *Journalism Practice* 13 (4): 493–508.

Watson, S., E. Bell, N. Rashidian, and A. Hartstone. 2018. *The Future of Advertising and Publishing.* New York: Columbia University Academic Commons.

Westlund, O., and S. C. Lewis. 2014. "Agents of Media Innovations." *The Journal of Media Innovations* 1 (2): 10–35.

Witschge, T., and G. Nygren. 2009. "Journalistic Work: A Profession under Pressure?" *Journal of Media Business Studies* 6 (1): 37–59.

Wojdynski, B. W., and N. J. Evans. 2016. "Going Native: Effects of Disclosure Position and Language on the Recognition and Evaluation of Online Native." *Journal of Advertising* 45 (2): 157–168.

Sponsored Content in Spanish Media: Strategies, Transparency, and Ethical Concerns

Dolors Palau-Sampio

ABSTRACT
Profound upheavals and the search for a viable business model have led the news industry to explore new sources of revenue. The mainstream Spanish media have set up special units to produce branded content, advertising that is integrated into editorial content. This article presents a multi-faceted approach to this practice in Spain, including interviews with branded content lab managers, a survey of journalists ($N = 170$), and content analysis of articles ($N = 331$) published by the six main legacy and digital native media companies in June and July of 2019. Results show inadequate disclosure, which makes it difficult for readers to distinguish between branded and editorial content. The journalists surveyed associate native advertising with the risk of losing credibility. This study reveals that the financial sector is the most active in supporting branded content productions, followed by energy and infrastructure, distribution and food industry, and phone companies. This research also unveils advertiser interest in connecting brand image to environment and sustainability values, together with a macro-issue encompassing well-being, sports, and health. This is consistent with the fact that the strongest role performance observed has been for service information, especially regarding tips for the economy, followed by those of the civic and infotainment categories.

Introduction

Over the last decade, the news industry has faced the combined effects of emerging digital technology and the turbulence caused by the search for a viable business model in the context of a global financial crisis (Franklin 2014). Profound disruption (Anderson, Bell, and Shirky 2014; Ryfe 2019) has significantly transformed not only production and consumption, but also the way in which a traditionally well-protected media industry is financed (Cozzolino, Verona, and Rothaermel 2018).

A drop in advertising expenditures along with a lower price in the digital environment (Picard 2004) has compelled legacy media to develop different survival strategies, yet none of them alone has been able to restore previous stability. The implementation of digital paywalls (Carson 2015; Arrese 2016), which have been scarcely effective considering the reluctance to pay (Newman et al. 2019), has been accompanied in other cases by the imposition of commercial strategies and infotainment solutions ahead of media quality (Picard 2004; Broersma and Peters 2013; Ferrer-Conill 2016). In this context, the advertising industry has also experienced a paradigm shift (Walmsley 2019), evolving from a product- to a consumer-centric perspective in which 'the pursuit of consumer brand engagement' is the key (Gambetti and Graffigna 2010, 801). New consumer expectations and habits, unprecedented commercial competition, the impact of media audience fragmentation, and digitization 'within changing media ecologies', have all reshaped the advertising industry over the last few years (Hardy, Powell, and MacRury 2018, xvi), which has been reflected in the media.

Involving emotional, cognitive and behavioural aspects (Kahn 1990), the concept of engagement is central to native advertising, one of the solutions adopted by digital media outlets to overcome the funding crisis. However, in its search for compelling messages, native advertising is also challenging the conventional divide, the so-called 'wall' (Coddington 2015) between editorial and commercial content. Thus, by allowing for mimetic advertising strategies and collaborating closely with content creation, media editors lend their own credibility to brands (Lynch 2018). Despite being a global trend, the implementation of branded content (Ferrer-Conill 2016) along with its laws and self-regulation rules (Lynch 2018) are influenced by national and regional culture and practice, and by the inherent characteristics of the media systems (Hallin and Mancini 2004; Hardy 2008).

Much research has examined branded content from the perspective of editors, business executives, lab managers, and professionals (Li 2019b; Serazio 2020; Hernández 2018; Carvajal and Barinagarrementeria 2019), as well as the content they produce and audience attitudes (Li 2019a; Campbell and Marks 2015; Wojdynski and Evans 2016; Krouwer, Poels, and Paulussen 2020). This study approaches the increasingly porous boundaries between the commercial and journalistic rationale in the Spanish context with a threefold objective: first, to analyse branded content articles and their disclosure in six digital media; second, to evaluate the media's reasons for adopting this type of content and its management; and third, to examine these practices from the perspective of the professional implications for journalists.

Literature Review

Branded Content Features and Disclosure

Under the umbrella term 'native advertising', many practices, including branded content, content recommendation, and sponsored content, refer to 'advertisements that are seamlessly integrated into editorial content' in order to be more effective than invasive digital advertising (Levi 2015, 649), and to avoid ad blockers. The evolution experienced by the advertising industry in recent years has led the IAB (Interactive Advertising Bureau) to include 'branded content' as one of the three main types of native advertising (IAB US. 2019). It is defined as 'paid content from a brand that is published in the same format as full editorial on a publisher's site, generally in conjunction with the publisher content teams themselves' (7).

Different attempts to describe branded content have stressed the relative absence of overt product promotion along with content that is 'relevant, entertaining or interesting' (IAB Spain 2019b, 64), which compels audiences to 'engage with the brand based on a [non-interruptive] pull logic due to its entertainment, information and/or education value' (Asmussen et al. 2016, 34).

In Spain, branded content is not explicitly regulated, but existing legislation does apply. Some examples include the General Law 34/1988 of Publicity, the Law 3/1991 on Unfair Competition, and the General Law 7/2010 on Audiovisual Communication, among others (IAB Spain 2019c, 5). However, there is no formal regulation on how to notify the consumer that these are paid ads. While the IAB US emphasizes that 'this content requires disclosure to the consumer that it is paid for/an ad' (2019, 7), the Spanish White Paper dismisses the explicit inclusion of the label 'advertising', and recommends 'strategies such as featured content, brought to you by...' (IAB Spain 2019b, 49).

Research recognizes the need to standardize the different national traditions in Europe (Lynch 2018), and emphasizes the fact that while the US Federal Trade Commission updated rules for native advertising in 2015, the European Union has not done likewise, and so the key regulation remains the Unfair Commercial Practices Directive 2005 (Hardy 2017). Proper identification involves the audience's right to transparency. This can avoid deception (Newman, Levy, and Nielsen 2015) and increase audience credibility (Campbell and Marks 2015; Krouwer, Poels, and Paulussen 2020, 17). Following these insights, we pose the next research question as follows:

RQ1a: How is branded content identified in digital news publications?

RQ1b: Are digital native news media more likely than legacy news media to publish branded content?

RQ1c: Which sectors of economic activity are commonly featured in published branded content?

RQ1d: Are branded content topics linked to a particular role performance (civic, service or infotainment)?

Labs and Sustainability

Influenced by antecedents including the patronage formula of radio soap operas during the 1920s and 1930s, branded content came into play at the beginning of the 21st century, with the BMW short film series *The Hire* in 2001–2002 amongst early examples (Serazio 2018). Even though this trend has appeared only recently in countries such as Spain (De Aguilera-Moyano, Baños-González, and Ramírez-Perdiguero 2015), it has become highly relevant: 92% of advertisers claim to use branded content – a third more than in 2013 – and investment grew by 41% (BCMA 2019, 34). Moreover, journalists and leading editors strongly believe that this option is likely to become one of the most important sources of digital revenue, both in Spain (APM (Asociación de la Prensa de Madrid) 2018) and around the world (Newman 2018).

However, the growing importance of branded content is not without controversy. A report sponsored by the Church of Scientology, published in *The Atlantic* in 2013, triggered alarms with regard to 'allowing an advertiser access to editorial space in a visual manner mimicking other news content' (Carlson 2015, 850). A number of studies have examined the erosion of the principle of separation between the editorial and advertising domains, and the establishment of practices and norms of integration in parts of digital native publishing (Coddington 2015; Carlson 2015; Artemas, Vos, and Duffy 2016; Hardy 2017; Cornia, Sehl, and Nielsen 2020). Scholars have analysed how powerful actors within the news publishing industry have advocated for native advertising as a means to ensure their continued existence (Couldry and Turow 2014; Ferrer-Conill 2016).

Unlike brand journalism (Bull 2013), produced by brands for publication in their own media (Arrese and Pérez-Latre 2017), branded content includes content hosted by media publishers and produced by the brand, by publishers, or jointly. Its pattern of production surpasses that of the four business models described by Sonderman and Tran (2013): Underwriting (sponsoring of normal reporting), Agency (custom content created in partnership with a brand), Platform (brands publish their own messages on a dedicated space provided by publishers), and Aggregated/repurposed (brands can use archived real journalism in a new package). While larger media companies have adopted the agency model, founded labs, and employed journalists and specialized writers to create brand stories (Sonderman and Tran 2013), branded content in smaller publications (Campbell and Lutostanski 2019) is mainly produced by the regular editorial staff (Bilton 2014). In both cases, the assistance of external staff is sometimes used (Laursen and Stone 2016). Considering the realignment of editorial and commercial boundaries involving branded content (Li 2019b), and the experience of branded content labs that have been launched by leading digital media in Spain since 2014, the next research question is set forth:

RQ2: What are the aims and principles governing the development of branded content labs?

Professional Identity, Ethics and Blurred Boundaries

Despite the current importance of native advertising as a source of revenue (IAB Spain 2019a), it is not without ethical controversy. Beyond the camouflaged strategies adopted and the deceptive appearance for audiences (Ferrer-Conill 2016; Han, Drumwright, and Go 2018), native advertising touches the heart of the professional journalistic identity (Kovach and Rosenstiel 2001; Deuze 2005). It weakens journalistic autonomy and contributes to the elimination of 'the distance between journalists and their funding sources, altering news practices' (Carlson 2015, 862).

Native advertising challenges the professional duties inspired by the social responsibility theory of the press (Siebert et al. 1956), which is 'to communicate to the public from the impartial perspective of the public good' (Ward 2005). Contrary to public interest, native advertising 'creates the risk that non-advertising content will be shaped in accordance with advertisers' wishes' (Hardy 2017, 83).

As in the case of advertorials designed to influence citizen opinion (Cooper and Nownes 2004; Hardy 2017), native advertising can be used as part of PR campaigns by governmental (Golan and Viatchaninova 2014) or commercial organizations. Research

Table 1. Triangulation method.

RQs	Aim	Method	Scope
1	Branded content characteristics	Content analysis	Items published ($N = 331$)
2	Production and management	Semi-structured interviews	Lab managers ($N = 5$)
3	Professional perceptions	Online survey	Journalists ($N = 170$)

Source: Compiled by the authors

on the ExxonMobile advertorials in the *NYT* warns of the misleading information (Supran and Oreskes 2017) that this form of 'outside lobbying' (Brown, Waltzer, and Waltzer 2001) might provide, and raises significant questions, particularly in a context of economic challenges. In this sense, Levi warns that 'native advertising will likely prove a Faustian bargain for the press' and 'may undercut the very journalism likely to promote democracy most robustly' (2015, 651).

Risk becomes especially dangerous when something presented as an option to ensure sustainability might turn into an unprecedented threat in terms of media trust and credibility (Amazeen and Muddiman 2018). Piety has suggested that native advertising 'threatens to kill the golden goose of editorial credibility' (2016, 100), leading consumers to distrust all content. When analysing the mid and long-term effects of blurring the boundary between native advertising and news, researchers refer to 'reputational' effects (Zeng 2018), 'negative perceptions of news credibility and quality' (Wojdynski and Evans 2016, 166), and ultimately, further erosion of public trust in the media (Ferrer-Conill 2016), which are key factors in the future of both the industry and journalists as well.

As the debate increasingly focuses on the transfer of editorial control to advertisers and its consequences for the standard exercise of journalism, we wanted to gain more insight from Spanish professionals, for which we pose the third research question:

> RQ3: How do journalists evaluate the adoption of branded content by the publications for which they work?

Methodology

A data triangulation method was used in order to analyse branded content management, production and professional perceptions in Spain by performing semi-structured interviews with labs directors, content analysis of published items, and an online survey of journalists (Table 1). The study focuses on six Spanish news websites, including legacy (*Elpais.com* [EP], *Elmundo.es* [EM], and *Lavanguardia.com* [LV]) and digital native media (*Elconfidencial.com* [EC], *Elespanol.com* [EE], and *Eldiario.es* [ED]), based on several business models, having implemented some kind of paywall (EM, EE, LV), membership (ED) or only advertising finance (EP, EC). These websites were ranked as having the highest number of unique users (PR Noticias 2019).

Content Analysis: Sampling Strategy and Coding

The first step of the research was to gain insight into branded content published by the six aforementioned media. Considering that such content is first showcased in each of the media's homepages, they were reviewed once a day – between 8 pm and

Table 2. Datasheet for content analysis.

Items	Options
Brand sector	Banking and Finance; Energy and Infrastructure; Distribution and Food Industry; Phone [companies]; Football, Health, Automotive Industry; Environment; Culture and Education; Others.
Issues	Environment and Sustainability; Economy; Well-being and Lifestyle; Sports; Technology; Health; Culture and Education; Rights and Social Issues; Entertainment; Housing; Others.
Role performance	-*Civic role*: Promotes citizen involvement in social, political, and cultural lives, with focus on underrepresented individuals. -*Service role*: Provides tips, advice and guidance. -*Infotainment role*: Appeals to audiences' emotions by story-telling tactics, including personalization.

Source: Compiled by the authors

10 pm – during June and July of 2019 to obtain the sample. As disclosure methods varied, the sampling strategy included a total of 889 items involving a variety of modalities rather than only traditional advertising. Ambiguous expressions were removed (i.e. advertorial, sponsored sections, content created by the brand for different media), which resulted from a comprehensive revision for the purpose of being consistent with the IAB definition of branded content (2019b) and concordant with the exchanges with the lab managers interviewed. After a second round and the removal of duplicates, the sample came down to 331 unique branded content articles from *Elpais.com* ($n = 95$), *Elmundo.es* ($n = 60$), *Lavanguardia.com* ($n = 56$), *Elconfidencial.com* ($n = 55$), *Elespanol.com* ($n = 29$), and *Eldiario.es* ($n = 36$). The links to these native advertisements were saved in an Excel file.

Content analysis of the final sample was carried out using a designed datasheet (Table 2) to identify: 1) brand sectors involved in branded content strategies; 2) the main topics of the items; and 3) the resulting role performance. We proceeded by associating the brand to a sector of activity, analysing the complete text to determine the main topic, and assigning a role performance. While the categories of Topic and Brand Sector were defined after the complete sample analysis was carried out, Role Performance used the codebook developed by Mellado (2015) and Mellado and Van Dalen (2017) as a reference, which has been applied in research on native advertising (Li 2019a). To guarantee reliability and consistency in the qualitative analysis, the only codifier performed a test-retest of 33% of the registers until complete agreement was reached before continuing to the entire data codification.

Once coded, the data was entered into the SPSS Spreadsheet and processed using R software. Various methods were employed. First, the Pearson chi-square test was used to test the strength of relationships between variables with a significance level of 5%. Second, through a log-linear model, we identified associations between the variables.

Interviews

The second step in the research involved semi-structured interviews with the branded content lab managers in order to deepen our knowledge regarding the production and characteristics of this content. The telephone interviews, which lasted between 45 min and one hour each, were conducted in September and October of 2019 with

Table 3. Branded content labs.

Media	Unit	Launch date	Team	Provides services to
EP	Prisa Brand Solutions	2014	100 professionals in the newsroom, product, and commercial departments	PRISA Group
EM	UE Studio	2014	20 professionals. *Profiles*: journalist, designer and creative, audio-visual production, analysts	Unidad Editorial Group
LV	BrandsLab	2015	12 professionals. *Profiles*: journalist, designer, SEO, reporting and analytics expert	Godó Group
EC	ECBrands	2015	12 professionals	*Elconfidencial.com*
EE	Marcas Ñ	2015	3 journalists supported by newsroom professionals	*Elespanol.com*
ED	ED Contenido Creativo	2016	—	*Eldiario.es*

Source: Compiled by the authors

the managers of EP, EM, LV, EC and EE; the team manager of ED did not respond to our request. Interviews were recorded and transcribed after carrying out an analysis and identification of quotations focussing on points of view regarding branded content and management of the units (Table 3).

Journalist Surveys

The third step in the research consisted of an online survey of Spanish journalists ($N = 170$), conducted during the first three weeks of October 2019. In order to gather their insight, we collaborated with a dozen professional associations[1] who distributed the survey in a Google formulary. The answers collected through the survey were reasonably balanced in terms of gender (56% men and 44% women) and years of experience (32% had more than 30 years, 38% between 16-30 years, and 30% 15 years or less). The survey sample included journalists working in radio and television (34%), print and digital newspapers and reviews (37%), or corporate communication (25%). Regarding their professions, 48% were newsroom journalists, camera operators or photographers, 23% were editors or section heads, and 23% were managers.

This research combines descriptive and inferential statistical analysis using the SPSS 25.0 programme. First, the chi-square test was used to check whether there was any significant association between the qualitative variables. Second, due to the nature of the data (not normally distributed variables) and the characteristics of the sample, the non-parametric methods Kruskal-Wallis and Mann-Whitney tests for comparing independent samples were used.

Results

Branded Content: Topics, Role Performance, Sectors Involved and Disclosure

RQ1a examined branded content disclosure in six Spanish media. Results showed a wide range of names that have been adopted to deliver branded content (Table 4). The most common are 'A project from' or 'Brought to you by', but the same media

Table 4. Branded content labels.

Media	Identification
EP	A project of [Un proyecto de], Content brought to you by [Contenido ofrecido por]
EM	A project of, UE Studio
LV	A project of, Powered by [sic], Brought to you by Brandslab
EC	Powered by, Brands balcony [El balcón de las marcas]
ED	Content brought to you by, ED Creative Content [Contenido Creativo]
EE	In partnership with [Con la colaboración de] MarcasÑ

Source: Compiled by the authors

Table 5. Sectors involved in branded content.

		Media*				Role Performance**					
		Legacy		Digital Native		Service		Civic		Infotainment	
		N	%	N	%	N	%	N	%	N	%
Banking & Finance	56	16.9	35	10.6	60	18.1	28	8.5	3	0.9	
Culture & Education	7	2.1	2	0.6	4	1.2	4	1.2	1	0.3	
Distribution & Food Ind.	24	7.2	13	3.9	23	7.0	5	1.5	9	2.7	
Energy & Infrastructure	28	8.5	19	5.7	7	2.1	40	12.1	0	0	
Environment	4	1.2	8	2.4	1	0.3	10	3.0	1	0.3	
Football	28	8.5	1	0.3	7	2.1	15	4.5	7	2.1	
Health	0	0	26	7.8	26	7.8	0	0.0	0	0	
Others	3	0.9	7	2.1	5	1.5	4	1.2	1	0.3	
Phone	33	10	3	0.9	23	7.0	10	3.0	3	0.9	
Services	16	4.8	6	1.8	18	5.4	4	1.2	0	0	
Sector of activity	Automotive Industry	12	3.6	0	0	8	2.4	4	1.2	0	0

Note: *Media & Sector: $x^2 = 90.02$, $d.f. = 10$, $p. < .000$
**Role Performance & Sector: $x^2 = 130.78$, $d.f. = 20$, $p. < .000$

often combine two or more labels, or even the name of the lab to identify this type of sponsored content.

Following RQ1b, legacy and digital-only news media were compared. During the period analysed, the three legacy media published two thirds ($n = 211$) of the branded content items gathered in June-July 2019, while online-only media provided 33.2% ($n = 120$). This reveals the strength of non-digital native media – particularly EP – in attracting emerging revenue sources in the digital environment. Furthermore, branded content has been adopted both by media that have implemented paywalls as well as and by those that are funded only by advertising.

This research aims to gain insight into the relationship between the media, sectors, topics, and role performance. Thus, a chi-square test was used to prove dependency by pairs. Considering that all p-values obtained were significant, a log-linear model was used to identify associations between the variables.

One of the purposes of RQ1c was to determine which sectors were more involved in branded content activity. The log-linear model did not find significant interactions between 'Media' and 'Sectors of activity'. However, it did identify relevant categories: banking and finance ($n = 91$), energy and infrastructure ($n = 47$), distribution and food industry ($n = 37$), phone ($n = 36$), football ($n = 29$) and health ($n = 26$) (Table 5).

When searching for dependency between 'Media' and 'Role performance', the log-linear analysis detected significant interaction between legacy media and Infotainment. In both types of media, service is the most noteworthy category, followed by civic and infotainment roles (Table 6).

Table 6. Media and role performance.

		Role performance					
		Service		Civic		Infotainment	
		N	%	N	%	N	%
Media	Legacy	111	33.5	78	23.6	22	6.6
	Digital Native	71	21.5	46	13.9	3	0.9

Note: $x^2 = 7000.2$, $d.f. = 2$, $p. < .003$

The results also revealed a relationship between the categories 'Sector of activity' and 'Role performance' (Table 5). In the first case, the log-linear model pointed to banking and finance, energy and infrastructure, and football as significant categories. Moreover, the two last, along with the environment sector, are most commonly associated with civic role performance.

Although the log-linear model did not find significant interaction between 'Issues' and 'Sectors of activity' (Table 7), some relevant variables were found in the last category: banking and finance, distribution and food industry, energy and infrastructure, football, health, and phone. Moreover, the category 'Topics' shows the following options to be meaningful: environment and sustainability ($n = 70$), economy ($n = 61$), well-being and lifestyle ($n = 53$), and sports ($n = 43$).

Considering the active supporters of branded content, we were interested in the issues presented in order to engage audiences. Brands revealed their links regarding environment and sustainability (21.1%), economy (18.4%), and a macro-issue involving well-being and lifestyle, sports, and health (37%). According to the results, energy and infrastructure, banking and finance, and the automotive industry are more inclined to present themselves as being associated with environmental and sustainability issues (73%). The distribution and food sector, however, tends to support articles dealing with well-being and sport (84%), while the banking and finance sectors are associated with the economy, and well-being and lifestyle (72.5%).

To answer RQ1d, we attempted to identify associations between 'Issues' and 'Role performance'. The log-linear model revealed that environment and sustainability, rights and social issues ($n = 17$), and sports are significant, as well as the interaction between service & economy, and service & environment and sustainability. The first case is where nearly 17% of service interactions are concentrated, while the second is most frequently associated with the civic role (17.5%) (Table 8).

Production and Management

Branded content units in the most influential Spanish digital media were launched between 2014 and 2016 as autonomous business units following the agency model (Sonderman and Tran 2013). The personnel running these branded content units were interviewed to answer RQ2, and they agreed that production and revenues have been rising continuously since 2017. ECBrands (ECB) confirmed that between 2017 and 2019, revenues increased six fold, from one million to six million euros. UE Studio (UES) estimated that the revenue received was approximately 12% of total revenues.

Prisa Brand Solutions (PBS) highlighted that big brands were crucial in boosting the power of branded content, as they considered it to be 'an interesting way to approach

Table 7. Topics and sectors of activity.

Sector of activity	Issues		Culture & Education	Economy	Entertainment	Environment & Sustainability	Health	Housing	Others	Rights & Social Issues	Sports	Technology	Well-being and Lifestyle
	Automotive Industry	N	0	0	0	9	0	0	0	2	0	1	0
		%	0	0	0	2.7	0	0	0	0.6	0	0.3	0
	Banking & Finance	N	2	43	0	7	0	5	1	4	1	5	23
		%	0.6	13	0	2.1	0	1.5	0.3	1.2	0.3	1.5	7
	Culture & Education	N	7	1	0	0	0	0	0	0	0	1	0
		%	2.1	0.3	0	0	0	0	0	0	0	0.3	0
	Distribution & Food Ind.	N	0	0	0	2	2	0	0	2	9	0	22
		%	0	0	0	0.6	0.6	0	0	0.6	2.7	0	6.6
	Energy & Infrastructure	N	3	0	0	35	0	0	1	2	2	3	1
		%	0.9	0	0	10.6	0	0	0.3	0.6	0.6	0.9	0.3
	Environment	N	0	0	0	12	0	0	0	0	0	0	0
		%	0	0	0	3.6	0	0	0	0	0	0	0
	Football	N	1	0	2	0	0	0	0	0	26	0	0
		%	0.3	0	0.6	0	0	0	0	0	7.8	0	0
	Health	N	0	0	0	0	22	0	0	0	2	2	0
		%	0	0	0	0	6.6	0	0	0	0.6	0.6	0
	Others	N	1	2	2	1	0	1	0	2	0	0	1
		%	0.3	0.6	0.6	0.3	0	0.3	0	0.6	0	0	0.3
	Phone	N	0	8	1	3	1	0	2	6	2	13	0
		%	0	2.4	0.3	0.9	0.3	0	0.6	1.8	0.6	3.9	0
	Services	N	1	7	3	1	0	0	1	0	1	2	6
		%	0.3	2.1	0.9	0.3	0	0	0.3	0	0.3	0.6	1.8

Note: $x^2 = 908.49$, $d.f. = 100$, $p. < .000$

Table 8. Issues and role performance.

Role Performance	Issues		Culture & Education	Economy	Entertainment	Environment & Sustainability	Health	Housing	Others	Rights & Social Issues	Sports	Technology	Well-being and Lifestyle
Role Performance	Service	N	8	56	4	11	25	6	4	0	13	22	33
		%	2.4	16.9	1.2	3.3	7.5	1.8	1.2	0	3.9	6.6	10
	Civic	N	6	5	2	58	0	0	1	17	18	5	12
		%	1,8	1.5	0.6	17.5	0	0	0.3	5.1	5.4	1.5	3.6
	Infotainment	N	1	0	2	1	0	0	0	1	12	0	8
		%	0.3	0	0.6	0.3	0	0	0	0.3	3.6	0	2.4

Note: $x^2 = 195.46$, d.f. $= 20$, $p. < .000$

the reader', which demonstrates 'their turning to this way to communicate' (UES). In this regard, one of the interviewees described the strength of branded content as a step forward in the brand journalism trend (Bull 2013), which started in 2015. Unlike brand platforms, media companies offer a showcase for branded content and 'provide value in addition to a communication strategy' (BrandsLab, BRL).

The understanding of what is involved in branded content required a considerable amount of 'evangelization work' (BRL). The people in charge of these departments agree that advertisers are increasingly conscious of its specificity and distinction from advertorials (Cooper and Nownes 2004; Hardy 2017), especially those of large corporations that consider it a suitable alternative to advertisements (PBS). The production of branded content starts with a briefing and is 'tailor-made' for the client (MAÑ). UES points out that a work team is set up according to the request submitted. Next, the team prepares a proposal for the client, which can often be redesigned with the client's own ideas. 'We organize our [branded content] units as an advertising agency with regard to professional methods and systems', stresses ECB, 'which has reduced the product return by the client to nearly zero'. The managers referred to branded content as 'interesting enough to be published, even if it is paid for' (MAÑ), or as content that is 'relevant to the reader and interesting to the brand' (PBS). Overall, they ensure that this content is on a par with editorial content in terms of reader attention and interest: 'The majority of the articles sponsored by brands are among those with a major readership ratio … They have been integrated into the newspaper ecosystem, thanks to stories that generate engagement' (ECB). UES expressed this in similar terms when explaining that branded content 'attracts new unique users and entices them to stay longer and retweet the content, which is positive for both [media and brands]. We have examples of resounding success; sometimes the digital edition director calls us to republish a video'.

When asked about the red lines drawn regarding publishing, PBS ensures that all content identified as branded content follows the *El País* style guide, and states that 'branded information material should be perfectly [equivalent] to organic content'. While MAÑ mentioned that branded content was subject to editorial criteria, BRL and UES referred to periodic meetings with the editorial staff responsible for branded content at *Lavanguardia.com* and *Elmundo.es* respectively, 'to inform them about sensitive content' (BRL), or to explain 'a new proposal for a client that will be heavily involved' (UES). In fact, the economic investment is significant: 'An advertising campaign of 50,000 euros can be effective. For branded content, however, you can do nothing with this same budget' (UES).

Among the potential risks of publishing branded content is editorial integrity (Sonderman and Tran 2013). One of the interviewees emphasized this particular relationship, since a brand 'decides to associate their name with a publication', but underscores the fact that the media 'needs to consider what they offer on the web page'. For example, 'If a product contains a lot of sugar and the brand wants to associate itself with a healthy lifestyle, we cannot compromise our name just because the content is sponsored. The newspaper also has a responsibility regarding what is published' (ECB).

Proper identification of branded content is fundamental for all five managers interviewed, who affirm that it is always identified in order to avoid deceiving the reader.

'Branded content that is undisclosed will not be found', declares Marcas Ñ (MAÑ), while ECB states: 'We are inflexible about not publishing [branded content] unless it is identified as sponsored'. However, when asked about potential confusion, UES revealed that the boundaries surrounding branded content are quite blurred, even for professionals, and encouraged IAB Europe to revise native advertising and content marketing, as the US Federal Trade Commission has done, which is in line with appeals by scholars for the standardization of rules (Lynch 2018; Hardy 2017).

According to the teams in charge, the amount of branded content that can be published in a digital issue is clearly defined by editors to ensure balance as well as 'content placement' (BRL). Managers admit that the branded content limit is set at a maximum of three (ECB) or five (BRL) spots on the homepage.

The importance of achieving results is demonstrated in some strategies implemented by the media. After 24 h on the homepage, content with larger budgets, or that which has not reached the expected number of views can be republished in special sections. 'Unlike agencies, we own the publishing surface, and when content needs more views, we change the title or the picture, or we try republishing' (UES).

Even if the size of branded content departments varies widely (Table 3), all of them have reported an increase in the number of employees. 'Work groups for the projects last longer than they did earlier, and we are required to grow' (UES). Units are expanding not only the number of professional profiles, but the variety as well, especially to reinforce the audio-visual, analytical, and reporting areas, as 'clients are no longer satisfied with the number of pages viewed and the reading time' (BRL).

Interviewees mentioned the recruitment of freelancers to handle the workload. This is compatible with the trend towards outsourcing media labour (Örnebring and Ferrer-Conill 2016), but also with the use of freelancers for assignments, 'where the editor wants to keep the organization at a distance' (Mathisen 2019, 647). However, some add that newsroom journalists offer support in searching for an approach on some issues. MAÑ and ECB highlighted the importance of journalistic specialization, as well as sharing the philosophy of the organization. In fact, some of the regular partners 'were former journalists of the media' (ECB).

In summary, branded content of the media companies interviewed is paid for by brands and produced by the publication in charge of the creative work. While only the publisher makes decisions regarding placement on the homepage, brands have the final word about the branded content sign off. Managers assert that proper identification of this content is provided (Coddington 2015), and they deny the risk to editorial integrity.

Professional Perceptions and Concerns

In answering RQ3, the journalists surveyed ($N = 170$) confirmed the regular presence of branded content in three-quarters of the media in which they are employed (Table 9). In fact, 44% of them work in media that always or frequently publish such content. Another relevant point is that branded content, according to those surveyed, is mostly created by the same newsroom journalists who produce the editorial content (46%), and to a lesser extent by an internal department [agency unit model] (17%), or a

Table 9. Journalists' perceptions.

Question	Possible answers	N	%	Mean	SD
Is branded content always clearly differentiated from editorial content in the Spanish media?	Yes, always	25	15		
	Not always	12	7		
	Seldom	54	32		
	No, it can be easily mistaken	79	46		
Does the media company for which you work publish branded content?	Yes, frequently	57	34		
	Yes, in each edition	17	10		
	Occasionally	57	34		
	Never	37	22		
Do you believe the newsroom should be asked for their opinion regarding the inclusion of branded content?	Yes	121	76		
	No	30	19		
	Other	8	5		
What is your opinion of branded content (Up to three options may be selected)	Acceptable if it offers quality content	43	25		
	This is against the basic principles of journalism	38	23		
	It weakens media credibility when mixing editorial and advertising content	82	48		
	This is an option to ensure financial viability	51	30		
	Other	7	4		
Assess from 1 (minimum) to 5 (maximum) your support of branded content	1	48	28		
	2	38	22		
	3	44	26	2.5	1.29
	4	24	14		
	5	16	9		
Assess from 1 (limited) to 5 (excessive) your perception of the presence of branded content in the Spanish media	1	8	5		
	2	14	8		
	3	60	35	3.5	1.04
	4	56	33		
	5	32	19		
Assess from 1 (minimum) to 5 (maximum) the overall support by your media company of branded content	1	34	22		
	2	23	15		
	3	65	42	2.7	1.25
	4	14	9		
	5	19	12		

third-party supplier [external staff] (27%). Disclosure is a key point in branded content. However, 85% of journalists who answered the survey believe that the Spanish media have not always established a clear distinction between branded and editorial content (Table 9).

According to the survey, the greatest threat from branded content is media credibility. In fact, those who selected this option were categorical and did not add a second alternative. Nearly a quarter of those surveyed consider that branded content practices go against the principles of journalism, and the majority fear a loss of credibility as well. Media sustainability appears to be the main reason to support branded content when this is an option to ensure financial viability, which precedes the consideration of quality. The ethical and professional concerns of branded content are evident among three out of four journalists surveyed, who agreed that they should be asked by the media for their opinion regarding its inclusion.

The survey aimed to identify not only journalists' support for branded content, but also their perception of its presence, as well as its perceived backing by their own media. For this reason, three of the questions asked the respondents to score each aspect on a scale of 1 to 5.

As the data was skewed, the Kruskal-Wallis test for comparing multiple groups was performed. It showed statistically significant results in six categories of the questions that asked for a ranking to be graded. Such was the case of the perceived support in their own media ($U=10.8$, $p < .028$), higher among those employed in the local media ($M=3.2$, SD $= 1.15$). Also significant was the position held when observing the perception of branded content ($U=8.1$, $p < .043$), as those in qualified positions or involved in corporate tasks saw it as being less excessive when compared to the view of newsroom journalists, camera operators, or photographers ($M=3.6$, SD $= 1.05$).

The Kruskal-Wallis test revealed a connection between working in a media company that publishes branded content and the perception of it being excessive ($M=4.2$, SD $= 1.02$), which was statistically significant ($U=10.3$, $p < .015$), in addition to having the highest perception of backing by their own media ($M=3.4$, SD $= 1.32$) ($U=48.3$, $p < .000$). We can also observe significant differences in the support for branded content according to the view of employees who back the idea of being asked about its use ($M=2.3$, SD $= 1.19$) ($U=29.2$, $p < .000$), compared to those who are less supportive and required consultation with the newsroom for its support. Likewise, with regard to the perception of pairs working in the same media ($M=3.4$, SD $= 1.10$), this was higher among those who dismissed the idea of consulting journalists ($U=8.5$, $p < .014$).

Finally, the chi-square test suggested no association between disclosure assessment and branded content support ($x^2 = 24$, $d.f. = 8$, $p < .002$). Personal assessment on the lack of disclosure noted significantly less support for it (63%).

Discussion and Conclusions

Prominent representatives of the media industry have adopted branded content as a solution to the funding crisis in journalism, which is at the heart of a paradigm shift in the advertising industry. Based on a triangulation method analysis, this study encompasses content, the perspective of journalists, and the views of lab managers. Furthermore, it focuses on Spain, a country where the economic crisis had an especially strong impact on the media industry and resulted in high unemployment among journalists (APM (Asociación de la Prensa de Madrid) 2018). The findings reveal a complex scenario in which formal regulations meet weak professional autonomy, together with increasing efforts by labs managers and editors to legitimise such content, which is viewed with suspicion by most journalists.

Embracing branded content as a vital lifeline, the media have explicitly blurred the symbolic dividing line between 'church and state' (Coddington 2015; Ferrer-Conill 2016; Cornia, Sehl, and Nielsen 2020). In Spain, it was formally articulated with a clear distinction between information and advertising in norms and codes of ethics (FAPE. 2020), and a separation between the newsroom and the commercial department (Nieto-Tamargo and Iglesias-González 2000).

Both the interviews with managers and the surveys with journalists have helped us to discover significant nuances regarding the production of branded content. While the leading Spanish media interviewed have launched internal units that are diverse in size and methodology, the agency model is not taking place consistently across the board. As the journalists surveyed stated, in most cases the same newsroom journalists are also in charge of the sponsored content. This is particularly threatening in a precarious context with weakened professional autonomy, as is the case of Spain (Goyanes and Rodríguez-Castro 2019), where many journalists are under pressure regarding content orientation (APM (Asociación de la Prensa de Madrid) 2018). In addition, with the current conditions of employment instability, these labs are recruiting former media journalists to carry out their activities. These findings are in line with research from the USA and Canada related to both newsroom journalists in charge of sponsored content, especially in small media (Bilton 2014; Campbell and Lutostanski 2019), and forced freelancing when stable employment is unattainable (Cohen 2016).

Interviews with lab managers reveal increasing efforts to accommodate and justify sponsored content. They claim that it offers interesting, practical content for audiences, or in other words, tips and advice about everyday life, as well as background information. This point is consistent with the content analysis carried out, which highlights that service and civic are the most prominent performing roles with regard to content type, in line with Li (2019a). While substantial differences were not found between digital and legacy media, surprisingly the role of infotainment appeared to be more closely associated with the latter. One explanation for this could be that our study only included general information media, and also the fact that brands seek features of more sophisticated storytelling.

Despite the insistence by lab managers that reader deception is avoided, this research has revealed problems of branded content disclosure. On the one hand, the media display it by using a variety of options, even in the same outlet, which can be ambiguous and difficult to identify for readers, as suggested by some research (Hoofnagle and Meleshinsky 2015; Wojdynski and Evans 2016). On the other hand, the vast majority of the journalists surveyed agreed that clear disclosure is not offered to readers.

Unlike lab managers, journalists display indications of unease and support for separation norms. In this regard, journalists believe that branded content is a major threat to media credibility, a consideration that is substantially ahead of the option of ensuring financial viability or providing quality content, which have emerged as major factors in the discourse emanating from managers of branded content units. The increase in branded content emphasized by the managers interviewed is consistent with the fact that nearly eight out of ten of the journalists surveyed are employed in media companies that offer this content. We observed a direct relationship between this fact and the rise in concerns about an excess of branded content in the Spanish media, or the need to listen to the newsroom regarding its inclusion. However, this finding clearly conflicts with the claim of some managers who deny differences between branded and media content.

The commitment and close relationship with brands, which is part and parcel of branded content according to what was expressed by the lab managers, implies significant risk to reputation (Zeng 2018; Wojdynski and Evans 2016). This especially occurs when sensitive sectors of activity pursue an association with certain values through this partnership. This creates a conflict with the rules of the profession and the social responsibility of the media, as nearly a quarter of the journalists surveyed believe when they state that branded content practices go against the basic principles of journalism. Moreover, the issue also involves the fact of their having to compete with their own editorial content, since brands often have large budgets to engage audiences. In fact, as revealed by our interviews with managers of branded content units, some branded content productions receive the same amount of attention from readers as those of the editorial department.

This research is not without limitations that should be addressed by future studies. First, considering brand sponsored editorial content in news publications, this study has only addressed one of the native advertisement options, while complete understanding would require other branded content formats that coexist in the digital ecosystem and whose boundaries are blurred. Second, this research sampled six Spanish publications over a two month period, which did not provide information from the entire media system, nor data regarding potential fluctuations throughout the year. Finally, this study analysed only the main topics and role performance of branded content productions. Future research should delve into the narrative through discourse and frame analysis, and focus on the sources mentioned. The current research could also be improved by including semi-structured interviews that would allow for a more nuanced approach to the viewpoints of journalists, as well as to expand those with branded content lab managers. Last but not least, these findings also suggest the need for further research in order to unveil whether involvement in branded content is also reflected in editorial content.

Notes

1. An email was sent to 17 Spanish professional associations, and 10 of them confirmed – either by answering the email or after receiving a call phone – their willingness to collaborate by distributing the online survey among the members through their newsletters or webpages. This was the case of the Colegio Vasco de Periodistas-Kazetarien Euskal Elkargoa, Colexio Profesional de Xornalistas de Galicia, Unió de Periodistes Valencians, Colegio de Periodistas de la Región de Murcia, Col·legi de Periodistes de Catalunya, Grup de Periodistes Ramon Barnils, and the Asociación de la Prensa of Madrid, Sevilla, Aragón and Alicante.

Acknowledgements

The author wishes to thank the editors and reviewers for their insightful and constructive feedback received through the official reviewing process.

Disclosure Statement

No potential conflict of interest was reported by the authors.

ORCID

Dolors Palau-Sampio (iD) http://orcid.org/0000-0001-9051-0239

References

Amazeen, Michelle A., and Ashley R. Muddiman. 2018. "Saving Media or Trading on Trust?" *Digital Journalism* 6 (2): 176–195.

Anderson, Charles W., Emily Bell, and Clay Shirky. 2014. *Post-Industrial Journalism: Adapting to the Present*. New York: Columbia Journalism School.

APM (Asociación de la Prensa de Madrid). 2018. *Informe Anual de la Profesión Periodística*. Madrid: APM. https://www.apmadrid.es/wp-content/uploads/2019/07/Informe-profesión-2018_baja.pdf.

Arrese, Ángel M. 2016. "From Gratis to Paywalls: A Brief History of a Retro-Innovation in the Press's Business." *Journalism Studies* 17 (8): 1051–1067.

Arrese, Ángel M., and Francisco J. Pérez-Latre. 2017. "The Rise of Brand Journalism." In *Commercial Communication in the Digital Age. Information or Disinformation?*, edited by Gabriele Siegert, Bjorn Von Rimscha, and Stephanie Grubenmann, 121–140. Berlin: De Gruyter Mouton.

Artemas, Katie, Tim P. Vos, and Margaret Duffy. 2018. "Journalism Hits a Wall: Rhetorical Construction of Newspapers' Editorial and Advertising Relationship." *Journalism Studies* 19 (7): 1004–1020.

Asmussen, Bjoern, Serena Wider, Ross Williams, Neil Stevenson, Elliot Whitehead, and Andrew Canter. 2016. "Defining Branded Content for the Digital Age." https://brandedentertainment.de/wp-content/uploads/2017/02/BCMA-Research-Report_FINAL.pdf

BCMA (Branded Content Marketing Association). 2019. "IV Content Scope Report." http://bcma.es/wp-content/uploads/2019/12/RESUMEN-IV-EDICIÓN-CONTENT-SCOPE.pdf

Bilton, Ricardo. 2014. "Meet the Publishers Who Ask Their Reporters to Write Native Ads." *Digiday*, June 5. http://digiday.com/publishers/publishers-enlist-reporters-write-native-ad-content/

Broersma, Marcel, and Chris Peters. 2013. "Introduction: Rethinking Journalism: The Structural Transformation of a Public Good." In *Rethinking Journalism*, edited by Chris Peters, and Marcel Broersma, 1–12. Abingdon: Routledge.

Brown, Herbert, Miriam B. Waltzer, and Clyde Waltzer. 2001. "Daring to Be Heard: Advertorials by Organized Interests on the Op-Ed Page of the New York Times 1985–1998." *Political Communication* 18 (1): 23–50.

Bull, Andy. 2013. *Brand Journalism*. New York: Routledge.

Campbell, Julia, and Emilie Lutostanski. 2019. "Branded Content Research: 13 Charts That Show How Local Media Approach and Profit from Sponsored Campaigns." https://www.localmedia.org/wp-content/uploads/2019/05/BCP_white_paper.pdf

Campbell, Colin, and Lawrence J. Marks. 2015. "Good Native Advertising Isn't a Secret." *Business Horizons* 58 (6): 599–606.

Carlson, Matt. 2015. "When News Sites Go Native: Redefining the Advertising – Editorial Divide in Response to Native Advertising." *Journalism* 16 (7): 849–865.

Carson, Andrea. 2015. "Behind the Newspaper Paywall–Lessons in Charging for Online Content: A Comparative Analysis of Why Australian Newspapers Are Stuck in the Purgatorial Space between Digital and Print." *Media, Culture & Society* 37 (7): 1022–1041.

Carvajal, Miguel, and Iker Barinagarrementeria. 2019. "Contenido de Marca en Diarios Españoles: Concepto, Organización y Retos de Los Periodistas Implicados." *Trípodos* 44: 137–152.

Coddington, Mark. 2015. "The Wall Becomes a Curtain: Revisiting Journalism's News–Business Boundary." *Boundaries of Journalism*, edited by Matt Carlson, and Seth C. Lewis, 67–82. Abingdon: Routledge.

Cohen, Nicole. 2016. *Writers' Rights: Freelance Journalism in a Digital Age*. Montreal: McGill-Queen's University Press.

Cooper, Christopher A., and Anthony J. Nownes. 2004. "Money Well Spent? An Experimental Investigation of the Effects of Advertorials on Citizen Opinion." *American Politics Research* 32 (5): 546–569.

Cornia, Alessio, Annika Sehl, and Rasmus K. Nielsen. 2020. "We No Longer Live in a Time of Separation': A Comparative Analysis of How Editorial and Commercial Integration Became a Norm." *Journalism* 21 (2): 172–190.

Couldry, Nick, and Joseph Turow. 2014. "Advertising, Big Data and the Clearance of the Public Realm: Marketers' New Approaches to the Content Subsidy." *International Journal of Communication* 8: 1710–1726.

Cozzolino, Alessio, Gianmario Verona, and Frank T. Rothaermel. 2018. "Unpacking the Disruption Process: New Technology, Business Models, and Incumbent Adaptation." *Journal of Management Studies* 55 (7): 1166–1202.

De Aguilera-Moyano, Joaquín, Miguel Baños-González, and, and Francisco Ramírez-Perdiguero, 2015. "Branded Entertainment: Entertainment Content as Marketing Communication Tool. A Study of Its Current Situation in Spain." *Revista Latina de Comunicación Social* 70: 519–538.

Deuze, Mark. 2005. "What is Journalism? Professional Identity and Ideology of Journalists Reconsidered." *Journalism* 6 (4): 442–464.

FAPE. 2020. "Código deontológico." https://fape.es/home/codigo-deontologico/

Ferrer-Conill, Raul. 2016. "Camouflaging Church as State: An Exploratory Study of Journalism's Native Advertising." *Journalism Studies* 17 (7): 904–914.

Franklin, Bob. 2014. "The Future of Journalism: In an Age of Digital Media and Economic Uncertainty." *Journalism Studies* 15 (5): 481–499.

Gambetti, Rosella C., and Guendalina Graffigna. 2010. "The Concept of Engagement: A Systematic Analysis of the Ongoing Marketing Debate." *International Journal of Market Research* 52 (6): 801–826.

Golan, Guy, and Evhenia Viatchaninova. 2014. "The *Advertorial* as a Tool of Mediated Public Diplomacy." *International Journal of Communication* 8: 1268–1288.

Goyanes, Manuel, and Marta Rodríguez-Castro. 2019. "Commercial Pressures in Spanish Newsrooms: Between Love, Struggle and Resistance." *Journalism Studies* 20 (8): 1088–1109.

Hallin, Daniel C., and Paolo Mancini. 2004. *Comparing Media Systems: Three Models of Media and Politics*. Cambridge: Cambridge University Press.

Han, Jiyoon (Karen), Minette Drumwright, and Wongun Goo. 2018. "Native Advertising: Is Deception an Asset or a Liability?" *Journal of Media Ethics* 33 (3): 102–119.

Hardy, Jonathan, Helen Powell, and Iain MacRury. 2018. "Introduction." In *The Advertising Handbook*, edited by Jonathan Hardy, Iain MacRury, and Helen Powell, xiii–xvii. Abingdon: Routledge.

Hardy, Jonathan. 2008. *Western Media Systems*. Abingdon: Routledge.

Hardy, Jonathan. 2017. "Commentary: Branded Content and Media-Marketing Convergence." *The Political Economy of Communication* 5 (1): 81–87.

Hernández, Rocío. 2018. "El 'Branded Content' o 'Periodismo de Marca', Nueva Fuente de Ingresos Para la Prensa." *Cuadernos de Periodistas* 35: 90–97.

Hoofnagle, Chris J., and Eduard Meleshinsky. 2015. "Native Advertising and Endorsement: Schema, Source-Based Misleadingness, and Omission of Material Facts." *Technology Science*. https://papers.ssrn.com/sol3/papers.cfm?abstract_id=2703824

IAB Spain. 2019a. *Inversión Publicitaria en Medios Digitales. Resultados 2018*. https://iabspain.es/wp-content/uploads/inversin-publicitaria-medios-digitales_2018_vreducida-2.pdf

IAB Spain. 2019b. *Libro Blanco de Branded Content y Publicidad Nativa*. https://iabspain.es/estudio/libro-blanco-de-branded-content-y-publicidad-nativa/

IAB Spain. 2019c. *Guía legal para branded content y figuras publicitarias afines*. https://iabspain.es/estudio/guia-legal-branded-content-y-figuras-publicitarias-afines/

IAB US. 2019. *IAB Native Advertising Playbook 2.0* [update]. https://www.iab.com/wp-content/uploads/2019/05/IAB-Native-Advertising-Playbook-2_0_Final.pdf

Kahn, William A. 1990. "Psychological Conditions of Personal Engagement and Disengagement at Work." *Academy of Management Journal* 33 (4): 692–724.

Kovach, Bill, and Tom Rosenstiel. 2001. *The Elements of Journalism: What Newspeople Should Know and the Public Should Expect*. New York: Three Rivers Press.

Krouwer, Smone, Karolien Poels, and Steve Paulussen. 2020. "Moving towards Transparency for Native Advertisements on News Websites: A Test of More Detailed Disclosures." *International Journal of Advertising* 39 (1): 51–73.

Laursen, Jesper, and Martha Stone. 2016. *Native Advertising Trends 2016: The News Media Industry.* https://nativeadvertisinginstitute.com/wp-content/uploads/2016/10/TrendReportNewsMedia16.pdf

Levi, Lili. 2015. "A Faustian Pact? Native Advertising and the Future of the Press." *Arizona Law Review* 57 (3): 647–712.

Li, You. 2019a. "The Role Performance of Native Advertising in Legacy and Digital-Only News Media." *Digital Journalism* 7 (5): 592–613.

Li, You. 2019b. "Contest over Authority: Navigating Native Advertising's Impacts on Journalism Autonomy." *Journalism Studies* 20 (4): 523–541.

Lynch, Lisa. 2018. *Native Advertising: Advertorial Disruption in the 21st-Century News Feed.* New York: Routledge.

Mathisen, Birgit Røe. 2019. "Ethical Boundaries among Freelance Journalists." *Journalism Practice* 13 (6): 639–656.

Mellado, Claudia, and Arjen Van Dalen. 2017. "Challenging the Citizen–Consumer Journalistic Dichotomy: A News Content Analysis of Audience Approaches in Chile." *Journalism & Mass Communication Quarterly* 94 (1): 213–237.

Mellado, Claudia. 2015. "Professional Roles in News Content: Six Dimensions of Journalistic Role Performance." *Journalism Studies* 16 (4): 596–614.

Newman, Nic, David A. Levy, and Rasmus K. Nielsen. 2015. *Tracking the Future of News.* Oxford: Reuters Institute for the Study of Journalism.

Newman, Nic, Richard Fletcher, Antonis Kalogeropoulos, and Rasmus K. Nielsen. 2019. *Reuters Institute Digital News Report 2019.* Oxford: Reuters Institute for the Study of Journalism.

Newman, Nic. 2018. *Journalism, Media, and Technology Trends and Predictions 2018.* Oxford: Reuters Institute for the Study of Journalism.

Nieto-Tamargo, Ángel, and Francisco Iglesias-González. 2000. *La Empresa Informativa.* Barcelona: Ariel.

Örnebring, Henrik, and Raul Ferrer-Conill. 2016. "Outsourcing Newswork." In *The Sage Handbook of Digital Journalism*, edited by Tamara Witschge, Christopher William Anderson, David Domingo, and Alfred Hermida, 207–221. London: Sage.

Picard, Robert G. 2004. "Commercialism and Newspaper Quality." *Newspaper Research Journal* 25 (1): 54–65.

Piety, Tamara R. 2016. "Killing the Golden Goose." In *Blurring the Lines. Market-Driven and Democracy-Driven Freedom of Expression*, edited by Maria Edström, Andrew T. Kenyon, and Maria Svensson, 101–108. Gothenburg: Nordicom.

PR Noticias. 2019. *ComScore febrero: 'El País' aventaja al 'El Mundo' en millón y medio de usuarios únicos.* https://prnoticias.com/2019/03/25/comscore-febrero-el-pais-ventaja-sobre-el-mundo/

Ryfe, David. 2019. "The Warp and Woof of the Field of Journalism." *Digital Journalism* 7 (7): 844–859.

Serazio, Michael. 2018. "Illuminating the Invisible: The Guerrilla Logic and Strategy of Digital Branded Content." *Advertising & Society Quarterly* 18 (4): 1–23.

Serazio, Michael. 2020. "Making (Branded) News: The Corporate Co-Optation of Online Journalism Production." *Journalism Practice* 14 (6): 679–696.

Siebert, Fred, Fred T. Siebert, Theodore Peterson, Theodore Bernard Peterson, and Wilbur Schramm. 1956. *Four Theories of the Press: The Authoritarian, Libertarian, Social Responsibility, and Soviet Communist Concepts of What the Press Should Be and Do.* Urbana: University of Illinois Press.

Sonderman, Jeff, and Millie Tran. 2013. "Understanding the Rise of Sponsored Content." *American Press Institute*, November 13. https://www.americanpressinstitute.org/publications/reports/white-papers/understanding-rise-sponsored-content/single-page/

Supran, Geoffrey, and Naomi Oreskes. 2017. "Assessing ExxonMobil's Climate Change Communications (1977–2014)." *Environmental Research Letters* 12 (8): 084019.

Walmsley, Ben. 2019. "The Death of Arts Marketing: A Paradigm Shift from Consumption to Enrichment." *Arts and the Market* 9 (1): 32–49.

Ward, Stephen J. A. 2005. "Philosophical Foundations for Global Journalism Ethics." *Journal of Mass Media Ethics* 20 (1): 3–21.

Wojdynski, Bartosz W., and Nathaniel J. Evans. 2016. "Going Native: Effects of Disclosure Position and Language on the Recognition and Evaluation of Online Native Advertising." *Journal of Advertising* 45 (2): 157–168.

Zeng, Yuan. 2018. "Native Advertising: Revenue and Acclaim or a Ruined Reputation?" *Media Asia* 45 (1–2): 21–24.

⏻ OPEN ACCESS

The Visual Boundaries of Journalism: Native Advertising and the Convergence of Editorial and Commercial Content

Raul Ferrer-Conill ⓘ, Erik Knudsen ⓘ, Corinna Lauerer and Aviv Barnoy ⓘ

ABSTRACT
This study investigates the visual objects that are used to either disclose or disguise the commercial nature of native advertising as news articles. We adopt a "material object" approach to explore the potential implications for journalism regarding transparency, trust, and credibility. Methodologically, this study used content analysis covering 21 publications in five countries: Germany, Israel, Norway, Spain, and Sweden. We analysed 373 individual native ads. The findings show that news outlets do not follow a consistent way to disclose native ads visually, negotiating the balance between transparency and deception. In this balance, news organizations do not boldly push for transparency and instead remain ambiguous. Our analyses show that both national and organizational characteristics matter when shaping the visual boundaries of journalism.

Introduction

This study explores the material visual objects digital news outlets use when publishing native ads and how they are created and disseminated internationally. By visual objects, we mean visual elements used in digital news websites to either disclose the commercial nature of native ads or to disguise them as news articles. These objects are the specific mechanisms by which news organizations negotiate the boundaries between advertising and editorial content. Their goal is to create ambiguous visual codes and conventions that audiences need to decode. Thus, the purpose of this study is to investigate how native ads are constructed to resemble news while disclosing that they are ads, exploring the instrumental elements that establish the form of news (Barnhurst and Nerone 2001). While our primary goal is not to compare media systems and their

This is an Open Access article distributed under the terms of the Creative Commons Attribution-NonCommercial-NoDerivatives License (http://creativecommons.org/licenses/by-nc-nd/4.0/), which permits non-commercial re-use, distribution, and reproduction in any medium, provided the original work is properly cited, and is not altered, transformed, or built upon in any way.

characteristics, this study also aims to compare whether the visual codes and conventions used in native ads are similar or varying in different countries and types of media. This is because journalism offers similarities and differences across national boundaries, not only regarding news making but also in financing and distribution models (Domingo et al. 2008; Hanusch 2009), which might determine how native ads are implemented. By doing so, this study identifies the visual elements used in native advertising production across countries and organizations, as a first step for identifying and deconstructing patterns that can lead to more systems-oriented future research.

As native advertising is a relatively new format, it is likely that news organizations' deployment strategies are still forming and changing. Unclear and ill-regulated forms of disclosure are responsible for readers' troubles in identifying native ads as commercial content (Amazeen and Wojdynski 2018). This, in consequence, has potential implications for journalism regarding transparency, trust, and credibility as readers may feel deceived when they realize content that looks like news is, in fact, advertising. It may also jeopardize the legitimacy of newsrooms (Sirrah 2019). Considering the theoretical and practical implications, it is surprising that, to the present day, there are few studies investigating the converging visual strategies used in native ads.

This study adopts an "object-oriented" approach to journalism (see Anderson and De Maeyer 2015) and draws inspiration from approaches proposed by Machin and Polzer (2015) by adding visual elements to quantitative content analysis. We analyse native ads on two levels – the in-feed homepage lead-item link and the full-page native ad – and compare these to regular news articles of the same outlet. We cover 373 native ads of 21 publications in five countries: Germany, Norway, Sweden, Spain, and Israel. The countries selected to match the researchers' expertise and to capture a broad range of different approaches to native advertising design.

The article starts by covering the literature on native advertising in journalism context and establishing the theoretical grounds for the use of material objects as the key components for the visual boundaries in journalism. We then turn to outline the methodological choices, followed by the results and discussion.

Visual Boundaries between News and Native Ads

The history of news media cannot be understood without the long-standing role of advertising as one of the main sources of revenue for news organizations (see Lauerer 2019). Native advertising is part of a broader phenomenon of increasing integration of the editorial and commercial sides within news media organizations (Cornia, Sehl, and Nielsen 2020) and has recently been implemented even by news organizations that used to criticize its use (Ferrer-Conill 2016; Wojdynski 2019). Fuelled by an inadequate regulatory framework (Casale 2015) and the increased influence of contemporary corporate capitalism in the news industry (Hardy 2016), native advertising keeps growing fast (Perrin 2019).

Native Advertising in Journalistic Contexts

In news media, native advertising can be defined as "a form of paid content marketing, where the commercial content is delivered adopting the form and function of editorial content with the attempt to recreate the user experience of reading news instead of advertising content" (Ferrer-Conill 2016, 905). In other words, "native advertising deliberately disables consumers' ability to recognize advertising elements on a website, rendering advertiser and publisher liable for deceiving consumers" (Wojdynski 2019, 1). This integration of advertising within journalism contradicts the long-standing normative tradition of keeping editorial and commercial content separate (see Ferrer-Conill and Karlsson 2018; Glasser, Varma, and Zou 2019), in which news organizations need to establish their authority and autonomy from commercial actors (Li 2019). Its deceptive nature sparks controversy, primarily as the industry increasingly advocates for its deployment (Carlson 2015). Such transgressions of commercial influence over editorial content are not a new development, but they have often been considered a questionable journalistic practice (Bagdikian 2004; Hamilton 2004) against the tenets of social responsibility, especially regarding autonomy, transparency, and deception (Schauster, Ferrucci, and Neill 2016).

To legitimize native advertising, news media managers argue that editorial-business collaboration should remain unproblematic as long as newspapers and news websites are transparent enough (Drew and Thomas 2017). However, transparency and deception remain the biggest concerns for native advertising use (Harro-Loit and Saks 2006; Ikonen, Luoma-Aho, and Bowen 2017) because they form an area of tension that is key to native advertising (Iversen and Knudsen 2019; Wojdynski 2016). This tension lies at the heart of native advertising because, on the one hand, deception is key to ensure readers perceive ads as a trusted source of information (Campbell and Marks 2015), and on the other hand, transparency is needed to circumvent regulation and avoid readers feeling deceived, jeopardizing the news outlet's credibility (Amazeen and Wojdynski 2018). In order to be effective, native advertising is embedded in the form of "shiny camouflage" that both mimics news appearance to lure readers while at the same time, labelling content to warn them (Ferrer-Conill and Karlsson 2018).

The attempt to "convince audiences" is demonstrated by scholarship in advertising journals focussing on the effectiveness of native ads (see Wang and Huang 2017; Campbell and Evans 2018; Wang, Xiong, and Yang 2019). Even when ads are disclosed, Wojdynski and Evans (2016), as well as Amazeen and Muddiman (2018), demonstrate that readers often fail to identify native ads' disclosure and that attitudes towards publishers and perceptions of their credibility declined. Amazeen and Wojdynski (2019) found that when digital news publishers were more transparent about the commercial nature of the content, news consumers were most receptive to native advertising. Making clear visual distinctions and increasing transparency should be an important goal for both news organizations and advertisers, as audiences favour specific cues that flag advertising. This is supported by Krouwer, Poels, and Paulussen (2020) who suggest that providing detailed disclosures about the authorship of native ads has a positive influence on the news website's credibility and that transparency does not only make readers more receptive to native ads, but it may also help to restore or sustain readers' trust in news websites.

However, the balance between transparency and deception also depends on the power asymmetries between news organizations' managers and the influence that marketers have over them (Hardy 2016). In fact, the controversial practice has sparked a debate about the issue of governance and legislation of native advertising. While Einstein (2015) claims that regulatory bodies have failed to regulate native ads, Ponikvar claims that "regulations would not solve the problem of deceptive advertisements any more effectively than do the current industry practices" (2015, 1210). The European regulatory framework of native advertising consists primarily of the Unfair Commercial Practices Directive (UCPD)[1] and the e-commerce Directive,[2] as well as several country-specific regulatory and policy structures (Hartsuiker 2016). In practice, the ill-equipped oversight relies on self-regulation by the European Advertising Standards Alliance (EASA) (Lynch 2018), which establishes operational standards for advertising self-regulatory systems. While a detailed account of the regulations of native advertising escapes the scope of this study, it certainly justifies the need for a visual inquiry of how news organizations create and disseminate native ads. The scope of regulations are based on "clear and conspicuous disclosure" with such factors as "placement of the disclosure in the ad," "the disclosure's prominence," or "whether other parts of the ad may distract a consumer's attention away from the disclosure" (Einstein 2015, 238–9). Similarly, the good practice recommendations proposed by EU regulators revolve around "clear identification," "label description," and "different visual demarcation," such as "shading, outlines, or borders" (Hartsuiker 2016, 6). Therefore, we proposed it is crucial to understand the material ways in which news media and marketers negotiate the disclosure of native ads.

Material Objects of Journalism as Interpretative Signals for Ad Recognition

Most literature on native advertising in journalism focuses on three fronts: the normative implications for journalism (Artemas, Vos, and Duffy 2018); the evolution of the practice (Iversen and Knudsen 2019); and the effects that native advertising has on its readers (Amazeen and Wojdynski 2018). The specific visual elements that are present in news websites' interfaces used to disguise or disclose native ads are practically unexplored. Adopting a "material sensibility" (see De Maeyer 2016) as a way to recognize the form of native advertising and the explicit design choices made by news organizations and advertisers helps us focus on what native ads are made of, visually. An "object-oriented" approach to journalism allows us to shine "an unusual light on the power dynamics of news production" (Anderson and De Maeyer 2015, 8) by looking at how news media and marketing try to impose their individual visual codes and conventions to acquire a journalistic form while providing commercial content. We refer to objects such as labels, titles, borders, logos, and their characteristics, such as typographies, colours, and sizes, that, while digital, remain purely material. Indeed, as Anderson and De Maeyer mention, "a resolute focus on materiality and objects is particularly useful for these kinds of genealogical expeditions; in an ontological sense, info-boxes and warning tags are purely digital objects, whose form is fluid and endlessly changeable" (2015, 7–8). The logos and labels that signal commercial content, as well as the similar typographies and colours of traditional news articles, establish the visual heuristic cues that help audiences interpret the text they are reading. These material objects of journalism function as ontological mechanisms to both imply an article is news and, at the same time, an ad. This negotiation is taking place at the

Krouwer, Smone, Karolien Poels, and Steve Paulussen. 2020. "Moving towards Transparency for Native Advertisements on News Websites: A Test of More Detailed Disclosures." *International Journal of Advertising* 39 (1): 51–73.

Laursen, Jesper, and Martha Stone. 2016. *Native Advertising Trends 2016: The News Media Industry.* https://nativeadvertisinginstitute.com/wp-content/uploads/2016/10/TrendReportNewsMedia16.pdf

Levi, Lili. 2015. "A Faustian Pact? Native Advertising and the Future of the Press." *Arizona Law Review* 57 (3): 647–712.

Li, You. 2019a. "The Role Performance of Native Advertising in Legacy and Digital-Only News Media." *Digital Journalism* 7 (5): 592–613.

Li, You. 2019b. "Contest over Authority: Navigating Native Advertising's Impacts on Journalism Autonomy." *Journalism Studies* 20 (4): 523–541.

Lynch, Lisa. 2018. *Native Advertising: Advertorial Disruption in the 21st-Century News Feed.* New York: Routledge.

Mathisen, Birgit Røe. 2019. "Ethical Boundaries among Freelance Journalists." *Journalism Practice* 13 (6): 639–656.

Mellado, Claudia, and Arjen Van Dalen. 2017. "Challenging the Citizen–Consumer Journalistic Dichotomy: A News Content Analysis of Audience Approaches in Chile." *Journalism & Mass Communication Quarterly* 94 (1): 213–237.

Mellado, Claudia. 2015. "Professional Roles in News Content: Six Dimensions of Journalistic Role Performance." *Journalism Studies* 16 (4): 596–614.

Newman, Nic, David A. Levy, and Rasmus K. Nielsen. 2015. *Tracking the Future of News.* Oxford: Reuters Institute for the Study of Journalism.

Newman, Nic, Richard Fletcher, Antonis Kalogeropoulos, and Rasmus K. Nielsen. 2019. *Reuters Institute Digital News Report 2019.* Oxford: Reuters Institute for the Study of Journalism.

Newman, Nic. 2018. *Journalism, Media, and Technology Trends and Predictions 2018.* Oxford: Reuters Institute for the Study of Journalism.

Nieto-Tamargo, Ángel, and Francisco Iglesias-González. 2000. *La Empresa Informativa.* Barcelona: Ariel.

Örnebring, Henrik, and Raul Ferrer-Conill. 2016. "Outsourcing Newswork." In *The Sage Handbook of Digital Journalism*, edited by Tamara Witschge, Christopher William Anderson, David Domingo, and Alfred Hermida, 207–221. London: Sage.

Picard, Robert G. 2004. "Commercialism and Newspaper Quality." *Newspaper Research Journal* 25 (1): 54 65.

Piety, Tamara R. 2016. "Killing the Golden Goose." In *Blurring the Lines. Market-Driven and Democracy-Driven Freedom of Expression*, edited by Maria Edström, Andrew T. Kenyon, and Maria Svensson, 101–108. Gothenburg: Nordicom.

PR Noticias. 2019. *ComScore febrero: 'El País' aventaja al 'El Mundo' en millón y medio de usuarios únicos.* https://prnoticias.com/2019/03/25/comscore-febrero-el-pais-ventaja-sobre-el-mundo/

Ryfe, David. 2019. "The Warp and Woof of the Field of Journalism." *Digital Journalism* 7 (7): 844–859.

Serazio, Michael. 2018. "Illuminating the Invisible: The Guerrilla Logic and Strategy of Digital Branded Content." *Advertising & Society Quarterly* 18 (4): 1–23.

Serazio, Michael. 2020. "Making (Branded) News: The Corporate Co-Optation of Online Journalism Production." *Journalism Practice* 14 (6): 679–696.

Siebert, Fred, Fred T. Siebert, Theodore Peterson, Theodore Bernard Peterson, and Wilbur Schramm. 1956. *Four Theories of the Press: The Authoritarian, Libertarian, Social Responsibility, and Soviet Communist Concepts of What the Press Should Be and Do.* Urbana: University of Illinois Press.

Sonderman, Jeff, and Millie Tran. 2013. "Understanding the Rise of Sponsored Content." *American Press Institute*, November 13. https://www.americanpressinstitute.org/publications/reports/white-papers/understanding-rise-sponsored-content/single-page/

Supran, Geoffrey, and Naomi Oreskes. 2017. "Assessing ExxonMobil's Climate Change Communications (1977–2014)." *Environmental Research Letters* 12 (8): 084019.

Walmsley, Ben. 2019. "The Death of Arts Marketing: A Paradigm Shift from Consumption to Enrichment." *Arts and the Market* 9 (1): 32–49.

Ward, Stephen J. A. 2005. "Philosophical Foundations for Global Journalism Ethics." *Journal of Mass Media Ethics* 20 (1): 3–21.

Wojdynski, Bartosz W., and Nathaniel J. Evans. 2016. "Going Native: Effects of Disclosure Position and Language on the Recognition and Evaluation of Online Native Advertising." *Journal of Advertising* 45 (2): 157–168.

Zeng, Yuan. 2018. "Native Advertising: Revenue and Acclaim or a Ruined Reputation?" *Media Asia* 45 (1–2): 21–24.

heart of news organizations. As Neff (2015, p.77) proposes, "focusing on objects can help show the lines of authority, the contexts of routines, and the richness of practices within organizations, including news organizations."

At the most basic level, objects in journalism can be defined as "something that can be seen and touched (…) it can be named and materially defined, it is often perceived as a tool, a device, or an artifact" (De Maeyer and Le Cam 2015, 87). Usher (2018) further divides these objects into hard and soft objects. The former relate to tangible objects such as buildings, newsrooms, or newspapers. The latter account for digital objects such as software, websites, or interfaces, which are the focus of this study. And while there is a clear separation between hard and soft objects, there are clear connections between both, as some "soft" objects try to emulate their "harder" counterparts. For example, many news websites tried to replicate traditional designs, aiming to emulate the newspaper look. Other researchers have looked into these "soft" objects that populate contemporary digital journalism, from the perspective of blogs and hyperlinks (De Maeyer and Le Cam 2015), analytics and metrics (Zamith 2018), popularity cues (Haim, Kümpel, and Brosius 2018), digital rewards (Ferrer-Conill 2017), or even chatbots (Belair-Gagnon, Lewis, and Agur 2020).

For our purposes, these material objects are the components of journalistic interfaces by which the current power asymmetries among different actors within media organizations and between news media and marketers become most apparent. In this context, these objects become the interpretative signals for ad recognition, devised and negotiated by management and advertisers, but essentially used by audiences as heuristic cues to interpret the content (Chaiken 1987). The combination of what we call coinciding objects (those used to camouflage ads as news) and disclosing objects (those placed specifically to signal commercial content) represents that struggle. We echo Usher's claim that "digital news products as objects of journalism are also sites where power is negotiated among the actors that use them, the actors that make them, and by the objects themselves, and in turn, invoke different claims about trust" (2018, 572). While the institutionalized negotiations are intended for actors across interacting social worlds (i.e. news outlets and advertisers), we believe users have an important role in these negotiations, as their interpretations are crucial to the nature of digital news products.

Visual Boundaries of Journalism

Lewis and Usher (2016) argue that objects of journalism have the power to visualize boundary work and the contours of journalism. If the material objects of journalism embedded in native ads have an ontological interpretative power for the audience to decide whether a piece is news or advertising, we argue that they can be used to establish the visual boundaries of journalism. The scale and granularity of material visual objects allow us to utilize the concept as a tool to organize and arrange the interface from the perspective of journalism and advertising.

As Machin and Polzer recognize, the visual aspect of journalism, in general, has been "conspicuously absent" from journalism studies. They argue that while it is clear that "content is collected and shaped to fit a newspaper or a website that has a clearly formed visual identity," the "visual aspects of news and journalism have tended to be sidelined as mere packaging" (2015, 1). However, there are notable exceptions. Barnhurst and Nerone (2001) conclude, through a historical account of the material form of newspapers, that the visual medium used to disseminate the news is what establishes the relationship between content and readers. In other words, it is through the material and visual form of the medium that the readers know news is news. This is corroborated by Grabe et al. (2000), who conclude that formal features associated with packaging in a tabloid or standard news programs on TV affect the processing and evaluation of information among the audience. Raeymaeckers (2004) further shows that layout also in print has a significant influence on readers. Schindler, Krämer, and Müller (2017) recently found that the visual appearance and layout style could influence the political slant attributed to a news article.

Moreover, innovation in visual technologies combined with programmatic advertising has the potential to traverse and redefine the boundaries that once may have only been apparent through content (Graham et al. 2011). News organizations establish visual codes and conventions for audiences to associate their products with journalism. However, while journalism employs a fairly homogenous visual communicative strategy across the globe (Machin and Polzer 2015), the visual codes shared by outlets and audiences may vary across types of publications (Coleman 2000) or cultural background (Hanusch 2009; Zhang and Hellmueller 2017). In the online environment, technological affordances affect the material construction of news sites (Pavlik 2000). The digital arena affords an increased mimetic isomorphism within digital journalism (Lowrey 2018) while still sustaining differences internationally (Domingo et al. 2008). This problem is exacerbated by the ongoing fluidity of online news. Multimodality, as a component of liquid news (Deuze 2008; Karlsson 2012), allows for malleable graphical elements of news websites. Templates and design layouts are in potential flux, yielding design choices (such as grids, fonts, and colours) to multimodal modes for communicating the news. Returning to the notion of objects of journalism, Usher points out that "these products are created with specific designs that make an argument about why journalism should be trusted; they enhance and limit the ability of journalists to do their work and also impact the ways that audiences and other actors access and engage with news" (2018, 573).

In the case of native advertising in digital newspapers, different visual objects of news items and native ads can be understood as tools for *disclosure transparency* (Tuchman 1972), referring to the degree of openness by news producers about how news is being produced. However, the specific case of native advertising requires adding the dimension of deception when considering the new rituals of transparency (Karlsson 2010). The tension between transparency and deception, mostly mediated through visual objects, will determine how organizations use native advertising in their digital newspapers. Our assumption is just like in other aspects of journalism, the visual objects of native advertising will sustain similarities and differences in various countries.

Therefore, we argue the visual boundaries between journalism and advertising materialize when examining how news organizations execute native advertising. The objects placed in their interfaces shed light on the material negotiations between news media and advertisers, and the decoding mechanisms for readers to identify transparency and deception. In our attempt to explore how the combination of coinciding and disclosing objects defines the visual boundaries between news and ads, and whether it changes across publications and cultural contexts, we extend our inquiry about how native advertising is being used in different national and organizational settings.

With such considerations, this study proposes the following research questions:

RQ1: What are the visual objects news outlets use most often in order to disclose or disguise native advertising?

RQ2: How does the use of these visual objects differ among various outlets in different countries?

Methodology

This study aims to identify and explore the material visual objects news organizations and advertisers use to either disclose or camouflage native advertising. Our goal is to capture a broad range of examples in different national and organizational contexts and find out possible similarities and differences. Moreover, the complexity of country-specific regulatory standards is an excellent incentive to study native advertising both within and across countries. Strategies on how to create native ads are at the early stages, and the performance at the visual level is evolving and potentially differing across news media. Thus, trying to capture the visual boundaries between news and native ads poses methodological challenges. We tried to overcome these issues following a two-step strategy.

First, following a similar approach to Domingo and colleagues (2008), the team of researchers selected native ads from the most popular news websites in four EU countries (Germany, Norway, Spain, and Sweden) and Israel. In this exploratory study, the selection of countries was mainly driven by the expertise and the language skills of the research team. These countries represent a sample of Western liberal democracies, in which Germany, Norway, and Sweden share a Democratic Corporatist Model, Spain operates under a Polarized Pluralist Model (Hallin and Mancini 2004), and Israel, while "remarkably similar to the west" (Hanitzsch et al. 2011, 287), follows a hybrid model that draws primarily from the Liberal Model but carries aspects of the other two models (Tenenboim-Weinblatt 2014). The five countries, though, share a similar trend: the way in which native ads are published is not necessarily decided by news reporters, but by executives and management to maximize profit. These "neoliberalization processes evident in Israel are typical of many additional media systems and labour markets around the world" (Davidson and Meyers 2016, 195). To select the news organizations, we applied two criteria. First, we selected the four news websites in each country that were ranked highest regarding visits in the traffic aggregator *Alexa*. Second, we checked those websites for their current use of native ads. This already revealed interesting insights. In Germany, for example, it was harder to find outlets, which regularly published native ads. In consequence, some of the most popular German websites had to be replaced by outlets with less traffic because they were not using native ads matching, and a fifth outlet (*Der Tagesspiegel*) was added to the German sample to increase the number of

Table 1. Sample of native advertising items by country and online news outlet.

	News Outlet	Type	Mode	website	Items
Germany	Bild	Mass-market	Legacy	bild.de	20
	Zeit	Up-market	Legacy	zeit.de	12
	Rheinische Post	Up-market	Legacy	rp-online.de	20
	Huffington Post*	Mass-market	Online only	huffingtonpost.de	20
	Der Tagesspiegel	Up-market	Legacy	tagesspiegel.de	8
Israel	Ynet	Mass-market	Legacy	ynet.co.il	20
	Calcalist	Mass-market	Legacy	calcalist.co.il	20
	Globes	Mass-market	Legacy	globes.co.il	20
	Haaretz	Up-market	Legacy	haaretz.co.il	20
Norway	VG	Mass-market	Legacy	vg.no	27
	Dagbladet	Mass-market	Legacy	dagbladet.no	11
	Aftenposten	Up-market	Legacy	aftenposten.no	8
	Nettavisen	Mass-market	Online only	nettavisen.no	34
Spain	El Mundo	Up-market	Legacy	elmundo.es	8
	El País	Up-market	Legacy	elpais.com	20
	ABC	Up-market	Legacy	abc.es	16
	El Confidencial	Mass-market	Online only	elconfidencial.com	13
Sweden	Aftonbladet	Mass-market	Legacy	aftonbladet.se	20
	Expressen	Mass-market	Legacy	expressen.se	20
	Dagens Nyheter	Up-market	Legacy	dn.se	20
	Svenska Dagbladet	Up-market	Legacy	svd.se	16

*The German publisher Burda Forward unexpectedly and without giving reasons closed the business of Huffington Post Germany (Huff Post Deutschland) on 31st of March 2019.

items. Thus, a total of 21 outlets were selected, capturing various types and modes. Regarding type, the sample includes almost as many mass-market (tabloid) outlets as up-market outlets (quality). Regarding the mode only three outlets are online-only publications, while the others are the online outlets of legacy media (see Table 1). All the outlets selected are owned by private companies and combine ad-based freemium models and partial paywalls as business models. We acknowledge that other factors, such as journalistic cultures, national regulation, managerial tradition, and technological affordances, may have an important role in the visual appearance of native ads. That is why this study explores and compares the same practices across a sample of publications from five countries, different news outlet type, and different modes of communication of these organizations as proxies for organizational differences, to identify potential patterns in the design of native ads.

In the second step, we selected and collected all the individual native ads published in all 21 outlets during the spring of 2017. A total of 373 native ads were identified and saved as an image screenshot for archiving purposes and simplifying the analysis. During the span of three months, each researcher analysed the websites of the publications in their countries, looking for new native ads. We analysed both the lead-items (in-feed links) on the homepage and the full-page native ads to which they linked. This is an important distinction. While some in-feed native ads suggest and promote recommendations to external sites, and some full native ads do not have in-feed lead-items on the homepage, we focussed on ads that had both an in-feed homepage lead-item and a full-page ad for our study. We considered the lead-item and the full-page item as two components of a single native ad, and accordingly, the analysis was done at both levels.

Following the definition of native ads, we decided to include only those ads that look like a news article and are labelled as advertising. We are aware that there are

Table 2. Visual objects according to the coinciding or disclosing nature.

Coinciding objects	Disclosing objects
Lead paragraphs	Advertiser name
Fonts (sizes/colours)	Advertiser logo
Background colours	Banners
Images	Labels
Pull quotes	Borders

paid articles without disclosure. The fact that they are not labelled, however, means that they are not native advertising (which requires some form of disclosure), and makes them practically impossible to identify. To select our native ads we specified three selection criteria. First, a lead-item on the homepage that presented some form of visual disclosure (such as a label or the advertiser's logo or name). Second, either the lead-item or the ad itself had to look similar to a regular news item. Third, the lead-item on the homepage had to be linked to an advertising page *within* the outlet's domain name. The reason to keep the items within the same domain name is to make sure the ad is published by the news outlet, instead of simply linking to external content as most banners do.

To analyse the sample, we used a quantitative content analysis incorporating visual elements, drawing inspiration from approaches proposed by Machin and Polzer (2015). Our codebook contained variables to analyse both the lead-items on the homepage and the full-page native ads. To measure how online newspapers differentiate between native advertisement and news content, our team of coders also collected regular homepage news items and standalone news articles for each publication as the baseline to which the native ad lead-items on the homepage and the full-page native ads were compared. These baseline homepages and news items allowed us to define the form of coinciding or disclosing objects in their original design (see Table 2). In this article, we present results on those variables that we consider to be most important visual objects: coinciding objects which help mimic the articles (use of lead paragraph, text size, text font, text colour, background colour, authorship bylines, banners), and disclosing objects, which were used to measure how native ads are disclosed (use of borders, number and explanation of disclosures, stating the advertiser and their logos). While this is not an exhaustive list of visual objects, we believe these are the most relevant objects to the contemporary visual mapping (Barnhurst and Nerone 2001) of contemporary native advertising in news media.

After pre-test adjustments to the codebook, we recruited and trained local coders to conduct five country-specific inter-coder reliability tests (Hopmann et al. 2016). The test results were another indicator of the diverse approaches to native advertising and the difficulty of having a unified understanding of the practice. After thoroughly revising the codebook and additional training with the coders, we conducted a second test with 16 items per country (approx. 20%). The mean reliability score (Krippendorff's alpha) for all variables in all countries was .90, and only one variable, i.e. the difference in background colour on the home page, had a mean reliability score below .66 (i.e. .6). For some variables, however, the intercoder reliability score returned a low score, although the coders only disagreed on one observation. Because of the rather low sample size for each country, Krippendorff's alpha returned a slim value. Arguably,

Table 3. Intercoder reliability tests (Percent of agreement [%] and Krippendorf's alpha [α]).

Variables	Coder_NO		Coder_SE		Coder_ES		Coder_IL		Coder_DE		Mean	
	%	α	%	α	%	α	%	α	%	α	%	α
Homepage level												
Use of border	100	1	100	1	100	1	100	1	100	1	100	1
Different background colour	94	0	100	1	100	1	100	1	94	0	98	.6
Stand out on homepage?	100	1	100	1	100	1	90	.76	94	.72	97	.9
Full-page ad level												
Amount of labels	75	.68	98	.91	97	.9	97	.89	100	1	93	.88
Disclosure of explanation	69	.53	94	.87	100	1	100	1	100	1	93	.88
Disclosure of sender	88	.67	100	1	100	1	94	.87	87	.74	94	.86
Authorship	87	.73	100	1	100	1	100	1	90	.78	95	.9
Use of lead paragraph	94	.77	100	1	94	.81	100	1	100	1	98	.92
Different title text font	94	77	100	1	94	.88	99	0	100	1	97	.73
Different title text size	88	.67	100	1	100	.1	100	1	100	1	98	.93
Different title text colour	100	1	100	1	100	1	100	1	100	1	100	1
Different background colour	69	.1	100	1	100	1	100	1	100	1	94	.82
Use of logo	100	1	100	1	100	1	94	.87	77	.6	94	.89
Use of banner ads for advertiser	100	1	100	1	100	1	94	.87	100	1	99	.97
Use of banner ads for other advertisers	100	1	100	1	100	1	100	1	100	1	100	1

however, one disagreement out of 16 items (99% agreement) is indeed a clear indication of a reliable result (see Table 3 for an overview of the reliability scores for all variables).

Following our two research questions, we organized our findings by first using descriptive statistics to show which are the material visual objects used by news organizations to mimic news articles and disclose native ads. Second, we use logistic regression models and Ordinary Least Square (OLS) regression models to analyse variance between countries and different types and modes of news outlets.

Findings

Material Visual Objects to Mimic or Disclose the Commercial Nature of Native Ads

Starting with our first research question, we investigate the *visual objects news outlets use most often in order to disclose or disguise native advertising*. Every native ad comprises a lead-item located on the homepage and the full-page ad to which the lead-item links. Figure 1 shows the descriptive statistics for the most often used objects at the homepage level. We observe that 69% of the articles do *not* include a border around the lead-item that distinguishes the ad from the editorial content, and 87% of the articles use a background colour that blends in with other content on the homepage. Despite not having borders, and showing similar colours, the majority (69%) of the lead-item of native ads overall are "somewhat different" from the lead-items to regular news articles on the homepage. While this assessment required a subjective evaluation from the coders of how much ads stand out, we believe this is the case, for example, because all the lead-items on the homepage presented a disclosing label. This means that, in general, across our sample, native ads are neither very different nor identical to the news items they share space with on the homepage. Needless to say, the lead-items have fewer visual objects to be coded because they take only a little space on the website.

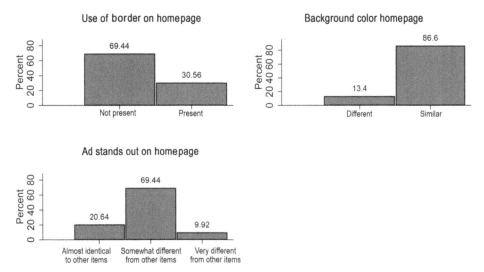

Figure 1. Visual objects at the homepage level.

In the analysis of the full-page ad, we first analysed the disclosing objects (see Figure 2). The first feature we observed was the number of labels in each ad page. Labels are arguably the most important visual objects disclosing that the full-page ad contains commercial content because they contain signal words like "sponsored," "paid by," or "advertising." The median amount of labels is one label per item, stretching from zero labels (10 percent) to a maximum of six labels within one item (0.3%). We analysed whether there was an explanation of the label, to clarify the type of ad. In other words, do the ads explain what labels such as "paid for" or "sponsored by" actually means? The majority (64 percent) of the ads did not contain information explaining what the disclosure label means. Only 33% of the ads offered such an explanation, and about 3% provided an external page with more information about what the labels meant. More than half the ad pages (55 percent) did not disclose who the advertiser paying for the ad is explicitly, for example, by displaying "sponsored by label X." A different take on disclosing the advertiser is only making an implicit connection by showing the advertiser's logo, but without clarifying the role of that organization. In fact, advertiser logos are a popular visual object, as in 68% of the ads presented the logo of the advertiser.

To code for coinciding objects that either mimic editorial content or differentiate commercial content, we compared several visual objects in the ads with regular news articles from the same publication that served as a baseline. This way, we could pinpoint whether these visual objects are different or similar in native ads and news articles from the same publication. Starting with the website's background colour (see Figure 3), the majority (82 percent) of the ads use a similar colour as the news articles. Most titles of the native ads use similar typography (62 percent), a similar font size (78 percent), and a similar font colour (78 percent) as regular news articles. More than half of the native ads (54%) use lead paragraphs to introduce their stories, just like the news articles in the respective publications. Another 23% is identical with the news articles in this regard as they do not use lead paragraphs, just like news articles in their publications do not. This means that about 77% of native ads mimic the use

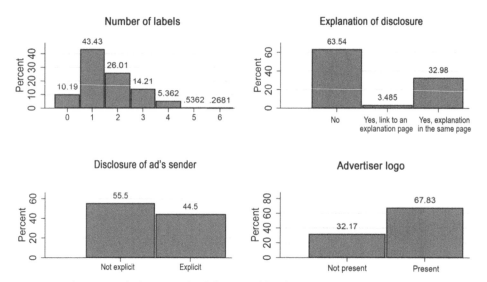

Figure 2. Disclosing visual objects at the full-page ad level.

or lack of lead paragraphs. Only 23% of ads dissent with the typical use of lead paragraphs in the articles of the respective news outlet: 12% of ads do not use lead paragraphs when news articles do, and 11% do use lead paragraphs when news articles do not. This is important because a lead paragraph is a staple of journalistic format, and native ads harness it as a coinciding object to resemble a regular news item.

Another staple of the journalistic genre is the disclosure of authorship. This is absent in 46% of the ads, while 54% explicitly specify the author as a person, news organization, or company. Finally, one visual object that is regularly present in the context of journalistic articles, namely banner ads surrounding the content, does not make its appearance in two-thirds (66 percent) of the full-page native ads. This probably indicates that, in most cases, news organizations offer undivided attention to the that advertisers run native ads.

Differences between Countries, Type, and Mode of the Outlets

In order to answer our second research question, we use logistic and Ordinary Least Square (OLS) regression models to analyse *the use of visual objects and whether they differ among various outlets in different countries.*

To get a clearer picture of how different forms of native ads manifest across the field, we have categorized the different news outlets by country, type of outlet (up-market or mass-market), and mode (legacy or online-only outlets). Table 4 shows these differences at the homepage level. Norway, online-only, and mass-market are the reference values for country, type, and mode, respectively. The first model shows the results from a logistic regression model where the presence of a border around the native ad on the homepage is the dependent variable. Because neither of the outlets in our sample from Norway and Spain use borders on the homepage, and because we observe minimal variation within countries, we do not include the country variable in the model. However, as there are substantial differences across countries, it is important to note that excluding or including

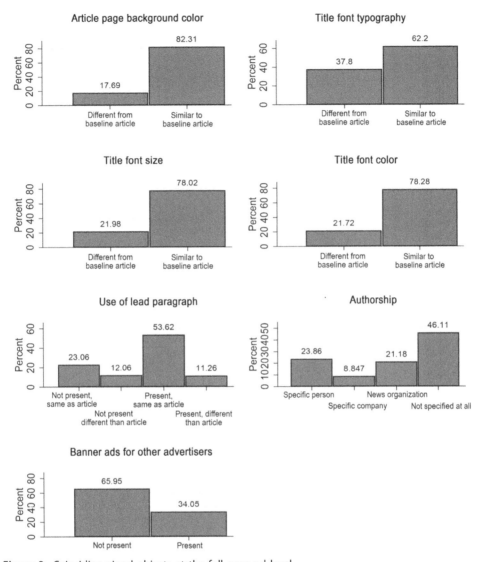

Figure 3. Coinciding visual objects at the full-page ad level.

countries as a control variable in the model does not matter for any of the results reported here. The first model shows that the type of outlet yields a statistically significant effect. Up-market outlets are more likely to use a border on the homepage than mass-market outlets. Similar to the first model, the second model in Table 4 does not include mode as a variable, because none of the online-only outlets in our sample use a different background colour to separate the ad from editorial content on the homepage. Model two shows that up-market outlets are statistically significantly less likely to use a different background colour compared to mass-market outlets. Turning to the third and last model in Table 4, we use an OLS regression model to estimate differences, but these results show an identical pattern if we instead use ordered logistic regression models. Because of the level of variation across countries present very little variation within some of the countries (e.g. all outlets in Norway stood out as "somewhat different" on the homepage), we

Table 4. Differences at the homepage level: Logistic and OLS regression models of differences between countries and newspapers.

	(Model 1) Use of frame on the homepage (1 = yes, 0 = no)		(Model 2) Background colour different (1 = yes, 0 = no)		(Model 3) Stand out on the homepage (0 = almost identical, .5 = somewhat different, 1 = very different)	
	b	se	b	se	b	se
Country:						
Norway					Ref.	(.)
Sweden					−.11*	(.042)
Germany					−.072	(.04)
Israel					.16***	(.041)
Spain					−.015	(.046)
Publication mode:						
Online only	Ref.	(.)			Ref.	(.)
Legacy	−.04	(.34)			.21***	(.039)
Publication type:						
Mass-market	Ref.	(.)	Ref.	(.)	Ref.	(.)
Up-market	.70***	(.25)	−1.06***	(.31)	.026	(.031)
Constant	−1.12***	(.18)	2.38***	(.24)	.38***	(.034)
Observations	373		373		373	
Adjusted R^2	.037		.057		.22	

Coefficients are unstandardized beta coefficients. Standard errors in parentheses.
*$p < .05$;
**$p < .01$;
***$p < .001$.
Logistic regression models (models 1 and 2) show Nagelkerke's R-square. All models are robust if we exclude or include countries as a control variable.

Table 5. Differences at the full-page ad level: Logistic regression models of differences between countries and newspapers.

	(Model 1) Similar title text font (1 = yes, 0 = no)		(Model 2) Similar title text size (1 = yes, 0 = no)		(Model 3) Similar title text colour (1 = yes, 0 = no)		(Model 4) Similar page background colour (1 = yes, 0 = no)	
	b	se	b	se	b	se	b	se
Country:								
Norway	Ref.	(.)	Ref.	(.)	Ref.	(.)		
Sweden	2.82***	(.44)	1.57***	(.44)	1.41***	(.46)		
Germany	3.98***	(.48)	2.23***	(.5)	3.71***	(.71)		
Israel	3.39***	(.47)	1.96***	(.45)	.27	(.38)		
Spain	2.43***	(.46)	1.29***	(.51)	2.35***	(.54)		
Publication mode:								
Online only	Ref.	(.)	Ref.	(.)				
Legacy	.74	(.44)	−2.23***	(.66)				
Publication type:								
Mass-market	Ref.	(.)	Ref.	(.)	Ref.	(.)	Ref.	(.)
Up-market	−1.79***	(.36)	−1.46***	(.051)	−2.165***	(.37)	−.96***	(.28)
Constant	−1.72***	(.19)	2.5***	(.6)	1.1***	(.26)	1.99***	(.21)
Observations	373		373		373		373	
Adjusted R^2	.417		.251		0.268		0.054	

Coefficients are unstandardized beta coefficients. Standard errors in parentheses
*$p < .05$;
**$p < .01$;
***$p < .001$.
Logistic regression models (all models) show Nagelkerke's R-square. All models are robust if we exclude or include countries as a control variable.

only use the country as a control variable in the analysis. We observe that native ads on the homepage of legacy newspapers are more likely to stand out than native ads on the homepage of online-only outlets. In sum, while there is limited variance within countries, we still observe substantial variance across countries, publication modes, and publication types regarding the use of visual objects on the homepage.

When it comes to the individual full-page ads, the first model in Table 5 shows the results from a logistic regression model with the difference between the regular news articles' title font and the native ads' title font as the dependent variable. We observe that, compared to Norway, all of the other countries are more likely to use a similar title font. While we do not observe any effect of mode, we observe that up-market outlets are less likely to mimic the regular news articles regarding title text font than mass-market outlets. In regards to the size of the title typography, the second model in Table 5 shows a similar pattern in terms of country differences and type differences. In contrast to the first model, however, we observe that the type also yields a statistically significant effect, as online-only outlets are more likely to use a similar text size than legacy outlets. Regarding text colour, the third model does not include outlet type as an independent variable as all of the online-only outlets in our sample use a similar text colour for the title text of the native ads. Controlling for country differences, the third model shows that up-market outlets are less likely to use colours in the title text that mimic the colour of the regular news articles. For the fourth and last model in Table 5, we again need to limit the analysis to include outlet type as the predictor, due to the same omitted variable bias reported for the analyses above. Regardless of whether or not we include country as a control variable, up-market outlets are more likely to use a different background colour, while mass-market are more likely to use a similar background colour, compared to the baseline articles.

Although our main intention of including countries in the models in Tables 4 and 5 is to control for country variations, we also observe that there are differences between countries regarding implementing native advertising. The strategies in using coinciding objects (especially on text size and colour, as well as background colour) are indeed different across countries. No country, however, predominantly designs native ads to look identical or very different from other news items.

Replicating the Visual Codes of Journalism – a Discussion

The findings show that, while news outlets have not reached – and may never reach – a consistent way to disclose native ads visually, the balance between transparency and deception is based on the combination of similar material visual objects. While they could make them look clearly different, most news outlets use coinciding visual objects in a similar way in both native ads and regular news articles. Because these objects diverge minimally, we believe coinciding objects are strategically used to camouflage native ads and pass them for regular news articles. At the same time, they use disclosing objects to signal their commercial status but not in an obvious manner. On the homepage, for example, native ads usually appear in the regular news flow, sharing space with editorial content. The prevalent choice is not to use a border or a different colour, but to add a small label as disclosure. Such a combination of visual objects provides support for Ferrer-Conill and Karlsson (2018) claim that native advertising functions as a "shiny camouflage," using design to hide and disclose its commercial nature at the same time. As Ikonen and colleagues (2017) suggest, the majority of visual objects in our sample attempt to maximize deception, and relatively few news outlets work towards transparency by making coinciding objects look different than news articles.

While this study only focussed on the visual composition of native ads in content analysis, it is possible to link our findings to studies investigating the production and consumption of hybrid ads. For example, those claiming that readers find it difficult to distinguish native ads (Wojdynski and Evans 2016; Amazeen and Muddiman 2018). This is because, as Wojdynski (2019) points out, native advertising purposefully combines the objects on the website to confuse readers. Studying native advertising with a "material object" approach (Anderson and De Maeyer 2015) is helpful in understanding what elements are used exactly. By breaking down native advertising into "soft objects" (Usher 2018) we can see how native ads try to replicate the visual codes of journalism in order to appropriate news media's clout (Ferrer-Conill and Karlsson 2018). By looking at them individually, we can see how news outlets use these material visual objects as a deliberate source of ambiguity for mimic and differentiation, and become the key factors of transparency and opacity. The combination of these visual objects often leaves it to the informed reader to decode that this is advertising. News organizations and advertisers know how to replicate the visual codes of journalism (Machin and Polzer 2015) and use the layout to influence readers (Raeymaeckers 2004; Schindler, Krämer, and Müller 2017).

Further, our results can be linked to studies on content production and on the negotiations among potentially involved actors (Usher 2018). Although this study offers no empirical evidence, we believe that these visual objects may offer an intuitive one: the visual boundaries between journalism are not universal but rather seem to depend on the negotiation between managers, journalists, and advertisers, and on how much a news organization is willing to risk declining trust in exchange for higher revenue. Moreover, if we consider the results instead of the process, our findings provide evidence to support the existence of power asymmetries (Hardy 2016), which suggests that in a case of direct clash, between commercial and editorial considerations, the former may get the upper hand.

The comparative aspect of this study reinforces our suspicion that while the visual boundaries of journalism and advertising are blurring across the field, the way in which native ads use visual objects are partly explained by their organizational cultural background (Hanusch 2009). However, this study provides evidence to suggest that the way in which a news organization disguises or discloses native ads is likely to be associated with its commercial market (type), and whether it is an online-only outlet (mode). Our findings show that the degree of transparency is not only contingent on national boundaries. Instead, online-only and mass-market publications tend to employ visual objects that facilitate mimicking content, while legacy and up-market outlets tend to favour transparency. This could be related to the fact that legacy media and up-market outlets have closer ties to the traditional understanding of journalism and may have a higher price to pay if they jeopardize their trust by not disclosing native ads clearly (Karlsson 2010; Krouwer, Poels, and Paulussen 2020). More importantly, what these significant differences among up-market and mass-market, digital-only and legacy, and their attempt to replicate the visual codes of journalism, is that material objects of native advertising represent the socially constructed visual identity of news and how marketers and news outlets shape them to communicate to their readers where the contours of journalism and advertising meet. Indirectly, the blurring of editorial and commercial content in terms of design requires additional markers that again separate the one from the other. These are signals that help news media, advertisers, and readers decipher the visual boundaries of digital journalism.

Negotiated Visual Boundaries of Journalism

This article has explored the material visual objects that news organizations use in their native ads and how the use of these objects varies across nations and publications. After analysing 373 native ads, we propose two main conclusions. First, while we found various approaches to native advertising design, there is a clear pattern across the board. Although coinciding and disclosing objects could be used to maximize transparency, native ads use coinciding objects to camouflage ads as much as possible and disclosing objects only to a minimal extent. This means that in the balance between transparency and deception, news organizations do not boldly push for transparency and instead remain ambiguous. We believe this suggests that in the negotiation between news organizations and marketers, the power asymmetries and needs for new forms of revenue pushes news media to integrate commercial and editorial content without clearly disclosing it. Furthermore, since the material visual objects act as a mechanism for readers to decode content is news or ads, their capacity to tell the two genres apart is intentionally diminished.

Second, while there are clear differences and similarities among the selected countries, there are also clear differences across the type and mode of news outlets. This indicates that differences within countries are more, or at least just as important as differences across countries. This could also imply that not only national regulatory frameworks but organizational settings shape the use of native ads. More concretely, we found mass-market organizations and online-only outlets tend to be less transparent. We believe this is because up-market and legacy organizations are often regarded as more trustworthy by the public, and therefore news outlets risk damaging their reputation and credibility to a greater extent (Wojdynski 2016). An alternative explanation (or perhaps a combination of both) is that up-market and legacy organizations have the economic and social capital to maintain power asymmetries more balanced and, therefore, can impose more transparent native ads.

The study contributes to journalism studies in various ways. First and foremost, it is the first attempt to visually compare how news organizations in different countries use native advertising. Focussing on the material visual objects, this study illustrates that the visual boundaries of journalism rest upon a few objects that, when tweaked, reveal or conceal the nature of commercial content. We contend that these boundaries, while they may be clear to practitioners, are certainly ambiguous and difficult to navigate by the audience, to which most scholarship on native advertising points. Thus, this set of visual objects are the primary markers for what is visually considered news and how native ads attempt to exploit those boundaries.

Despite the apparent celebratory rhetoric of news media managers (Ferrer-Conill 2016), practitioners in marketing and in news media organizations that have influence over how native ads look like should strive to establish a cohesive visual strategy that clearly discloses ads – at least within one market. Both coinciding and disclosing objects should be used in that effort. We know regular journalists may have little to no control over how native ads appear on websites, and that these decisions reside in the hands of management, marketers, and technical people. However, we believe that if native advertising is the site of contestation of journalistic power, a strong push by journalists should be taken to maintain visual clarity over journalistic jurisdiction.

The findings of this study are shaped not only by the countries we covered but by the decision to analyse the "most visited" news websites. With the rapid change of native advertising and the differences of implementation, these results should be interpreted as an initial snapshot of the practice internationally, and not as a generalizable practice in all news media. While our choice of method proved to be the best for the purpose of the study, it comes with limitations. The first one is about the possibility of missing those native ads that are disclosed extremely opaquely. Another issue is the "shelf life" of the designs we captured. Native advertising may be a rapidly changing practice due to technological innovation, regulatory changes, and the evolution of the advertising industry. While we believe that these objects reflect a negotiation of power (Usher 2018), we are aware that our data, collected in 2017, only cover visual elements present in the digital layout, and therefore relies on our interpretation of the use and meaning of visual objects. In itself, studying visual objects is a moving target that is contingent on the time of data collection. Our analyses, however, show that these tendencies exist in the outlets we studied, and we believe they paint a familiar picture. While specific combinations of visual objects may vary across the board, our aim was to bring to the fore the importance of the material construction of native ads and to visualize how fragile the visual boundaries of journalism become in a digital environment. Future research could complement this study by looking into how actors within news media actively negotiate the visual output of native ads. A thorough account of the adequacy of regulatory frameworks but also how news organizations address the use of visual elements in their policies could inform current compliance with regulations. Further, longitudinal studies that attempt to scrutinize the evolution of these strategies and mechanisms of disclosure and camouflage could continue to expand our knowledge about the visual boundaries of journalism.

Notes

1. UCPD – Directive 2005/29/EC (https://eur-lex.europa.eu/LexUriServ/LexUriServ.do?uri=OJ:L:2005:149:0022:0039:EN:PDF)
2. E-Commerce Directive 2000/31/EC (https://eur-lex.europa.eu/legal-content/EN/TXT/PDF/?uri=CELEX:32000L0031&from=EN)

Acknowledgments

We would like to thank all our colleagues who volunteered for the daunting task of coding native ads or provided feedback to improve our coding guide. Special thanks to Michael

Karlsson for the dedicated and thorough feedback he offered in the early (and later) stages of this study.

Disclosure Statement

No potential conflict of interest was reported by the author(s).

Funding

Raul Ferrer-Conill's research is supported by the Ander Foundation: Anne Marie och Gustav Anders Stiftelse för Mediaforskning. Aviv Barnoy's work on this article is supported by ISF grant 650/18.

ORCID

Raul Ferrer-Conill (iD) http://orcid.org/0000-0002-0501-2217
Erik Knudsen (iD) http://orcid.org/0000-0002-7046-9424
Aviv Barnoy (iD) http://orcid.org/0000-0002-6067-7094

References

Amazeen, Michelle A., and Ashley R. Muddiman. 2018. "Saving Media or Trading on Trust? The Effects of Native Advertising on Audience Perceptions of Legacy and Online News Publishers." *Digital Journalism* 6 (2): 176–195.

Amazeen, Michelle A., and Bartosz W. Wojdynski. 2018. "The Effects of Disclosure Format on Native Advertising Recognition and Audience Perceptions of Legacy and Online News Publishers." *Journalism: Theory, Practice & Criticism*.doi:10.1177/1464884918754829.

Amazeen, Michelle A., and Bartosz W. Wojdynski. 2019. "Reducing Native Advertising Deception: Revisiting the Antecedents and Consequences of Persuasion Knowledge in Digital News Contexts." *Mass Communication and Society* 22 (2): 222–247.

Anderson, C. W., and Juliette De Maeyer. 2015. "Objects of Journalism and the News." *Journalism: Theory, Practice & Criticism* 16 (1): 3–9.

Artemas, Katie, Tim P. Vos, and Margaret Duffy. 2018. "Journalism Hits a Wall: Rhetorical Construction of Newspapers' Editorial and Advertising Relationship." *Journalism Studies* 19 (7): 1004–1017.

Bagdikian, Ben H. 2004. *The New Media Monopoly*. Boston, MA: Beacon Press.

Barnhurst, Kevin G., and John C. Nerone. 2001. *The Form of News: A History. The Guilford Communication Series*. New York: The Guilford Press.

Belair-Gagnon, Valerie, Seth Lewis, and Colin Agur. 2020. "Failure to Launch: Intrapreneurs, News Organizations, and Non-Adoption of Chatbots." *Journal of Computer-Mediated Communication* 25 (4): 291–306.

Campbell, Colin, and Nathaniel J. Evans. 2018. "The Role of a Companion Banner Ad and Sponsorship Transparency in Recognizing and Evaluating Article-Style Native Advertising." *Journal of Interactive Marketing* 43: 17–32.

Campbell, Colin, and Lawrence J. Marks. 2015. "Good Native Advertising Isn't a Secret." *Business Horizons* 58 (6): 599–606.

Carlson, Matt. 2015. "When News Sites Go Native: Redefining the Advertising–Editorial Divide in Response to Native Advertising." *Journalism: Theory, Practice & Criticism* 16 (7): 849–865.

Casale, A. J. 2015. "Going Native: The Rise of Online Native Advertising and a Recommended Regulatory Approach." *Catholic University Law Review* 65 (1): 129–154.

Chaiken, Shelly. 1987. "The Heuristic Model of Persuasion." In *Social Influence: The Ontario Symposium*, edited by Mark P. Zanna, James M. Olson, and C. P. Herman, 3–39. Hillsdale, NJ: Lawrence Erlbaum.

Coleman, Renita. 2000. "Use of Visual Communication in Public Journalism." *Newspaper Research Journal* 21 (4): 17–37.

Cornia, Alessio, Annika Sehl, and Rasmus Kleis Nielsen. 2020. "'We No Longer Live in a Time of Separation': A Comparative Analysis of How Editorial and Commercial Integration Became a Norm." *Journalism* 21 (2): 172–190.

Davidson, Roei, and Oren Meyers. 2016. "Toward a Typology of Journalism Careers: Conceptualizing Israeli Journalists' Occupational Trajectories." *Communication, Culture & Critique* 9 (2): 193–211.

De Maeyer, Juliette. 2016. "Adopting a 'Material Sensibility' in Journalism Studies." In *Handbook of Digital Journalism*, edited by Tamara Witschge, C.W. Anderson, David Domingo, and Alfred Hermida, 460–476. London, UK: Sage Publications.

De Maeyer, Juliette, and Florence Le Cam. 2015. "The Material Traces of Journalism." *Digital Journalism* 3 (1): 85–100.

Deuze, Mark. 2008. "The Changing Context of News Work: Liquid Journalism for a Monitorial Citizenry." *International Journal of Communication* 2 (5): 848–865.

Domingo, David, Thorsten Quandt, Ari Heinonen, Steve Paulussen, Jane B. Singer, and Marina Vujnovic. 2008. "Participatory Journalism Practices in the Media and beyond: An International Comparative Study of Initiatives in Online Newspapers." *Journalism Practice* 2 (3): 326–342. doi:10.1080/17512780802281065.

Drew, Kevin K., and Ryan J. Thomas. 2017. "From Separation to Collaboration: Perspectives on Editorial? Business Collaboration at United States News Organizations." *Digital Journalism* 6 (2): 196–215.

Einstein, Brandon R. 2015. "Reading between the Lines: The Rise of Native Advertising and the FTC's Inability to Regulate It." *Brooklyn Journal of Corporate, Financial & Commercial Law* 10 (1): 225–248.

Ferrer-Conill, Raul. 2016. "Camouflaging Church as State: An Exploratory Study of Journalism's Native Advertising." *Journalism Studies* 17 (7): 904–914.

Ferrer-Conill, Raul. 2017. "Quantifying Journalism? A Study on the Use of Data and Gamification to Motivate Journalists." *Television & New Media* 18 (8): 706–720.

Ferrer-Conill, Raul, and Michael Karlsson. 2018. "Native Advertising and the Appropriation of Journalistic Clout." In *The Routledge Handbook of Developments in Digital Journalism Studies*, edited by Scott Eldridge, II and Bob Franklin (pp. 463–474). New York, NY: Routledge.

Glasser, Theodore L., Anita Varma, and Sheng Zou. 2019. "Native Advertising and the Cultivation of Counterfeit News." *Journalism* 20 (1): 150–153.

Grabe, Maria Elizabeth, Shuhua Zhou, Annie Lang, and Paul David Bolls. 2000. "Packaging Television News: The Effects of Tabloid on Information Processing and Evaluative Responses." *Journal of Broadcasting & Electronic Media* 44 (4): 581–598.

Graham, Connor, Eric Laurier, Vincent O'Brien, and Mark Rouncefield. 2011. "New Visual Technologies: Shifting Boundaries, Shared Moments." *Visual Studies* 26 (2): 87–91.

Haim, Mario, Anna Sophie Kümpel, and Hans-Bernard Brosius. 2018. "Popularity Cues in Online Media: A Review of Conceptualizations, Operationalizations, and General Effects." *Studies in Communication | Media* 7 (2): 186–207.

Hallin, Daniel C., and Paolo Mancini. 2004. *Comparing Media Systems: Three Models of Media and Politics*. Cambridge, UK: Cambridge University Press.

Hamilton, James T. 2004. *All the News That's Fit to Sell: How the Market Transforms Information into News*. Princeton, NJ: Princeton University Press.

Hanitzsch, Thomas, Folker Hanusch, Claudia Mellado, Maria Anikina, Rosa Berganza, Incilay Cangoz, Mihai Coman, et al. 2011. "Mapping Journalism Cultures across Nations: A Comparative Study of 18 Countries." *Journalism Studies* 12 (3): 273–293.

Hanusch, Folker. 2009. "A Product of Their Culture. Using a Value Systems Approach to Understand the Work Practices of Journalists." *International Communication Gazette* 71 (7): 613–626.

Hardy, Jonathan. 2016. "Money, (Co)Production and Power. The Contribution of Critical Political Economy to Digital Journalism Studies." *Digital Journalism* 5 (1): 1–25.

Harro-Loit, Halliki, and Kertu Saks. 2006. "The Diminishing Border between Advertising and Journalism in Estonia." *Journalism Studies* 7 (2): 312–322.

Hartsuiker, Chris. 2016. IAB Europé Guidance. How to Comply with EU Rules Applicable to Online Native Advertising. IAB Europe.

Hopmann, David Nicholas, Frank Esser, Claes H. de Vreese, Toril Aalberg, Peter van Aelst, Rosa Berganza, Nicolas Hubé, et al. 2016. "How We Did It. Approach and Methods." In *Comparing Political Journalism*, edited by Claes H. de Vreese, Frank Esser, and David Nicolas Hopmann. London: Routledge.

Ikonen, Pasi, Vilma Luoma-Aho, and Shannon A. Bowen. 2017. "Transparency for Sponsored Content: Analysing Codes of Ethics in Public Relations, Marketing, Advertising and Journalism." *International Journal of Strategic Communication* 11 (2): 165–178.

Iversen, Magnus Hoem, and Erik Knudsen. 2019. "When Politicians Go Native: The Consequences of Political Native Advertising for Citizens' Trust in News." *Journalism* 20 (7): 961–918.

Karlsson, Michael. 2010. "Rituals of Transparency: Evaluating Online News Outlets' Uses of Transparency Rituals in the United States, United Kingdom and Sweden." *Journalism Studies* 11 (4): 535–545.

Karlsson, Michael. 2012. "Charting the Liquidity of Online News: Moving towards a Method for Content Analysis of Online News." *International Communication Gazette* 74 (4): 385–402.

Krouwer, Simone, Karolien Poels, and Steve Paulussen. 2020. "Moving towards Transparency for Native Advertisements on News Websites: A Test of More Detailed Disclosures." *International Journal of Advertising* 39 (1): 51–73.

Lauerer, Corinna. 2019. "Advertising and Journalism." In *Oxford Research Encyclopedia of Communication*. Oxford University Press.doi:10.1093/acrefore/9780190228613.013.775.

Lewis, Seth C., and Nikki Usher. 2016. "Trading Zones, Boundary Objects, and the Pursuit of News Innovation: A Case Study of Journalists and Programmers." *Convergence: The International Journal of Research into New Media Technologies* 22 (5): 543–560.

Li, You. 2019. "Contest over Authority: Navigating Native Advertising's Impacts on Journalism Autonomy." *Journalism Studies* 20 (4): 523–541.

Lynch, Lisa. 2018. *Native Advertising: Advertorial Disruption in the 21st-Century News Feed*. New York, NY: Routledge.

Machin, David, and Lydia Polzer. 2015.*Visual Journalism*. New York, NY: Macmillan Education, Palgrave.

Neff, Gina. 2015. "Learning from Documents: Applying New Theories of Materiality to Journalism." *Journalism: Theory, Practice & Criticism* 16 (1): 74–78.

Pavlik, John. 2000. "The Impact of Technology on Journalism." *Journalism Studies* 1 (2): 229–237.

Perrin, Nicole. 2019. "US Native Advertising 2019. Display Budgets Keep Flowing to New Formats." eMarketer.

Ponikvar, Anthony B. 2015. "Ever-Blurred Lines: Why Native Advertising Should Not Be Subject to Federal Regulation." *North Carolina Law Review* 93 (4): 1187–1210.

Raeymaeckers, Karin. 2004. "Newspaper Editors in Search of Young Readers: Content and Layout Strategies to Win New Readers." *Journalism Studies* 5 (2): 221–232.

Schauster, E. E., P. Ferrucci, and M. S. Neill. 2016. "Native Advertising is the New Journalism: How Deception Affects Social Responsibility." *American Behavioral Scientist* 60 (12): 1408–1424.

Schindler, Johanna, Benjamin Krämer, and Philipp Müller. 2017. "Looking Left or Looking Right? Effects of Newspaper Layout Style on the Perception of Political News." *European Journal of Communication* 32 (4): 348–366.

Sirrah, Ava. 2019. "Guide to Native Advertising." Tow Center for Digital Journalism. https://www.cjr.org/tow_center_reports/native-ads.php

Tenenboim-Weinblatt, Keren. 2014. "Producing Protest News: An Inquiry into Journalists' Narratives." *The International Journal of Press/Politics* 19 (4): 410–429.

Tuchman, Gaye. 1972. "Objectivity as Strategic Ritual: An Examination of Newsmen's Notion of Objectivity." *American Journal of Sociology* 77 (4): 660–679.

Usher, Nikki. 2018. "Re-Thinking Trust in the News. A Material Approach through 'Objects of Journalism'." *Journalism Studies* 19 (4): 564–578.

Wang, Pengyuan, Guiang Xiong, and Jian Yang. 2019. "Serial Position Effects on Native Advertising Effectiveness: Differential Results across Publisher and Advertiser Metrics." *Journal of Marketing* 83 (2): 82–97.

Wang, Ruoxu, and Yan Huang. 2017. "Going Native on Social Media: The Effects of Social Media Characteristics on Native Ad Effectiveness." *Journal of Interactive Advertising* 17 (1): 41–50.

Wojdynski, Bartosz W. 2016. "The Deceptiveness of Sponsored News Articles: How Readers Recognize and Perceive Native Advertising." *American Behavioral Scientist* 60 (12): 1475–1491.

Wojdynski, Bartosz W. 2019. "Native Advertising." *Oxford Research Encyclopedia of Communication*. Oxford University Press. doi:10.1093/acrefore/9780190228613.013.842.

Wojdynski, Bartosz W., and Nathaniel J. Evans. 2016. "Going Native: Effects of Disclosure Position and Language on the Recognition and Evaluation of Online Native Advertising." *Journal of Advertising* 45 (2): 157–168.

Zamith, Rodrigo. 2018. "Quantified Audiences in News Production: A Synthesis and Research Agenda." *Digital Journalism* 6 (4): 418–435.

Zhang, X., and Lea Hellmueller. 2017. "Visual Framing of the European Refugee Crisis in Der Spiegel and CNN International: Global Journalism in News Photographs." *International Communication Gazette* 79 (5): 483–510.

"It's in the Air"—Sponsored Editorial Content as a Path for Stealth Government Propaganda: The Case of Israeli Media

Anat Balint

ABSTRACT

This article explores the rise of government-sponsored content, a recent development in the branded content model, in which government agencies assume the role of sponsors of editorial content. Theoretically, branded content blurs the boundary between strategic messages and communicative ones. As such, it embodies an inherently manipulative essence. By examining three case studies of government-sponsored content deals in the Israeli market (2014, 2016, 2017), the article seeks to understand the implications of such blurring once government agencies adopt this practice. Based on triangulation of sources (government documents, media content and reports in the press) the study follows the formation of these deals and dissects the consequences of their implementation. Findings suggest that government-sponsored content promotes the infliction of new types of harm that differ from those customarily associated with commercial sponsorship. It impels media bodies to adopt the role of government agencies at the formation stage. Subsequently, it allows these government campaigns to establish a ubiquitous presence within media space. Most important, the deals open a path for stealth propaganda, either for personal promotion of politicians or advancement of political agendas concerning controversial topics. As such, they corrupt both media outlets and the public sector.

Introduction

In late 2016, a documentary film broadcast on Channel 2, Israel's most popular channel at the time, sparked a heated debate. The presenter, a prominent journalist, announced in a grave voice that the Jewish people are on the verge of extinction. Many Jews, he argued, are "vanishing" because of the high rate of intermarriage among diaspora Jews. This claim touched a sensitive nerve and drew the attention of television critics. A brief disclosure at the corner of the screen—"in cooperation with the Ministry of Diaspora Affairs"—shed light on a silently rising phenomenon in Israeli media: deals with leading media outlets for government-sponsored content (GSC).

The present article is an exploration into a recently emerging development in the *branded content* (BC) model, wherein commercial sponsors are replaced by government ministries. Such evolution reflects the tendency of this financial model to expand into new, previously less commercialized territories.

The article explores the implications of GSC on the organizational culture and professional conduct of digital journalism outlets as well as the eventual impact on journalistic outputs. More broadly, it explores the ways in which changes in the economic ecosystem of journalism in the digital age may affect the flow of information to the public and raises fundamental questions as to the possible harms for democracy.

Theoretically, I suggest that the BC model (that includes *native advertising* (NA) on digital platforms) relies on the presentation of strategic messages as communicative ones, revealing its inherent manipulative essence (Habermas 1984).

Indeed, scholars have identified the blurring effect at the heart of BC, dissecting its potential harm to the media's integrity, independence and public trust therein, particularly in the context of journalism (Balint 2012, 2016; Carlson 2015; Conill 2016; Conill and Karlsson 2018; Couldry and Turow 2014; Einstein 2016; Goodman 2006; Hardy 2016; Iversen and Knudsen 2017). In recent years, researchers focussed their attention on audiences' ability to identify stealth advertising and its consequent impact on their attitudes (Amazeen and Muddiman 2017; Amazeen and Wojdynski 2018; Boerman and Van Reijmersdal 2016; Hyman et al. 2016).

To date, this emerging funding model for media content, in which government agencies are assuming the role of sponsors but their identity as the source of the message is blurred with that of the media outlet (hence the stealth nature of the content), has not been studied academically. The present article aims at bridging the gap in data and analysis by critically dissecting the rise of GSC in the Israeli media market.

The Israeli case provides an interesting landscape for a more thorough view of this new BC manifestation. Policymaking and enforcement of BC in this country have been inconsistent and contradictory. Despite repeated attempts, regulators failed to institute a change that would establish clear boundaries for BC and obligate proper disclosure of sponsorship. Against this background, BC remains formally prohibited, yet continues thriving and expanding into new terrains—one of them GSC. Between the years 2015-2019, approximately 222 GSC deals were implemented across various Israeli media outlets (TV, radio, press and digital) at an overall expense of approximately US$14 million[1] in taxpayers' money (Appendix A:20).

The current article seeks to shed light on the rise of GSC in this context by asking two questions:

1. How are these agreements made and arranged under conditions that place them in the grey zone of legality?
2. In what ways does the implementation of GSC deals with media outlets allow for new forms of blurred demarcations surrounding editorial content?

The Fluid Nature of Branded Content

Since the early 2000s, BC has been emerging as a dominant but controversial[2] financial model for production of media content. Its global emergence—an outcome of the interplay between the global neo-liberal order and the introduction of digital technologies—reflects a significant change in the media economy (Baltruschat 2011; Hardy 2017, 2018).

The model is defined as the integration of a third party, commercial or otherwise, into media content—that is not its producer, broadcaster or distributor—on the basis of material recompense and without clearly identifying such transactions as advertising (Balint 2016). The various names ascribed to this phenomenon reflect the different perspectives of its stakeholders: In media and advertising jargon, BC is prevalent as a general term and NA[3] is used in the context of digital environments. Both these terms were adopted by research scholars as well (Carlson 2015; Einstein 2016; Conill and Karlsson 2018; Iversen and Knudsen 2017). In critical discourse, some of the expressions used are *stealth marketing* (Goodman 2006) and *embedded branding* (Balint 2012, 2016). Another term, with a more neutral orientation, is *sponsored content* (Boerman and Van Reijmersdal 2016). In this article, BC will refer to the general phenomenon, while GSC will designate its sub-category that is at the heart of the present work. Furthermore, I will use NA to refer to BC on digital content platforms.

One palpable characteristic of BC is its fluid nature—that differentiates it from historical practices of commercialization, such as product placement and sponsorship (Barnouw 1978; Newell, Salmon, and Chang 2006; Segrave 2004; Turow 2006). This refers both to its propensity to assume abstract representations—as well as its tendency to expand into new territories, across geographical markets, media platforms and genres.

Historically, commercialization of content was focussed on the integration of products and brand names. Over the past few decades, however, the dominance of branding processes led practitioners to emphasize abstract representations of sponsors in content, implemented through the integration of values, worldviews and brand graphic design. This trend lead to the ubiquitous presence of brands in media content (Balint 2016).

Second, industry reports (Adyoulike 2015; Quinn and Kivijarv 2018) point to the remarkable global expansion of BC—and NA in particular—within only one decade.

Third, this model shifted rapidly from old media (primarily television) to digital media, leaping across genres from entertainment content in the early 2000s (Jenkins 2006) to the news industry a decade later. In 2014, it became an integral part of the financial model of the online editions of quality newspapers such as *The New York Times* (Somaiya 2013), *The Guardian* (Moses 2014a), *The Washington Post* (Sebastian 2013) and *The Wall Street Journal* (Moses 2014b).

This study focuses on what appears to be yet another turn in the expansive nature of BC: The emergence of "cooperation deals" between private media outlets and government agencies. This new manifestation of BC shifts the source of sponsorship from the private sector (corporations) to the public one (Ministries) and presents a new path of content subsidy. The most distinctive feature of this model is the blurring between the source of the strategic message (the governmental sponsor) and the outlet that mediates it to the public as 'editorial content'. This is the phenomenon I call GSC.

Understanding the Distinction between Content and Advertising: A Theoretical Framework

Blurring of boundaries between editorial content and advertising stands at the heart of the BC model. Those who profit from implementing these deals tend to celebrate this convergence (Heyer 2003) and argue that the two categories were never distinct and that their traditional separation through regulation, ethical codes or cultural norms is quickly eroding and may cease to exist. Nevertheless, critics of the model perceive blurring of advertising and editorial to be detrimental.

Three theories of harm are commonly mentioned to justify public regulation in this field. The first relates to reduced competition in the media market (by distorting the editorial process in favour of sponsors rather than the public), the second to concern about over-commercialization of media content, in the spirit of the No Logo critic (Klein 2000) and the third focuses on deception of consumers, who are led to believe that advertising is an outcome of an editorial choice (Goodman 2006). However, it is Habermas' notion of the public sphere (1989)—and particularly his *Theory of Communicative Action*—, which introduce the distinction between *communicative action* and *strategic action* (Habermas 1984) that provides a useful theoretical framework for understanding the fundamental distinction between advertising and content and—most importantly—the damage brought upon the ethics of public discourse by their blurring.

According to Habermas's typology of action, the actors in communicative action aim at reaching an understanding "in order to coordinate their actions" (Habermas 1984). Their mutual agreement must have a rational basis and rely on "validity claims"—common convictions that are best understood as "truth" (Goodman 2006). Thus, communicative action refers to a dialogue in which the speakers are able to reach agreement by influencing each other's thoughts, values, opinions and ultimately behaviour. Such decision-making resembles editorial choices concerning the work of content creators (e.g., journalists, scriptwriters). In strategic action, by contrast, actors seek to gain influence over others for their own ends, rather than attempting to achieve consensus. The speaker's views in this case cannot be changed, and arguments are merely instrumental in achieving a desired goal. Practically speaking, this is the essence of advertising and other marketing communication. Another important distinction concerns intention: In communicative action, the speaker's aim is apparent in the meaning of what is said. This is not the case regarding strategic action. Here, "we identify their meaning only in connection with the intentions their authors are pursuing and the ends they want to realize" (Habermas 1984).

The BC model blurs the line between these two actions by presenting a strategic action as a communicative one. Habermas perceives this as *concealed strategic action*—"the result of a confusion between actions oriented to reaching understanding and actions oriented to success" (Habermas 1984, 332). When this effort is deliberate, as in the case of BC, "... at least one of the parties behaves with an orientation to success, but leaves others to believe that all the presuppositions of communicative action are satisfied." This, in Habermas's view, is nothing but "conscious deception" or simply: "manipulation" (Habermas 1984, 332). To put it simply, the people who are behind BC deals intentionally manipulate users by concealing the strategic intent behind the content and presenting it as the bearer of a communicative mission. Ofcourse, critics of Habermas' Deliberative Democracy theory challenge some of his basic assumptions. Most notably, in the context of his discourse ethics, Mouffe argues that an ideal speech situation is "conceptual impossibility" (Mouffe 2000, 33). According to Mouffe, the idea of a coercion-free deliberative sphere cannot be fulfilled and that a decision can be achieved only through the dominance of a master siginifier and the exclusion of others (Mouffe 1999). Thus, there is space for further explore the implications of BC from Mouffe's Agnostic Pluralism theory or other critics of Habermas.

Concerns about Branded Content by Commercial Sponsors

The deceptive nature of BC has been a focus of concern in recent critical literature. Scholars follow one of two principal paths: The first concerns the growing erosion of content/advertising differentiation, often referred to as "church and state" in the context of journalism and its ethics. Scholars who uphold this view underscore the damage to journalism's professional norms, autonomy and integrity, as well as the possibility of a subsequent decline of public trust in the media (Balint 2012, 2016; Carlson 2015; Conill 2016; Conill and Karlsson 2018; Couldry and Turow 2014; Einstein 2016; Goodman 2006; Hardy 2016; Iversen and Knudsen 2017). After the U.S. Federal Trade Commission instituted new regulatory guidelines mandating clear disclosure of such advertising on digital platforms (FTC 2013),[4] other scholars examined audiences' ability to identify NA and its impact on users' attitudes. Generally speaking, research shows that only a minority of users successfully identify the commercial nature of NA (Amazeen and Muddiman 2017; Amazeen and Wojdynski 2018; Boerman and Van Reijmersdal 2016; Hyman et al. 2016). For example, only 17% of participants correctly identified the *sponsored content* label—the term with the most recognizable language of all (Amazeen and Muddiman 2017; Wojdynski and Evans 2016). Correct identification depends not only on the characteristics of the disclosure (Amazeen and Wojdynski 2018; Boerman and Van Reijmersdal 2016; Wojdynski 2016; Wojdynski and Evans 2016; Wu et al. 2016), but also on audience characteristics. Younger, more educated audiences who engage with news media for informative purposes were more likely to identify NA as such (Amazeen and Muddiman 2017).

The Rise of Government-Sponsored Editorial Content: The Israeli Case

The case of Israel's media landscape provides a good starting point for exploring the rise of GSC, as this funding model has become a notable and controversial phenomenon in this market since the mid-2010s.[5] From 2015 to 2019, approximately 222 GSC deals were implemented across various Israeli outlets: 84 in digital outlets, 65 in commercial television, 57 in commercial radio and 16 in the press. The overall government expenditure for these deals was approximately US$14 million: $3.6 million for digital outlets, $8.1 million for commercial television, $1.15 million for commercial radio and $1 million for the press (Appendix A:20). Thus, GSC in Israel was then most prevalent on digital outlets, but more costly on commercial television, reflecting the stronger impact attributed by sponsors to broadcast television. There are sporadic examples of somewhat similar practices in other countries, such as the case of Irish government advertorials for the Ireland 2040 plan in local and national newspapers, that evoked a public uproar (Power, 2018). The Israeli case, however, constitutes a unique landscape in which media outlets cooperate with government arms to blur the line between the identity of the source of the strategic message and that of the platform carrying it (media outlet), i.e., GSC. This has turned into a systematic and comprehensive phenomenon throughout the 2010s.

The rise of the GSC model should be understood within the context of this market's development and regulatory climate. Israeli media have undergone rapid transformation since the late 1980s, as part of the country's comprehensive shift from a socialistic welfare state toward a neo-liberal economy, that began in 1978. Within 15 years, Israel progressed from protracted domination of a state-controlled broadcast authority (single television channel and a number of radio stations) into a predominantly privatized landscape with abundance of outlets: two commercial broadcast channels, cable and satellite multichannel platforms, commercial local radio stations and print and online news outlets, alongside a reformed public broadcasting corporation.

Specifically, BC—the presentation of advertising as content—is formally prohibited in Israel according to audiovisual media laws (Appendix A:19,3) and rules (Appendix A:18), as well as the Consumer Protection Law, that is not medium specific[6] (Appendix A:4). Since the mid-2000s, however, as the media outlet crisis intensified, BC boomed as a new source of revenue (Balint 2012). Israeli media regulators enforced existing laws inconsistently and all efforts at determination of a new and clearer policy in this field failed repeatedly (Balint 2012; Shwartz-Altshuler and Chesler 2014).[7] Regulators' incompetence in setting clear policies should be understood within the context of the overall disempowerment of media regulation in Israel. This occurred due to the neo-liberal turn but at the same time, due to growing political control over the media during Benjamin Netanyahu's era as PM.[8] This trend proved beneficial to stakeholders in this case: Revenues outnumbered random penalties and the BC market kept thriving within the grey zone of legality. This ambiguous landscape has become even more perplexing recently. While stakeholders in commercial television and radio pushed for a change in the Second Authority Law that would allow BC but obligate its disclosure,[9] the Attorney-General filed a formal position paper in response to a class action suit against the popular online news outlet YNET, stating that the practice clearly violates the Consumer Protection Law by presenting deceptive advertising (Persico 2018).

At the same time, a regulatory path for GSC was established. SATR rules (for licensees) and Ministry of Finance guidelines (for all Ministries) independently allow Ministries and media outlets to embrace content collaborations that are not of a commercial or political nature (Appendix A:18, 15).[10] This led to a dual regulatory mechanism: SATR approves these agreements for commercial media outlets, while the Government Advertising Agency (GAA) manages transactions for government ministries, referring each to a bid committee.

Ongoing failure in establishing a coherent and comprehensive policy eventually led to transfer of the issue from policymakers to the justice system. Several class-action lawsuits regarding BC by commercial sponsors were filed in Israeli courts, as well as an appeal to the High Court of Justice in the matter of GSC (Benzaquen 2019). The High Court of Justice decided to accept the case of GSC, despite the objection of SATR licensees and the Attorney General (Appendix A:20), but legal procedures have not begun to date (Benzaquen 2020). In the meantime, market forces shape the landscape, and the phenomenon, with both commercial and governmental sponsors, continues to thrive. Both *Keshet*[11] and *Yedioth Ahronoth*,[12] two leading players in the Israeli market to be described below, are being sued for BC while simultaneously relying on it as a vital source of income.

For these reasons, I chose the Israeli case for my primary exploration of GSC and its potential harms. I will ask two research questions:

1. How are these agreements made and arranged under conditions that place them in the grey zone of legality?
2. In what ways does the implementation of GSC deals with media outlets allow for new forms of blurred demarcations surrounding editorial content?

Methodology

To approach the research questions, I chose to conduct a qualitative analysis of three case studies of GSC deals in the Israeli market. I used a multiple methods approach, i.e., triangulation (Berg and Lune 2012; Denzin and Lincoln 2011), relying on three sources of empirical data:

1. Documents from the formation stage of these deals (requests to the regulator, bid protocols, contracts, internal research reports, etc. (Appendix A).
2. Media materials concerning the implementation of these deals (websites, documentaries, newspaper articles, short videos) (Appendix B).
3. Various newspaper articles that reflect public discourse on these deals after their implementation (investigative articles and television critiques).

This approach not only adds rigour to the case study methodology (Yin 2009) but also, in the context of this research, enables us to trace the deals from their initial formation to their final implementation.

I then applied thematic coding to analyse the empirical materials of each case study in relation to the research questions. The findings are thus organized according to the relevant themes, indicating the respective case studies from which they derive.

As detailed below, I chose case studies that involved various Ministries and topics, seeking to portray the rise of this phenomenon over time (2014, 2016, 2017). Another consideration in the choice of case studies was the abundance of empirical data that these cases offered, based on documents obtained by journalists and NGOs through Israel's Freedom of Information Law. These documents provided a valuable resource and a considerable methodological advantage over deals with commercial sponsors, who are not bound by mandatory transparency. Nevertheless, this choice does embody some inherent bias: The case studies drew public attention because they raised legal and ethical questions. Thus, they provide a sound opportunity for exploring the problematic aspects of GSC but do not necessarily represent similar deals that may have been less controversial.

Case 1: No Texting While Driving (2014)

In March 2014, the Israel Ministry of Transportation and Road Safety (MoTRS) launched a two-month campaign warning against texting while driving. Inspired by Oprah Winfrey's No Texting campaign (2010), its aim was to make the public aware of the problem and change drivers' behaviour (Appendix A:1).

The chief promotional activity was a *cooperation* deal with Keshet. Most activity concerned integration of the campaign's messages in various Keshet programs on Channel two and on its digital platform, Mako. The contract between the GAA and Keshet was detailed: It listed the Keshet programs slated to integrate the campaign's messages, alongside regular 30-second slots. It also specified exposure via the Mako online service. For example, Keshet committed to produce various clips for the campaign and integrate them in current affairs programs: The morning show, late news show and a pre-prime time program. It also agreed to produce a long documentary on the topic (Appendix A:9). The overall costs of this deal came to $550,000 (Appendix A:10).

Case 2: Connecting Israelis with the Jewish Diaspora (2016)

In March 2016, the Israel Ministry of Diaspora Affairs (MoDA)[13] launched a campaign to promote awareness and knowledge about diaspora Jewry, aimed at "making Israeli citizens feel they are part of the collective of the Jewish People" (Appendix A:6). The campaign comprised sponsored content alongside some traditional advertising and involved several television, internet and print media outlets. The chief partnering body was Keshet, that stands at the centre of this analysis. As in the previous case study, this deal included integration of the campaign's messages in a variety of Keshet programs on Channel 2, a special one-hour documentary and a special Mako section (Appendix A:13).

Another deal was signed with a BC agency known as *Grey Content*.[14] Other partners in the MoDA's campaign were media outlets that target right wing and religious Jewish audiences.[15] Overall, the MoDA invested approximately $2,000,000 in the Israeli side of this campaign, of which Keshet's share was $570,000 (Appendix A:14).

Case 3: Pro-Israel Advocacy Online (2017)

In mid-2017, the Israel Ministry of Strategic Affairs and Public Diplomacy (MoSA) launched an extensive campaign to fight the BDS movement and create a pro-Israel advocacy network online. The principal platform for this activity was the website *4il*,[16] a content hub that invites activists to take part in fighting attempts at Israel's delegitimization online. The Ministry invested considerable effort in building and promoting this platform spending approximately $2,000,000 to cover the costs of the platform, social media advertising, public events and BC in Israeli media (Benzaquen 2017d). The two primary BC deals were struck with Yedioth ($100,000) and Keshet ($157,000). These transactions will constitute the focus of our analysis (Appendix A:8).

Findings

Coming Together: The Formation of Branded Content Deals with Government Agencies

As the empirical data suggests, the formation of cooperation deals between media outlets and government offices requires an initial blurring between the roles of each party to the deal, so that they appear to be conducting a joint mission, as equal partners. This occurs when each side "lends" part of its role to the other. The blurring process takes place in two stages: In the first, the media body voluntarily assumes a public or national mission, as if it were a government body. Ministries' strategic goals are presented to regulators by licensees as a communicative mission (Habermas 1984). In the second, the media outlet "lends" its editorial independence to the governmental partner, allowing the Ministry the last word regarding the content they sponsor. Below, I present this process as reflected in the case studies.

Joint National Mission

Formal requests submitted by licensees to SATR preliminary approval, provide a glimpse at the media outlets' rationale for cooperating with various government agencies.

In the No Texting campaign, Keshet presented the problem as a "national mission" and also a "countrywide plague" that it is determined to fight and defeat.

> We believe that preventing cellular phone use while driving has **turned into a national mission**. As part of this battle, Keshet would like to cooperate with the Ministry of Transportation and the National Road Safety Authority to raise this topic on the public agenda and **spearhead authentic change among the Israeli driving public**[17] (Appendix A:1).

In the campaign linking Israelis with diaspora Jewry, sponsored by the MoDA, the rationale called on Israeli citizens to play a more active role in halting the rise of assimilation among diaspora Jews, a trend presented as an "existential threat."

> … Keshet would like to cooperate with the Ministry of Diaspora Affairs **to make Israeli citizens** aware of the **growing existential problem** of diaspora Jewry (i.e., assimilation, as mentioned earlier in the document [A.B.]) and to **make viewers aware of the need for greater Israeli involvement** in diaspora affairs and in activities that foster connections among all the world's Jews …

> As part of this cooperation, **we will provide the Israeli public with information and activity guidelines** for recruiting members of the audience to face the challenge (Appendix A:13).

The idea of recruiting Israelis for the online battle against BDS, in cooperation with the MoSA, was presented to the regulator as an urgent need for Israeli citizens' participation in an *existential* national mission:

Throughout Israel's 69 years of existence, various interest groups, from within or outside the state, **have taken action to question Israel's right to exist**. In most cases, these elements know only one side of the story. They were not exposed to other sides or to any contending narratives ...

Consequently, to **make viewers aware of the ways in which they can improve Israel's public diplomacy and serve as Israel's ambassadors on the web**, Keshet would like to cooperate with the Ministry of Strategic Affairs in this campaign (Appendix A:2).

It can be argued that these rationales were strategically formulated to comply with regulations prohibiting cooperation with organizations of a political or commercial nature[18] (Appendix A:18). These documents, however, provide an inside view of the justifications that executives use to explain these deals. They immerse the media outlets they lead into the role of the relevant government agencies, adopting the agency's perspective, goals and mission. Consequently, they strive to "educate" members of their audience in the desired directions, ultimately motivating them to take action in the real world (e.g., "do not text while you drive," "get involved in fighting BDS").

Outsourcing Editorial Independence

Formal BC contracts provide plentiful insight into field, but are rarely exposed.

The contract for the No Texting campaign is an exception. It was signed between the GAA (representing the MoTRS) and Keshet, and later made public (Benzaquen 2016b). It clearly accords the sponsoring entities the right to have the last word regarding broadcast and online content. Section 13 of this contract states:

Keshet will make its best efforts to send the GAA the lineup and content of the items. Keshet commits to show the program/vignettes to the GAA and the Ministry (MoTRS [A.B.]) before broadcasting (Appendix A:9).

There is strong supporting evidence that commitment to granting sponsors the final say has become the norm for BC deals in Israel with commercial and non-profit enterprises alike (Balint 2016). Indeed, former GAA manager Gadi Margalit confirmed that such conditions were standard in BC contracts, explaining:

This relates to pre-confirmation of the content outline. There are cases of disputes in which broadcasters ask for what you call "independence," such as the one we had (in the No Texting campaign) regarding the documentary film presenter's identity (Benzaquen 2016b).

Hence, in the formative stages of these cooperation deals, the roles of the respective parties appear to have amalgamated: Media outlets adopt Ministries' missions in their designated fields, while the Ministries assume editorial authority. Instead of two terrains that are separate and even oppositional, in the spirit of the Habermasian notion of the public sphere (Habermas 1989), the two spheres tend to unify and become subject to the sponsors' strategic goals.

This empirical data suggests that looking at stage of the formation of BC deals is essential to understating how the blurring between the source of the message and the media platform that carries the message, occurs.

Blurring the Line: Implementation of Branded Content Deals with Government Agencies

Empirical data from the three case studies provides evidence that GSC deals tend to blur the line between previously distinct categories of media content.

To address this issue, I begin by discussing four structural aspects of these deals: use of multiple forms of advertising; cross platform presence; amalgamation of genres and shared copyrights. I contend that when combined, these aspects engender a multifaceted blurring effect that helps the campaigns establish ubiquitous presence across media space.

I then examine the ways that GSC deals are implemented into media content. Here, blurring occurs between the formal goals of these governmental campaigns and strategic, stealthy objectives, whether personal or political. I maintain that the purported "editorial content" introduced through GSC deals paves the way toward use of public funds for the personal promotion of politicians and—in some cases—for stealth political propaganda concerning controversial issues.

Taking over Media Space
From Advertising Slots to Sponsored Editorial Content. Empirical data sheds light on the often complex structure of GSC deals, including involvement of various advertising tools. As the contract of the No Texting campaign shows, on television, the deal included regular 30-second advertising slots alongside promotional content vignettes[19] and integration of the campaign in several of Keshet's programs. In the digital arm, *Mako*, the contract specifies a list of banners across various sections of the website, along with a special content section dedicated to the campaign.

As such, the deal is not just about sponsored editorial content, but offers an array of promotional tools, ranging from traditional advertising to surreptitious advertising within media content. Deals of this type ultimately assist in obscuring the line between advertising and content. The final experience for users is that of continuous exposure to the campaign's messages across time and space.

Flow across Platforms. All three campaigns were implemented across multiple platforms— television, digital media and print. Both Keshet and Yedioth could offer multiple platforms under the same ownership, allowing audience flow from one platform to the other. Such convergence appears to be a significant consideration for sponsors: The minutes of the GAA Bid Committee meeting regarding the No Texting campaign include a clear statement by a GAA professional, indicating that Keshet was to be preferred over its competitors because "the campaign is based on integration of screen and digital [media]," a specialty regarding which Keshet's proposal surpassed all others (Appendix A:5).

Content flow did not end there. Both Keshet and Yedioth organized public events in cooperation with the MoSA in its efforts to fight the boycott movement. This Ministry became a partner in Keshet's annual global television conference[20] (Appendix A:11,12). Yedioth organized an international conference for its subscribers, in cooperation with the Ministry, entitled *Fighting the Boycott* (Benzaquen 2016a). These events marked the culmination of a full campaign cycle, from the mediated sphere to the real world.

Amalgamation of Genres. The data show that GSC deals with leading media bodies pave the way toward integration of stealth advertising in different programing formats within these bodies, promoting a blurring effect among genres and their specific ethics. The Keshet case demonstrates this tendency clearly. Advertisers are regularly offered a "package" of current affairs programs for integration of sponsored content (Appendix B:16). In the MoTRS and MoDA campaigns, the deals included, in addition, a special documentary dedicated to the campaign's theme.

Indeed, the involvement of a prominent journalist in a documentary sponsored by the MoDA aroused harsh criticism of Keshet and the journalist, who were accused of ethical misconduct (Alpher 2016; Schiff 2016).[21] In another instance, the No Texting campaign contract included the promise of a sketch in the highly respected satirical show *Eretz Nehederet* [Hebrew: A Marvellous Land] (Appendix A:9).[22] This promise encouraged the GAA to approve the deal with Keshet without looking at competitive offers (Appendix A:5), even though it was never fulfilled (Benzaquen 2016c).

The outcome of this sponsored content flow across genres, is the blurring of their distinct characteristics and consequent potential erosion of their respective professional norms and ethics. As one television critic concluded regarding the MoDA's controversial "documentary": "If this is what the most popular TV channel presents as a 'documentary,' we may better be off with *Big Brother*" (Schiff 2016).

Shared Copyrights. Yet another aspect of blurring is evident in the No Texting campaign. As the contract (Section 11.4) indicates, Keshet has agreed to allow the MoTRS and the GAA to make further use of editorial content for the Ministry's strategic needs and the GAA's promotional platforms—website and YouTube channels—for an unlimited time (Appendix A:9). This means that although Keshet holds the copyrights for this content, they are shared with the sponsors for all intents and purposes. What was presented to audiences as "editorial" at first turned into promotional material for the sponsors, on their own platforms.

The combination of these elements accords government campaigns ubiquitous presence in media space, eroding distinctions between advertising and content and differentiation among platform, genre and content ownership. Audiences thus become surrounded with strategic messages and may experience difficulty identifying them as such.

Turning Public Service Campaigns into Personal and Political Agendas

Below, I analyse the implementation of the three deals. Specifically, I discuss the ways in which the so-called "public" premise of these campaigns was shifted covertly, through manipulation of editorial content, into one that promotes individuals or political agendas, despite explicit prohibitions stipulated in government guidelines and media regulations (Appendix A:15,16).

Personal Promotion. The empirical data suggests that GSC opens the way for personal promotion of politicians and senior executives. In the No Texting campaign, then Minister of Transportation Israel Katz gained dominant presence in the campaign, both on television and online, thanks to cooperation with Keshet. To a great extent, Katz became the face of the campaign. He was interviewed on all current affairs programs included in the deal and in the special documentary on the topic. The Minister also wrote a personal op-ed piece for the special Mako section dedicated to the campaign (Appendix B:2). In the interviews and column, his work was mentioned alongside that of Oprah Winfrey concerning the same issue.

In a response to the press, the Ministry spokesperson denied that the interviews were sponsored, claiming that the Minister was invited to talk about the campaign after the deal was signed and independently of it (Benzaquen, 2015). In the case of the Ministry of Diaspora Affairs, one of the Ministry's executives was interviewed for the "documentary" that was part of the deal, alongside representatives of a Jewish organization that the Ministry helped sponsor (Benzaquen 2017a).[23] Similarly, executives from the Ministry of Strategic Affairs and representatives of Jewish organizations were interviewed by Ynet's political reporter as part of the deal concerning the anti-BDS campaign (Benzaquen 2017b).

Political Propaganda. Two of the case studies demonstrate how BC deals involving government agencies can become a vehicle for embedding political framing of topics at the heart of public debate. Both campaigns—pro-Israel advocacy online and connecting the Israeli public with the Jewish diaspora—touch on controversial issues within Israeli society.

In the first case, although objection to calls for a boycott of Israel is widely consensual among Israelis, the decision to present the BDS movement as a strategic threat to the state— and specifically, the attempts to unite Israelis around this cause—became highly controversial. The Ministry's actions were criticized from the left as an attempt to divert attention from the internal Israeli debate over the occupied territories, to impair Palestinian political freedom and to blur the line between political criticism of Israel and antisemitism (Editorial 2019). In particular, the cooperation deals with Yedioth and Keshet were criticized as a new form of "stealth propaganda" (Benzaquen 2017d). An opposition Knesset member claimed these deals are "unethical for both sides" (Benzaquen 2017c).

Keshet's sponsored editorial section on the topic indeed became a blunt form of nationalistic propaganda: The site, called *Love Israel*, was branded with Israeli flags in the background, with part of the Star of David at their centre designed as a heart (Appendix B:4). It presented headlines such as "The people who did wonderful things for the state" and "Love Israel? Tell us what you've done for it"[24] (Appendix B:6,3). A comparative analysis of Ynet and *Haaretz* online coverage of the anti-BDS campaign during the first half of 2016 displayed a clear bias. Ynet's coverage of the topic was more extensive, but the framing of its reports was manipulative. It presented events in a manner favourable to Israel and avoided any criticism of the government (Loycker 2017).

In the second case, the political bias was even more elusive. Although the sense of mutually assured solidarity among the Jews as a people is consensual in Israel, there is an overt disparity between religious conservative Israelis and secular liberal ones in their attitudes toward the Jewish diaspora. The results of preliminary research conducted by the GAA for the MoDA demonstrated this gap. Generally, while the former camp tends to espouse collectivist Zionist attitudes resembling the Israeli national ethos of the early decades of the state combined with religious values, the latter tends to maintain more individualistic stands and uphold secular values. Thus, for example, when asked about intermarriage, both groups agreed it should be considered a national problem, but secular Jews, unlike their religious counterparts, were far more open to intermarriage at the individual level.[25] Consequently, the GAA austerely recommended that the future campaign should focus on a unifying consensual message of mutual responsibility among all Jews, the sense of being one large family, while avoiding more divisive topics: Jewish identity, judgmental Zionist points of view[26] and intermarriage (Appendix A:7).

In practice, the campaign with Keshet took precisely the opposite path. While the title of the special Mako section was *Mishpocheh* [Yiddish (from Hebrew): a Family], in the spirit of the GAA's recommendations, its content primarily bore an overtly nationalistic religious agenda, resembling that of the right-wing Minister of Diaspora Affairs at that time, Naftali Bennett. The various "articles" not only presented Israel as the "best" and "safest" place for the Jews, but also appropriated the success of diaspora Jews, emphasizing the controversial religious notion of "the Chosen People" (Appendix B:1,5). Several video clips presented stories of Jews who decided to come to Israel as a result of projects conducted by Jewish organizations that the Ministry helped sponsor (Appendix B:7). At the peak of the campaign, the sponsored documentary *Vanishing* aired on Channel two during prime time. Hosted by a prominent journalist, it presented intermarriage as a "second Holocaust" that leads the Jewish people to the brink of extinction. It caused a public uproar and called public attention to the problematic aspects of GSC. One television critic argued that Bennett became "Channel 2's supervising editor" (Alpher 2016), while another referred to the documentary as "Government advertising against assimilation with a journalist as its presenter" (Schiff 2016). A *Haaretz* editorial defined the piece as "Jewish Orthodox racist propaganda" that is part of Bennett's broader "incitement against secularism" (2019).

Politicization was evident in yet another aspect of the campaign: The Ministry choose to follow the GAA's recommendations to target audiences more amenable to the campaign's goals, i.e., Conservative Jews. As such, budgets were streamed to right wing and religious media outlets, as mentioned earlier, sending the Minister's electorate the messages they wanted to hear (Appendix A:7). Thus, in both cases, campaigns that began with the premise of a public service became—in the guise of editorial content—a tool for straightforward political propaganda.

Conclusions

This study is an initial exploration of an emerging form of BC: The collaboration of private media outlets and government offices. It adopts a critical approach that considers the blurring of boundaries between advertising and content, between strategic action and communicative action, to be manipulative (Habermas 1984). By examining three case studies taken from the Israeli market, it seeks to elucidate the problematic aspects of this phenomenon in two stages: The initial, formative stage and subsequent implementation.

As the empirical data analysis shows, the blurring effect at the heart of GSC is broader and deeper than the disparity between advertising and content. Based on the stealth essence of this form of advertising, blurring extends to other terrains serving the sponsors' strategic goals, yielding new forms of audience manipulation and possible harm.

First, at the formative stage of these deals, the two sides tend to merge their roles: Private media outlets "willingly" adopt the public and even national role of government agencies by committing themselves to convey certain strategic messages to the public and advocate for change in behaviour. At the same time, they subject their editorial voice to their government partners. The outcome is not that of roles being exchanged, but rather, both sides join to execute the strategic mission of these governmental entities. These findings add to current literature (Carlson 2015; Conill and Karlsson 2018; Conill 2016; Iversen & Knudsen 2017) by suggesting that the formative phase of BC deals is crucial to understanding how the practice works to change professional and ethical norms within media outlets.

Second, at the implementation stage, the fluid nature of this model and its manipulative essence become even more evident and bear new types of damage. The case studies show that these deals tend to establish ubiquitous presence for the campaigns across media space. The agreements involve various promotional tools, offer cross-platform presence, blur among genres and allow sponsors further use of the editorial content on their own promotional platforms. This means that audiences become surrounded with strategic messages that are hard to detect and approach critically. The findings support the understanding of BC as a central phenomenon in the new media economy, an outcome of a neo-liberal globalized media arena in which digitalization results in growing commercialization of content (Baltruschat 2011; Hardy 2017, 2018). Moreover, the study offers tools to dissect and understand the process of commercializing content, i.e., how sponsors gain ubiquitous presence through these deals.

In a more alarming manner, under the guise of editorial independence, GSC paves the way toward use of public funds for personal promotion of politicians and dissemination of overt political propaganda, despite regulatory restrictions.

This is probably the most harmful outcome of this new form of BC. What is presented as editorial content can become a vehicle to embed a certain political framing in issues at the heart of public debate, thereby impairing the media's role as a public sphere (Habermas 1989). More simply stated, the model corrupts both sides, as government agencies may use public money for personal and political propaganda, while media outlets erode their editorial independence by flagging such propaganda as though it were an expression of their editorial voice rather than an outcome of financial constraints and contractual obligations. This observation provides evidence of the practice's fluid nature—its migration from the market to the state, resulting in new forms of harm.

These findings present BC in general and GSC in particular as concerning phenomena in the rapidly changing economic ecosystem of digital journalism. Both models indeed open new paths for funding digital journalism; however, they raise grave questions as to their ethical implications and consequent sustainability. Particularly, GSC pushes journalism outlets to assume the role of government arms and eventually results in content that bears manipulative essence and has ubiquitous presence across media space. The economic necessity of adapting to the digital environment, thus, seems to result in pushing online journalism bodies to become vehicle of stealth propaganda by the state around political issues, thus distorting the editorial process that is at the basis of any democratic public debate.

The findings presented here are relevant to all who struggle with the BC phenomenon in general and specifically its recent expansion into government-sponsored deals: Lawmakers, regulators and activists. It is particularly useful for educators who seek to promote media literacy in an age in which finding one's way through the clutter of information becomes a daily struggle. There is an overt need, however, for further research on GSC that would allow for the extension of scholarly knowledge beyond the Israeli case. While the Israeli case currently stands out regarding the extent to which GSC was embedded into regulatory systems, the fluid nature of BC may suggest that other markets may follow. Small countries that shifted drastically from welfare state to neo-liberal economies may be particularly vulnerable. Consequently, research on GSC in other markets could contribute significantly to critical debate in this field. Furthermore, while this article placed GSC within the scholarly discourse on BC, there is a need for further elaboration of this market practice's adoption and its implications for the broader and complicated terrain of state and media relations and interdependency.

Notes

1. All amounts cited here appear in Israeli currency in the original documents and were converted to US dollars at an exchange rate of NIS 3.50 = US$1.00.
2. See, for example, John Oliver's satirical commentary on the topic (Oliver 2014).
3. NA is defined as "the practice of online publishers accepting payment from particular advertisers to publish customized content that looks very similar—in terms of tone, presentation, and functionality— to the independently produced news, editorial, and entertainment content on the site" (Bakshi 2015).
4. The EU also updated its rules on commercial communications (television, advertising, teleshopping, sponsorship and product placement) in 2018. While emphasizing the need for disclosure in commercial communications, the European Audiovisual Directive, unlike the FTC, defines sponsorship and product placement as two different practices. In addition, the Directive does not relate to online platforms (Audiovisual and Media Services Policy Team, 2018), possibly explaining why research on NA followed in the footsteps of FTC policymaking more than that of the European Directive.
5. Before 2015 there were sporadic cases of GSC and their monitoring was not systematic.
6. The first two laws pertain to television and radio, while the Consumer Protection Law is medium-independent and entails a comprehensive prohibition on deceptive advertising (Section 7C).
7. The failure to establish a consistent policy is partly an outcome of this market's fragmented regulatory structure: One regulating body for multichannel television and another for commercial radio and television broadcasting. All attempts at instituting a unified media regulator, in the spirit of British Ofcom or the American FCC, have failed so far.

8. Israeli PM Benjamin Netanyahu was indicted for bribery, fraud and breach of trust in three criminal cases in January 2020, all related, directly and indirectly, to his attempts to control Israeli media. A report by the State Comptroller of Israel published in May 2020 uncovered the ongoing disempowerment of both SATR and the Cable and satellite Broadcasting Council because of ongoing political involvement (Appendix A:17).
9. This change was approved by the Knesset (Israel's Parliament) on February 19, 2018. Nevertheless, the SATR did not publish its rules for proper disclosure of BC as the law required. Consequently, the new legislation is not valid in practice and the status quo remains in force.
10. Israeli Consumer Protection Law's definition of "advertising" (section 1 to the law) is limited to commercial advertising. Thus from a legal perspective it is debatable if GSC can be seen as a violation of this law.
11. Keshet Media Group began with a franchise for the former Channel 2 and currently is a licensee of Channel 12 and the owner of Mako website and of Keshet International.
12. The Yedioth Media Group owns one of Israel's oldest daily newspapers—*Yedioth Ahronoth*—and the popular digital news service Ynet. The group has many other media holdings: Magazines, a publishing house, local newspapers, etc.
13. This Ministry, first established in 1999, is responsible for fostering the connections between the State of Israel and the Jewish Diaspora.
14. This agency produced one-minute clips documenting the daily lives of Jews around the world. —The clips were broadcast daily over all three commercial channels before the main news programs. For an example, see https://www.youtube.com/watch?v=1yvOAkOqa9w.
15. *Israel Hayom* daily newspaper, *Makor Rishon* weekly, *Channel 7* digital radio and the *Channel 20* cable and satellite television channel.
16. See https://4il.org.il/.
17. All emphases in these citations were added by the author (A.B.).
18. Section 13 Alef-1-Het of the rules.
19. These vignettes are short clips, hybrids of programming and advertising that serve as a loophole to expand commercial time.
20. The Ministry paid $71,000 for this partnership in 2017 and $54,000 in 2018.
21. The *Haaretz* television critic wrote: "If only Yoav Limor (the journalist leading the documentary team) had the minimal professional integrity and journalism ethics that a democratic press ordinarily displays. But he does not … This is how democracies erode. Channel 2 acts as if it were representing the Government" (Alpher 2016).
22. A popular satirical sketch show somewhat inspired by *Saturday Night Live*.
23. This incident has turned into a dispute between the legal advisors of the Ministry of Diaspora Affairs and the GAA regarding approval of the senior executive's participation in the documentary. Neither side agreed to accept responsibility.
24. Both pieces mentioned here were oriented to encourage engagement and action. The first was a short story competition and the second was a contest for online activists who defend Israel online.
25. As the GAA researchers concluded: "In this collision between the Jewish national ethos and the liberal individual ethos that is oriented towards maximizing personal happiness, individual happiness overcomes tribal affiliation" (Appendix A:7).
26. In the Zionist narrative typical of the early decades of the state, life in the Diaspora was viewed as inferior to national fulfillment of one's Jewish identity by living in Israel.

Disclosure Statement

The author declared no potential conflicts of interest with respect to the research, authorship and/or publication of this article.

Funding

The author received no financial support for the research, authorship and/or publication of this article.

References

Adyoulike 2015. *Native Advertising Set to Double by 2018*. December 18. Accessed October 12, 2019. https://www.prnewswire.com/news-releases/native-advertising-set-to-double-by-2018-562919861.html

Alpher, R. 2016. "Hitler, I shrunk the Jews: How Bennett became the supervising editor of Channel 2." *Haaretz*, December 21. https://www.haaretz.co.il/gallery/television/news/.premium-1.3167034 [Hebrew]

Amazeen, M. A., and A. R. Muddiman. 2017. "Saving Media or Trading on Trust?: The Effects of Native Advertising on Audience Perceptions of Legacy and Online News Publishers." *Digital Journalism* 6 (2): 14–2019.

Amazeen, M. A., and A. R. Muddiman. 2018. "The Effects of Disclosure Format on Native Advertising Recognition and Audience Perceptions of Legacy and Online News Publishers." *Digital Journalism* 6 (2): 176–195.

Bakshi, A. 2015. "Why and How to Regulate Native Advertising in Online News Publication." *Media Law and Ethics* 4 (3–4): 1–47.

Balint, A. 2012. *Inside the Box: Embedded Branding in Israeli Commercial Television*. Jerusalem: Israel Democracy Institute.

Balint, A. 2016. *Branded Reality–The Rise of Embedded Branding ('Branded Content'): Implications for the Cultural Public Sphere*. London: University of London.

Baltruschat, D. 2011. "Branded Entertainment and the New Media Economy." In *The Propaganda Society: Promotional Culture and Politics in Global Context*, edited by Gerald Sussman, 45–60. New York: Peter Lang.

Barnouw, E. 1978. *The Sponsor: Notes on a Modern Potentate*. New York: Oxford University Press.

Benzaquen, I. 2020. "High Court of Justice will hear the appeal against covert government propaganda." *The Seventh Eye*.

Benzaquen, I. 2015. "Nationwide plague." *The Seventh Eye*, October 13. https://www.the7eye.org.il/170818 [Hebrew]

Benzaquen, I. 2016a. "Boycott bonanza." *The Seventh Eye*, April 4. https://www.the7eye.org.il/199173 [Hebrew]

Benzaquen, I. 2016b. "Paid for content? You've got veto rights." *The Seventh Eye*, June 29. https://www.the7eye.org.il/206206 [Hebrew]

Benzaquen, I. 2016c. "The wonders of native advertising." *The Seventh Eye*, July 4. https://www.the7eye.org.il/207013 [Hebrew]

Benzaquen, I. 2017a. "We did not approve." *The Seventh Eye*, January 3. https://www.the7eye.org.il/230775 [Hebrew]

Benzaquen, I. 2017b. "When the campaign hires the editorial team." *The Seventh Eye*, December 18. https://www.the7eye.org.il/268283 [Hebrew]

Benzaquen, I. 2017c. "What I see here is a campaign for the Ministry of Strategic Affairs, not a fight to debunk BDS." *The Seventh Eye*, December 21. https://www.the7eye.org.il/274019 [Hebrew]

Benzaquen, I. 2017d. "Israel's truth forces." *The Seventh Eye*, December 24. https://www.the7eye.org.il/272146 [Hebrew]

Benzaquen, I. 2019. "Appeal to the High Court of Justice: Stop stealth advertising by government agencies." *The Seventh Eye*, September 2. https://www.the7eye.org.il/342947 [Hebrew]

Berg, B. L., and H. Lune. 2012. *Qualitative Research Methods for the Social Sciences*. 8th ed.; Intl. ed. Boston and London: Pearson.

Boerman, S. C., and E. A. Van Reijmersdal. 2016. "Advertising in New Formats and the Media: Current Research and Implications for marketers." In *Informing Consumers about "Hidden advertising: A Literature Review of the Effects of Disclosing Sponsored Content,"* edited by P. de Pelsmacker, 115–146. London, UK: Emerald Group Publishing. https://doi.org/10.1108/978-1-78560-313-620151005.

Carlson, M. 2015. "When News Sites Go Native: Redefining the Advertising–Editorial Divide in Response to Native Advertising." *Journalism: Theory, Practice & Criticism* 16 (7): 849–865.

Conill, R. F. 2016. "Camouflaging Church as State: An Exploratory Study of Journalism's Native Advertising." *Journalism Studies* 17 (7): 904–914.

Conill, R. F., and M. Karlsson. 2018. Native Advertising and the Appropriation of Journalistic Clout. In *The Routledge Handbook of Developments in Digital Journalism Studies*. London: Routledge. https://doi.org/10.4324/9781315270449-36.

Couldry, N., and J. Turow. 2014. "Advertising, Big Data and the Clearance of the Public Realm: Marketers' New Approaches to the Content Subsidy." *International Journal of Communication* 8: 17.

Denzin, N. K., and Y. S. Lincoln. 2011. *The Sage Handbook of Qualitative Research*. 4th ed. Thousand Oaks, CA: Sage.

Editorial 2019. "Ministry of Strategic Damages." *Haaretz*, June 13. https://www.haaretz.co.il/opinions/editorial-articles/.premium-1.7363111

Einstein, M. 2016. *Black Ops Advertising: Native Ads, Content Marketing, and the Covert World of the Digital Sell (Reprint)*. New York: OR Books.

FTC. 2013. *Disclosures: How to Make Effective Disclosures in Digital Advertising*. Washington, DC: Federal Trade Commission.

Goodman, E. 2006. "Stealth Marketing and Editorial Integrity." *Texas Law Review* 85: 83–152.

Habermas, J. 1984. *The Theory of Communicative Action*. Vol. 1. Cambridge: Polity.

Habermas, J. 1989. *The Structural Transformation of the Public Sphere: An Inquiry into a Category of Bourgeois Society*. Cambridge: Polity.

Han, J. (K.), M. Drumwright, and W. Goo. 2018. "Native Advertising: Is Deception an Asset or a Liability?" *Journal of Media Ethics* 33 (3): 102–119. https://doi.org/10.1080/23736992.2018.1477048/.

Hardy, J. 2016. Resourcing a viable digital journalism. In *The Routledge Companion to Digital Journalism Studies*, edited by B. Franklin and S. Eldridge II. Abingdon, Oxon: Routledge. https://www.routledge.com/9781138887961

Hardy, J. 2017. "Commentary: Branded Content and Media-Marketing Convergence." *The Political Economy of Communication* 5 (1): 1.

Hardy, J. 2018. "Branded Content: Media and Marketing Integration." In *The Advertising Handbook*, edited by J. Hardy, H. Powell, & I. Macrury, 102–122. 4th ed. Abingdon, Oxon: Routledge.

Heyer, S. J. 2003. "Steven Heyer's manifesto for a new age of marketing." February 5. https://adage.com/article/news/steve-heyer-s-manifesto-a-age-marketing/36777

Hyman, D. A., D. J. Franklyn, C. Yee, and M. H. Rahmati. 2016. "Going Native: Can Consumers Recognize Native Advertising? Does It Matter?" SSRN Scholarly Paper No. ID 2816655. Retrieved from Social Science Research Network website: https://papers.ssrn.com/abstract=2816655

Iversen, M. H., and E. Knudsen. 2017. "When Politicians Go Native: The Consequences of Political NA for Citizens." *Journalism* 20 (7): 961–978.

Jenkins, H. 2006. "Convergence culture: Where old and new media collide." http://www.loc.gov/catdir/enhancements/fy0730/2006007358-d.html

Klein, N. 2000. *No Logo: No Space, No Choice, No Jobs, Taking Aim at the Brand Bullies*. London: Flamingo.

Loycker, A. 2017. "Good for the Jews." *The Seventh Eye*, January 19. https://www.the7eye.org.il/232913 [Hebrew]

Moses, L. 2014a. "*The Guardian*'s unusual take on native ads." Adweek, February 13. http://www.adweek.com/news/press/guardians-unusual-take-native-ads-155715

Moses, L. 2014b. "*The Wall Street Journal* launches native ad studio." Adweek, March 10. http://www.adweek.com/news/press/wall-street-journal-launches-native-ad-studio-156212

Mouffe, C. 1999. "Deliberative Democracy or Agonistic Pluralism?" *Social Research; New York* 66 (3): 745–758.

Mouffe, C. 2000 *The Democratic Paradox*. London, New-York: Verso.

Newell, J., C. T. Salmon, and S. Chang. 2006. "The Hidden History of Product Placement." *Journal of Broadcasting & Electronic Media* 50 (4): 575–594.

Oliver, J. 2014. "Native advertising." http://www.hbo.com/last-week-tonight-with-john-oliver/episodes/01/13-august-3-2014/video/ep-13-clip-native-advertising.html?autoplay=true

Persico, O. 2018. "The Attorney-General is also against making stealth advertising 'kosher'." *The Seventh Eye*, December 8. https://www.the7eye.org.il/312013 [Hebrew]

Quinn, P., and L. Kivijarv. 2018. "Global branded entertainment marketing forecast 2018." Accessed October 16, 2019, from PQ Media | Custom Media Research website: https://www.pqmedia.com/product/global-branded-entertainment-marketing-forecast-2018/

Schiff, E. 2016. "TV Critic: *Vanishing*, Channel 2, 10:00 PM." *Yedioth Ahronoth*, December 20. https://www.yediot.co.il/articles/0,7340,L-4895589,00.html [Hebrew]

Sebastian, M. 2013. "*The Washington Post* starts selling native ads for print." Advertising Age. http://adage.com/article/media/washington-post-starts-selling-native-ad-units-print/243851/

Segrave, K. 2004. *Product Placement in Hollywood Films: A History*. http://www.loc.gov/catdir/toc/ecip0417/2004008626.html

Shwartz-Altshuler, T., and T. Chesler. 2014. "Regulating branded content in the Israeli media." https://www.idi.org.il/media/7791/regulating_branded_content.pdf

Somaiya, R. 2013. "Times publisher sets out plan for "native" ads." *The New York Times*, December 19. http://www.nytimes.com/2013/12/20/business/media/publishers-letter-explains-limits-on-branded-content-at-the-times.html?_r=0

Sterling, G. 2018. "Native will dominate display spending in 2018." *Marketing Land*, April 11. https://marketingland.com/native-will-dominate-display-spending-in-2018-238081

Turow, J. 2006. *Niche Envy [Electronic Resource]: Marketing Discrimination in the Digital Age*. http://site.ebrary.com/lib/aberdeenuniv/Doc?id=10173665

Wojdynski, B. W. 2016. "The Deceptiveness of Sponsored News Articles: How Readers Recognize and Perceive Native Advertising." *American Behavioral Scientist* 60 (12): 1475–1491.

Wojdynski, B. W., and N. J. Evans. 2016. "Going Native: Effects of Disclosure Position and Language on the Recognition and Evaluation of Online Native Advertising." *Journal of Advertising* 45 (2): 157–168.

Wu, M., Y. Huang, R. Li, D. S. Bortree, F. Yang, A. Xiao, and R. Wang. 2016. "A Tale of Two Sources in Native Advertising: Examining the Effects of Source Credibility and Priming on Content, Organizations and Media Evaluations." *American Behavioral Scientist* 60 (12): 1492–1509.

Yin, R. K. 2009. *Case Study Research: Design and Methods*. 4th ed. London: Sage.

Appendix A: Hebrew-Language Documents

1. Barda, V. 2014. "Content Collaboration Request, Ministry of Transportation—Prevention of texting while driving." March 5. https://cdn.the7eye.org.il/uploads/2015/08/keshet-transportation-ministry-sponsored-content2014.pdf
2. Barda, V. 2017. *Content Collaboration Request*. Ministry of Strategic Affairs.
3. Communications Law (Telecommunications and Broadcasting). 1982. https://www.nevo.co.il/law_html/Law01/032_002.htm
4. Consumer Protection Law. 1981. https://www.nevo.co.il/law_html/Law01/089_001.htm
5. GAA. 2014. "Bid Committee Protocol: No Texting Campaign, in cooperation with Keshet." February 11. https://docs.google.com/viewerng/viewer?url=https://cdn.the7eye.org.il/uploads/2016/06/lapam-protocol-keshet1122014.pdf&hl=iw
6. GAA. 2016. "Bid Committee Protocol: Connecting Israelis and Diaspora Jews Campaign, in cooperation with Keshet." August 21. https://cdn.the7eye.org.il/uploads/2017/03/diaspora-marketing2017.pdf
7. GAA. 2017a. "Research: Tightening Israeli-Diaspora Relationships—Research and Recommendations." January. https://cdn.the7eye.org.il/uploads/2017/07/diaspora-ministry-recommendations-lapam-32016.pdf
8. GAA. 2017b. "Bid Committee Minutes: Online Activists against Israel's De-Legitimization Campaign, in cooperation with Keshet." April 6. https://cdn.the7eye.org.il/uploads/2017/12/lapam-msa2018.pdf
9. GAA-Keshet. 2014. "Contract between the government of Israel and Keshet Broadcasting Ltd.: Ministry of Transportation Campaign." https://cdn.the7eye.org.il/uploads/2016/06/keshet-transportation-ministry-campaign-contract2014.pdf
10. Kilshtok, E. 2014. "Media expenses by the Ministry of Transportation 2012-2014." June 12. https://cdn.the7eye.org.il/uploads/2015/10/transportation-ministry-advertising2014.pdf
11. Krakovsky, R. 2017. "Professional opinion with regard to contracting Keshet as an exclusive vendor." February 7. https://cdn.the7eye.org.il/uploads/2017/03/232321.pdf
12. Krakovsky, R. 2018. "Professional opinion with regard to contracting Keshet as an exclusive vendor." January 29. https://cdn.the7eye.org.il/uploads/2017/12/261095.pdf
13. Lahav, A. 2016. *Content Collaboration Request*. July 17. Ministry of Diaspora Affairs.
14. Ministry of Diaspora Affairs. n.d. "Media expenses by the Ministry of Diaspora Affairs: Campaign for Connecting Israelis to Diaspora Jewry 2015-2016." https://cdn.the7eye.org.il/uploads/2017/07/diaspora-ministry-advertising2015-2016.pdf
15. Ministry of Finance Directives: Non-Commercial Government Publications. 2018. June 11. https://mof.gov.il/takam/Pages/horaot.aspx?k=15.3.0.2
16. The Second Authority for Television and Radio. 2019. "Approved Content Collaborations with Government Agencies and NGO's on Israeli Commercial Television 2015-2018. Reply to Freedom of Information request by The Seventh Eye." May 22.
17. The State Comptroller and Ombudsman of Israel. 2020. "70th Annual Report, Part 2, Ministry of Communication, Independence of Broadcast Regulation Bodies" (in Hebrew). May 4. https://www.mevaker.gov.il/sites/DigitalLibrary/Pages/Reports/3285-23.aspx
18. Second Authority. 2009. "The Second Authority for Television and Radio Regulations (Programming by Franchisees)." http://www.rashut2.org.il/editor/UpLoadLow/b-116.pdf
19. The Second Authority for Television and Radio Law. 1990. http://www.rashut2.org.il/editor/UpLoadLow/B-55.pdf
20. Sephadi-Atilla, E. 2019. "General Attorney's response to Higher Court of Justice Appeal on GSC: Bagatz 5664/19." https://cdn.the7eye.org.il/uploads/2019/12/30122019-566419.pdf

Appendix B: Hebrew-Language Media Materials

1. "Hatred, defamation and antisemitism: World Jewry has a hard job coping." 2017. January 24. Retrieved from Mako website: https://www.mako.co.il/special-Jewish-people-family/Article-87f645f3ccfc951006.htm?sCh=781d36a288d37510&pId=885471177
2. Katz, I. 2014. "Texting while driving is like driving after four shots of alcohol." March 13. Retrieved from Mako website: https://www.mako.co.il/special-no-sms/articles/Article-68e547d853bb441006.htm
3. Love Israel Editorial. 2017. "Love Israel? Tell us what you did for the country." September 6. Retrieved from Mako website: https://www.mako.co.il/special-love-israel/articles/Article-19efbfdbf762d51006.htm?sCh=1b13a3b0545e2510&pId=25483675
4. Love Israel [government-sponsored content]. n.d. Retrieved from Mako website: https://www.mako.co.il/special-love-israel/articles?partner=SecondNav
5. "One of Us: The 20 greatest Jews in the world." 2016. *Mako*, September 21. https://www.mako.co.il/special-Jewish-people-family/Article-403724cd35c4751006.htm?sCh=781d36a288d37510&pId=173113802
6. Senior-Shneor, N. 2019. "The people who did great things for Israel: The winning stories of the What You Did for Israel [Love Israel] contest." September 20. Retrieved from Mako website: https://www.mako.co.il/special-love-israel/articles/Article-a92bc3f099e9e51006.htm?sCh=1b13a3b0545e2510&pId=25483675
7. Shoham, Y. 2017. "Jewish moms shift momentum." *Mako*, February 26. https://www.mako.co.il/special-Jewish-people-family/Article-2ef06497bb97a51006.htm?sCh=781d36a288d37510&pId=885471177

Native Advertising in the Chinese Press: Implications of State Subsidies for Journalist Professional Self-Identification

Dan Wang and Steve Zhongshi Guo

ABSTRACT

This article reports a case study on how government-sponsored native advertising influences everyday practices of journalism and journalists' role identification in China. The process is the result of the state attempt to centralize control in response to digitalization that is, changing the press landscape. Building on social identity theory, we undertook an ethnographic fieldwork in a local party newspaper to observe how news organization and journalists make sense of the changes. Analyses show that, in addition to gains in material resources, the politics of native advertising also symbolizes new salient values for journalists whose professional identity swings between idealism and realism. The complexity of the phenomena under study reveals a plurality of meanings of the interplay among native advertising, journalistic routines, and the ever-shifting state-media relationship in China.

The proliferation of digital media has threatened, for better or for worse, the monopoly of legacy media in the information market all over the world (Wang and Sparks 2019b). In response, legacy media are forced to adapt to the Internet infrastructure to reclaim authority and the lost territory (Lewis 2012; Wang and Sparks 2020). Market potentials are turning native advertising into a global phenomenon, making it an increasingly routine affair for media bent on securing revenue (Iversen and Knudsen 2019; Ornebring and Conill 2016). While considerable scholarship is concerned with the possible erosion of media autonomy and the age-cherished professional role by native advertising (Carlson 2015; Hardy 2017), few studies closely contrast the old and new media-adverting relationships at the macro-level and examine their implications on individual journalists at the micro-level in liberal and non-democratic political systems. Despite the seemingly commercial nature of the transition, the impact is mainly political for the Chinese media. This article interrogates this problem at both conceptual and practical levels.

News has always had an uneasy relationship with advertising. By the mid-20th century, norms of separation of advertising and editorial were institutionalized across news media in many parts of the world. The obligation of soliciting advertising was departmentalized to sales staff and detached from the editorial office, at least in theory (Ornebring and Conill 2016). In China, too, journalists have upheld principles of this segregation by hinging on values of social responsibility (Zhao 2008; Chen and Hu 2016), professional ethics (Xu 2016) as well as journalistic career definition and aspiration (Pan 2000). Professionalism-minded journalists who saw themselves as a reputable instrument serving public interests were willing to sacrifice personal interests for greater ideals where no room was left for advertising (Shirk 2011; Tong 2015).

Moreover, editorial-advertising separation was first introduced officially in the *Provisions on the Administration of Newspaper Publication* dating back to 2005 (General Administration of Press and Publication 2005) and later singled out as a mandate for media under the direct control of the central government in 2016 following a speech by country's president Xi Jinping (Cai 2016; General Administration of Press and Publication 2017; Chinese Journalist Association 2020). The course of event took an ironic turn at about the same time when the state issued the directive on news-advertising separation in 2016. Paid advertising, which started off under the label or logo of promotional materials made clear to audiences, is now semi-institutionalized, blending into news and editorials without the knowledge of the reading public. Native advertising refers to "promotional messages that match the form and behaviour of the digital media in which they are disseminated [...] in news feeds, publishers' websites, search results, posts in social media, email and other digital communications" (Hardy 2017, 13). On cyber media platforms, news and ads become undifferentiated and their merging is forcibly imposed on the audience (Carlson 2015).

Digital native advertising in China burgeoned in a different socio-political context. Although it is difficult to pinpoint the exact date of the first formal appearance of branded content, it is clear that Xi's speech on media convergence in 2014 officially set the practice in motion (Xi 2014, 2018). It not only afforded state-sponsored advertising full legitimacy, but also drove traditional commercial advertising out of the news space. With state power and money on its side, native advertising emerged as a new form of political propaganda. That is why rather than contradicting the policy on editorial-advertising separation, native advertising has consolidated the state-media mutual reliance. Seen this way, the directive on convergence, initiated to contain diverse sources of information on the Internet (See: CNNIC 2019; Yao and Jin 2017), serves the dual functions of stretching the reach of ideological intervention on the Internet and realigning the business models of legacy media (Jaros and Pan 2018; Wang and Sparks 2019a; Xiong and Zhang 2018).

Operationally, the tightened ideological grip on propaganda pressures political bureaux at various rungs of the administrative ladder to boost publicity (CNNIC 2019; Repnikova and Fang 2018). As a concomitant move, the Ministry of Finance began to allocate massive subsidies to local press groups to support digitalization and funds to local governments to finance publicity. In effect, regulations on advertising-news separation have pulled media closer to state financed propaganda because the rules have restricted the access of (local) media to non-state sources of funding (see: Xiong, Liu, and He 2021). Therefore, one distinguishing factor that separates the West and China is that native adverting in the latter is driven politically while it is mainly rooted in the market for the former. Since state subsidies in China make any alternative sources of funding prohibitive, a new relationship has formed whereby *news* and *advertising disguised as news* coexist. In sum, native advertising is the result of combined influences of policy for media convergence, state mandate for increased local government publicity, and a new business model for traditional media to cope with financial difficulties in the digital age.

The studied newspaper organization started a new sponsored content model called *TeKan* (literally "special issue" or soft news *RuanWen*) in response first to the financial crisis brought by the digital technologies and later to the political directive from the central government. *TeKan,* formalized in 2013 in the studied newspaper, turned native advertising into part of the responsibility of journalists whose job now includes soliciting government paid-for content and giving it a "news feel." In return, staffers are promised both symbolic (e.g., status in the organization) and financial rewards. As a spinoff of its predecessor of paid news (*youchang xinwen*, see: Zhang 2009; Li 2013), *TeKan* breaches all the traditional boundaries of the media advertising relationship (e.g., signature, page, soliciting practices). Whereas whether or not to solicit paid news was an individual choice in the past, native advertising is now an institutional behavior. Whereas it was not mandatory for individual journalists to solicit and produce paid news before, except for fringe personal gain on the side, making *TeKan* now is part of a series of semi-institutionalized practices that are obligatory in the organizational operation and culture. The new system of practice looms large on young staffers, since digital technologies tend to distance their job performance from their editors and managers. The ability to solicit *TeKan* is now seen as a mark of professional competence. In every sense of the word, *TeKan* is native advertising with Chinese characteristics.

In several major ways, the rise of native advertising has uprooted the conventional notion of professionalism in journalism (Artemas, Vos, and Duffy 2018; Atal 2018; Conill 2016). Concerned scholars view the rise of native advertising as an abnormality in the professional conduct of journalism, which has fallen from its traditional grace (Li 2019). Valid as they may be, these views have overlooked individual journalists' responses to their changing identity, neglecting the nuanced nexus of structure-agency negotiations as well as political contestations at the micro-level.

Inspired by Grubenmann and Meckel (2017) work, we adopt the social identity theory (SIT) to explain the negotiation and self-identification process wherein individual journalists react to changes brought by the formalization of native advertising. Central to our analysis is how journalists make sense of their role, build their identity, and achieve self-actualization through allegiance to new group membership when they have to accept native advertising as a fact of life in the business of news making.

The locus of our research is a party newspaper in China and the context is its special issue *TeKan*, or extra in the newspaper lingo. The research findings are expected to contribute both to the cultural understanding of native advertising in the Chinese context and to the theoretical extension to self-categorization in SIT.

Professional Identification and Journalism

Scholars have explicated the notion of media professionalism from diverse perspectives. They all, however, recognize the core characteristic of professionalism as the ability to distinguish itself from other (similar) professions (Abbott 1988; Lewis 2012), suggesting that professional identity is more than just a market product and that the people within a profession hold propriety controls over resources reserved more or less exclusively for that profession (Hotho 2008). Journalists differentiate themselves from other information producers by claiming ownership of rhetorical and material resources such as objectivity, fact-checking and power reliance (Tong 2018; Tuchman 1978). This applies to both Western countries as well as China (De Burgh 2003; Lu and Pan 2002).

The formation of professional identity involves a series of cognitive negotiations between the individuals and their profession and constant interpretations by the individuals of the changing contexts. From the constructivist viewpoint, Gioia et al. (2013) argued that professional identity arises from the process of members' collective sense-making and sense-giving. Sveningsson and Alvesson (2003) looked at the social processes through which individuals construct the sense of self. Both studies ignored individual choices and how individuals interact with the structure. In the field of journalism studies, scholars share an expanded view of professional identify which occurs at individual, organizational and institutional levels (Shoemaker and Reese 2014). Scholars of Chinese journalism studies are more interested in the gap, or cognitive dissonance, between individual aspirations and organizational goals in the formation and change process of journalistic identification (He 2000).

In his social identity theory (SIT), Tajfel (1978) bridged the micro- and macro- perspectives in professional identification from an individual perspective, arguing that one's social identity is an output of both structure and agency. Different from other theories that deal with the structure-agency duality, SIT emphasizes human practices as being determined by social cognition (Hotho 2008). With the focus on individual self-categorization strategies, SIT sees professional identity as a process of forming "individual knowledge that he [or she] belongs to certain social groups together with some emotional and value significance to him [or her] of this group membership" (Tajfel 1972 cited in Grubenmann and Meckel 2017, 2). Knowledge from group communication theory has informed us that individual's self-categorization into a group not only fuels the "in-group" and "out-group" identity, but also facilitates the "in-group" individuals to internalize the group values and ideas as part of their own self-conception (Terry and Callan 1998; Turner et al. 1987).

At any given point in time, different journalists could absorb different role-conceptions (Hassid 2011; Willnat, Weaver, and Wilhoit 2019) whose dynamics are reflected in their amenability to change (Carlson 2015; Lewis 2012; Nielsen 2016), a phenomenon suitably analysed in the SIT framework. In their study, Grubenmann and Meckel (2017) discovered that traditional journalists treated digital journalists as members of an inferior outgroup due to the low quality of their work. In China, studies found that journalists who categorize themselves as belonging to the advocacy or objectivity groups felt superior to those who subscribed to the mouthpiece role (Shirk 2011; Tong and Sparks 2009). The underlying rationale is that journalism attached to public interest appeals to higher professional principles than compliant journalism serving authorities (Tong 2018). The advent of native advertising in China presents a new context for journalists to categorize or re-categorize themselves into different identity groups as both political and economic resources from the state increase.

Journalistic Professionalism, Advertisement, and Changes in China

In China, the advent of advertising and penetration of the market logic in the media industry were viewed with a mixture of hospitality for the sake of financial sustainability and hostility because of its potential to threat the party-state control over media (Pan 2000; Lu and Pan 2002). Since the marketization of the country's media industry in 1979, media organizations started to produce diverse forms and content of journalism to cater to the taste of audiences (Lee 2000; Stockmann 2013).

During the press commercialization period (1980s to 2010s), the market acted as a counter-force to the authoritarian control (Stockmann 2013). Journalists identifying subscribing to the "American value" were more willing to push the ideological boundary. Those who believed in the mouthpiece role of media pale in contrast (Tong 2007). In fact, state subsidies are not new to Chinese media. Although the state "weaned" its financial support for media since 1979 and granted financial self-determinism to media organizations, Chinese media have never been entirely free from funding channelled out of the state coffers. Media organizations in China received preferential policies ranging from tax reduction, forced subscription, property ownership to special funding meted out under a variety of labels (Lee, He, and Huang 2006; Xiong and Zhang 2018). Yet, not until recently did the state funding become a fixture in the form of sponsored political content (Wang and Sparks 2020).

The Case Study

The studied title experienced financial difficulties in 2012 with no signs of recovering. The managerial board decided to rely on government subsidies and political native advertising in 2013 in the face of drastic declines in circulation (XX news organization 2013). For that purpose, they issued an internal regulation requesting all journalists to include soliciting and producing native advertising as part of their job responsibility.

Traditionally, the party press was the main channel through which local governments demonstrate their achievements to higher authorities. *TeKan* has inherited that practice. As a municipal newspaper, the title in this study started to publish political advertising for district and lower level government offices since 1982 (head of editorial office, 2016). In order to maintain institutional prestige while adhering to the party line at the same time, the title devoted one independent print page called "*TeKan*" (literally "Special Issue") only for political advertising that was mainly solicited by staffers from advertising departments (traffic beat editor, 2017). The editorial norm for political advertising is that they publish whatever the local government's publicity officers feed them at the last page of the newspaper without bylines. But, as mentioned above, that was more of an individual choice rather than organizational one.

Today, the special page of *TeKan* still exits for print paper, but the practice has changed for current staffers. In terms of routines, the making of *TeKan* involves mandatory solicitation of content and production of a news-like content within a journalist's beat column and byline. This newsroom rule necessitated downsizing of the advertisement department whose staffers were encouraged to retire early or reconsider their career path since 2014 (Deputy Chief Editor, 2017). Staffers capable of soliciting more *TeKan* contracts earn greater respect from peers and superiors. This is particularly true in the digital age since many journalists choose to work outside of the newsroom (Journalist E, 2016). Competition in the digital newsroom no longer revolved around attracting more audience. "The beat editors encourage us to convince our government clients to purchase bots to like our articles if necessary for the digital version" (Journalist E, 2017). This is because a *TeKan* deal will rake in a lot more reward to the organization than a single advertisement.

To be sure, political advertising continues to exist but marginalized to the periphery of advertising business and the minds of staffers who feel belittled by efforts devoted to its production. At the time this article was written, the political title charged RMB100,000 (about US$14,000) per page with a commission up to 10% of the value of any government contract the journalists succeed in soliciting. In keeping with the state call for media convergence, local governments have also increased their publicity budget (for evidence, see: Wang and Sparks 2020). As such, *TeKan* formally gained official recognition and centrality in the organization's business strategy.

Journalists in the newspaper hold different attitudes towards blending *TeKan* and news, partly because of the contradiction between the idea of *TeKan* and their beliefs in media professionalism (interviewee A, 2018) and partly because of inequality in distribution of funds (interviewee D, 2018). "Police and political beats always get more contracts than us," said a cultural beat journalist. Guided by SIT that analytically connects the structural changes with individual cognitions, we raise the following research questions:

Q1: What changes have *TeKan* brought about in the everyday practices of journalists?

Q2: How do journalists interpret the changes?

Q3: How do journalists categorize or re-categorize their group membership in the changing context?

Methods

We combined inductive methods of participant observation, archival study and in-depth interviews to capture the two key elements in journalism identity: role perception and role performance (Hanitzsch 2017).

The lead author spent seven months in the traffic police beat of the studied municipal party title in a southern metropolis of China from 2016 to 2017. Access to the newsroom was made possible through the introduction of the author's acquaintance in the organization. An attempt was made to follow up the fieldwork in 2021 to update the findings. The studied newspaper belongs to a press group ranked "outstanding" in the industry. It received direct state subsidy for building its digital centre. The choice of the traffic police department was made with the knowledge that the local police bureau invests the most on native advertising that year mainly because the bureau boasted a higher publicity budget than any other government organizations in town.

A field note akin to a daily journal was kept of the work and interactions at work. Since WeChat (an equivalent of WhatsApp) has become the most widely adopted social media platform for business and personal use, the contents of journalistic identity presentation on WeChat Moments were recorded and analysed with respondents' consent. In order to have a better grasp of the changing dynamics of the news organization, the author also collected and analysed internal documents and historical records from the organization's archive. In-depth interviews of 15 staffers were conducted to discern interpretations and explanations of journalistic practices that were related to their identity (for justification, see: Scheurich 1995) during and after the fieldwork in 2017 and 2018. Among the 15 interviewees, six were traffic police beat journalists, two were traffic police beat editors and the rest were editors and managers. Note that although the number of interviewees is small, their network at work constitutes a map of productive relations within the organization as well as between media and their sources.

All respondents were aware of the status of the author and requested anonymity. Although anonymity has its drawbacks in social research, promise of it is the best way to secure honesty in the context of political life in China. Therefore, all information that reveals the city, the organization or the respondents was removed.

Findings

Including TeKan into the Work Structure

RQ1 deals with the changes brought by *TeKan* in journalists' everyday work life. Participants' perceptions of *TeKan* varied significantly in terms of both their discourses and actions. Taken as a whole, *TeKan* tasks are far from being a mere extension of conventional work. The additional responsibilities generate new values and routines that challenge the existing structure and newsroom culture. Analyses of discourses and documents that contrast the "before" and "after" effects of *TeKan* yielded two themes characterizing the new working conditions and norms in the organization: *boundary erosion* and *investor uniformization*. They constitute a new force that changes the job perceptions and practices as well as judgements of news.

Boundary erosion. Similar to digital media in the West (Carlson 2015), the operational logic of native advertising (sponsor pays and controls the news-like content) has crossed the line of the editorial- advertisement division in the news organization under study. But the effect was primarily on journalists who work for the print paper. Journalists who work only for the digital platform are not involved in the *TeKan* system because their job is to reproduce secondhand stories from official sources. From the structural viewpoint, one can argue that digital technology is not the core force in the rise of native advertising in China. Instead, it functions as a catalyst for a business model imposed by the central government to enforce the political directive of media convergence (Wang and Sparks 2020).

Specific to this study, the erosion manifests itself in two aspects. First, it has become a common practice for the editors to publish *TeKan* on news pages. The field notes recorded multiple times when the chief editor ordered staffers to take down news stories in order to vacate space for *TeKan* stories. "To do this, journalists would need to make the two kinds of stories look the same," said the deputy chief editor. Government sponsored publicity is to be written in the format of news stories with bylines. Journalist E from the traffic police beat explained, "Nowadays, we need to dig out news values [from government-initiated events or publicity] where there is none."

A typical example of *TeKan* would be the monthly City Safety Index in the *City News* (*Bendi xinwen*) column which records crime rate in each district, an arrangement that earns roughly 300,000 RMB per year since 2016. Before the formalization of *TeKan*, the local police bureau had to use *guanxi* (social capital) or create pseudo-events (e.g., police office open day) to obtain favourable news coverage. But now since *TeKan* became a semi-institutionalized arrangement, the local police bureau uses their information fee to purchase news coverage in the form of native advertising. In 2016, when the city government localized President Xi Jinping's ideas of the "rule of law" (Nesossi 2016) and "enhancement of national security" (12th National People's Congress, 2015), it launched the "urban management and regulation year" scheme (Mayor 2016). In line with this theme, the city's police bureau made enhancing public security the focus of its work in 2016 (2016 CityX Police Bureau Work Report). These moves were reflected in the articles published by the studied title. According to a police beat journalist, over 50% of income of the organization in 2016 was from *TeKan*, comparing to less than 5% in the early 2000s.

Second, soliciting *TeKan* became an unwritten rule for (beat) journalists in 2014. Journalists and editors had to encorporate *TeKan* related practices and values into their everyday work, even if this means putting public events that meet traditional news values to secondary considerations. Usually, the required quota of *TeKan* contract is calculated by the Finance Office in accordance with both the tax payment of the beat's responsible source, and the native advertising income from previous year. According to one traffic police beat journalist:

> Every journalist is assigned with an annual quota of TeKan contracts. [...] Different beats will get different target quota and commission based on a set of standards such as previous years' native advertising contracts from the beat, the tax paid by the source and so on. We will lose our job if we fail to fulfil it.

With the threat of job loss looming large, individual journalists who work under the new routine conjure up ingenious ideas to solicit *TeKan*. For instance, the annual report of this press group recorded that over half of the income of one commercial title in the press group was from government's official accounts on social media (XX Press Group 2017). Journalist N from the political beat resorted to personal family connections with the major's office for more *TeKan* contracts. The deputy chief editor jokingly commented that "in the future, having personal connections with the government should be on the job description." Her script reveals that the formalization of *TeKan* forged increasing dependence on government, power reliance, at both organizational and personal levels.

Investor uniformization. Increased reliance on *TeKan* engenders a tendency for the newspaper organization to gradually detach itself from the commercial advertisements and gravitate to the market logic of *TeKan*. In so doing, patrons of sponsored content are narrowed to a group of government agencies that share common vested interest. A deeper impact of investor uniformization is the disability for journalists and their organizations to distinguish themselves from other information workers through their unique products. Reliance on official sources for news has led to news articles being modified or rephrased in line with government publicity. This does not only happen to the traffic police beat in one press, but to almost all journalists from different media in the city on the traffic police beat. "We used to discover interesting events in the city to report. But now, with all the *TeKan* pressure, writing conventional news is just a side work for many of us" said the party title traffic police beat editor.

Since senior journalists are already equipped with the necessary skills and resources needed in traditional news writing, they devote most of their energy to soliciting and producing *TeKan*. Strategies like taking turns to write news among journalists from the same beats and modifying public notices from the government became norms in the newsroom. Traditional news is considered interchangeable with public notices from the government. Taken together, the structure of formalization of *TeKan* has deprived the profession of what little autonomy it once enjoyed (Tong and Sparks 2009).

Group Conflicts and Fluid Self-Categorizations

RQ2 and RQ3 are concerned with the interpretation and identification process of individual journalists in the *TeKan* era. In Deuze's (2005) view, core values in journalism are important because it can help the institution to build its own social cement; and the interpretations of these core values are equally important because individual practices reinforce and perpetuate them. *TeKan* brings a new set of knowledge that journalists have to acquire in order to (re)-socialize into the changed work environment. The aforementioned boundary erosion and investor uniformization are the main features distinguishing *TeKan* from paid news identified in previous studies (see: Zhao 1998). What makes *TeKan* unique is its blending of market logic with power reliance. Although treating government agencies as client is not new to press industry (see: Lee, He, and Huang 2006), pushing it into the core operational strategy is. As a result, the once limited discursive space for different voices and professional imagination (Shirk 2011), is practically reduced to zero.

Consequently, *TeKan* created and heightened conflicts between old and new work values. Looking closely into the data, we identified that our participants were caught in two groups of conflicts, with three dimensions on each side: church vs. state, news vs. -un-news, and power congruence vs. incongruence. Based on group characteristics, we named one groups "the ideal group" and the other "the realistic group." The ideal group values traditional professionalism, whereas the realistic group stresses the utilitarian connotations which are at odds with the pursuit of professionalism.

Traditionally, group membership means members in one group would reject that of membership of the other (Terry and Callan 1998). Yet, the three pairs of dilemmas laid the foundation for identity switching whereby journalists find themselves having to engage in identity hopping between two groups. That is to say, different from previous studies on group membership and SIT (Hotho 2008; Grubenmann and Meckel

Group Membership	
Ideal	*Realistic*
Independence from *TeKan*	*TeKan* solicitation
Quality news	*TeKan* news
Distance from power	Alignment with power

Figure 1. Self-categorization mechanism in group membership identification.

2017), our data show that journalists' group categorization is situation-oriented. Instead of sticking to one group, journalists must move between groups, blending "us" and "them" in the process. The fluidity of the self-identification points to the instability of the new structure brought by *TeKan*, suggesting a certain degree of resistance against the new values.

Figure 1 pits the ideal group against the realistic group across three dimensions. Data gathered from field work provide compelling evidence in support of our argument about journalists' identity dilemmas. By definition, independence from *TeKan* can only reside in journalists' mind as an ideal. Even the hardcore believers have to solicit *TeKan* against their will to earn their keep in the institution. The shift from exception to rule of *TeKan* solicitation led to the formation of a new routine. Our interviewees did their best "to get the job done" with minimal efforts (Journalist A, 2017). Yet, even if they do not need to produce *TeKan*, chances of publishing professional work are slim because of the shrinking press space for traditional work of quality (Journalist C, 2016).

Soliciting TeKan. Subscribers to the ideal group expressed negative attitudes towards soliciting *TeKan*. The prevailing sentiment was that their rights for making choice have been deprived in the structural change. They were only being compliant because the new routine is nothing short of a coerced commitment (journalist B, 2016). According to the deputy chief editor of the organization, before *TeKan* became a formal responsibility, journalists and editors also solicited *TeKan*, but they did so purely for extra income. A traffic police journalist D explained:

> Politically speaking, Chinese journalists do not have too much freedom. [...] But it was up to us to decide whether we wanted to tread the grey line of TeKan. Different news staffers hold different conceptions of the profession. Some of them chose to distance themselves from TeKan to show their respect for professionalism. The formalization of TeKan deprived us of that.

In the perception of journalist D, the deprival of choice in the daily routine has designated working journalists a role much like that of a robot. Moreover, given that the sponsors of the native advertising are government organizations, journalists are working under the dual pressures of following propaganda obligations and seeking state financial rewards. Viewed this way, the lapdog-watchdog dilemma proposed by Zhao (2004) is rendered irrelevant in explaining the current media ecology.

Disciples of the ideal group do not summarily reject the values of the realistic group because *TeKan* promises personal gains in social network, income and access to government resources. Now, the average monthly salary of a working journalist could barely keep up with the rising cost of living in the city. In the words of journalist B:

> Our basic wage is RMB3,000 (about US$420). Every month, we have to publish 15 news articles. We are promised a bonus for additional articles. During public holidays, we have to be on duty in case of breaking news. For that, we could get three to five times the usual daily payment. In all, we could roughly get RMB7,000 (about US$980) per month, which is far from enough in this town. That's why we need TeKan.

Clearly, the utilitarian values have their appeals, particularly so under increasingly precarious working conditions for journalists in China (Peng 2017; Wang et al. 2020) who fit into the "workaday" identity in Hassid's (2011) role typology. To save time so that they could reach more *TeKan* resources, journalists used WeChat as the sole platform to exchange news sources and their finished articles. By doing so, news production has become a side-business, whereas *TeKan* soliciting is the core responsibility, regardless journalists' attitudes to the change.

News quality. Members of the ideal group strengthen their identity through constant reference to various definitions of good journalism as an in-group cohesive. Part of what they do is to construct a mental image of *TeKan* as a threat to professional standard. They pride themselves for being able to use diverse sources and engage in creative forms of writing rather than acting like a copycat of official press releases as in the case of *TeKan* writers. This finding was consistent with previous studies on the cognitive dissonance of Chinese journalists who aspire to Western media professionalism but work under the supervision of the party (He 2000; Zhao 2004).

When the same group of journalists have to produce *TeKan*, they expressed contempt for the task, deeming it non-journalistic and inferior. For example, senior staffers showed reluctance to describe *TeKan* as news. "News costs money. *Tekan* makes money" (deputy chief editor, 2017). Another journalist put it somewhat differently, "*Tekan* is coverage of events created by the government. News to me is coverage of events as they happen. Otherwise, we'd be no different from public relations officers." The term "salesperson" was mentioned in the interview of all our participants when discussing *TeKan*. As "begging for *TeKan* contracts" enters the routine, journalists also felt a drop of disrespect from the source:

> The police used to treat us as equal or even superior because they wanted us to cover positive stories about them. Now they just treated us as a puppy without the fear of retaliation. [...] the power relationship has reversed.

When the discourse extends to roles outside of journalism, an inferiority complex sets in, thanks to *TeKan* which, among others, devaluates the professional work by journalists. The law enforcement force, which used to be a source of news like all other institutions, now takes on the additional role of being a client to be serviced and pleased.

Power reliance, when manifested as an exclusive press-government relationship, makes for another reason for the idealist respondents to express distain. As our interview data show, *TeKan* has exacerbated tensions between journalists who flaunt power resources and those who stick to power supervision and social responsibility (journalist A, 2016). The fact that the utilitarian journalists tend to take advantage of their access to official resources for personal gains adds to the lowering of their status in the eyes of idealists. Our observations confirmed this speculation. It is very common for members of the realistic group to flaunt their close connections with government source on social media (WeChat Moments, an equivalence of Twitter) and in everyday conversation.

That said, we found that the values of the two groups sometimes converge. Our interviewees recognized the necessity of self-branding through exhibition of power resources (e.g., "I have connections in the law enforcement"). According to the marketing research literature, an important part of identity branding is to distinguish oneself from others, especially those in the same field (Molyneux, Holton, and Lewis 2018). The only platform where journalists responsible for online content could demonstrate their work and their efforts at building power networks is WeChat Moments as they barely see their boss at work due to the digitalization of work (most work can be done via various platforms. For evidence, see: Wang and Sparks 2020). The fate of online journalism, assigned the bottom place in the institutional pecking order, is testimony to disproportional attention paid to *TeKan* production on the print side.

Ironically, although the ideal group members make a habit of criticizing the power reliance value, they sometimes actively engage in using it as a leverage to negotiate with or even circumvent existing rules. For instance, one idealist participant posted a scoop on her WeChat Moments together with her personal interpretations before her organization made it public. This, as she explained, is her way to establish herself as a professional journalist. Power-relevant resources are not only capable of upgrading a journalist's status and persona in the workplace, but can also be used as a bargaining chip for journalists to negotiate with their organizations when breach of rules is at stake. The same journalist also often presents her privilege of not showing up for work during the work time. For her, the absence would not incur displeasure from editors because she has connection with the police officers and thus a better chance to acquire *TeKan* contracts.

Discussions and Conclusions

Inclusion of *TeKan* as a job responsibility has changed the work value and culture in the newsroom. In a more abstract sense, the segregation between the ideal and the realistic groups re-affirms the long-standing normative-utilitarian (or practical) contestation. *TeKan*, being a state policy, is not up for negotiations, leaving little room for noncompliance. The only space individual staffers have is their perceptions. In an environment that values utilitarian pursuits over ideal ones, journalists can do little to resist the new norm. All these lead to a clear indication that the rise of *TeKan* is not a matter of journalism going astray. It is a new form of highly politicized journalism. If anything, it is a manifestation of combined influences of policy for media convergence, state mandate for increased local government publicity, and new business model for traditional media to cope with the financial difficulties in digital age.

With SIT as our main theoretical framework, we closely examined the linkage between macro-level changes in media industry and the society to micro-level self-identification of journalists in China. Results of our fieldwork reveal the full complexity of *TeKan*. Similar to the West, the rise of native advertising has changed boundaries between editorial and advertising content (Carlson 2015). The Chinese case is special in at least two senses. First, motives underpinning the emergence of native advertising in China are overwhelmingly political rather than commercial. Instead of following the market logic of free competition, native advertising in China is monopolized by political offices, to the exclusion of other social institutions and interests. Second, and related to the monopoly, native advertising in China is fully subsidized by the state. Media's growing dependence on *TeKan* makes it clear that news organizations have lost their entitlement to financial self-determination and freedom to choose among advertisers. With subsidies serving as a sugar-coated incentive, finally and definitively, the entirety of journalism practice in China fell within government controls.

For individual journalists, our study identified two types of negotiation mechanism by two very different groups of journalists. As discussed, tensions between the two groups are ultimately normative vis-à-vis utilitarianism in nature (Pan 2000; Stockmann 2013; Zhao 2004). Our contribution to this line of theorizing lies in our discovery and description of nuances in the confrontation as reflected in the fluidity of self-grouping among journalists. In this regard, we offer three explanations. First, *TeKan,* as the new and unstable factor contributing to the organizational structural changes, is likely to trigger resistance at the onset from habitus journalists have built on the old structure (Ryfe 2012). Second, *TeKan* strips journalists of what limited editorial space granted to them in the pre-*TeKan* days. Regardless of personal beliefs and values, journalists who have to produce *TeKan* for a living. Hopping between two ideal and realistic groups serves as a cognitive dissonance reduction strategy for them. Third, the prevailing influence of utilitarianism is gradually taking the upper hand over professionalism ideals in the newsroom, especially among new recruits (Peng 2017; Wang et al. 2020; Zhou, Xu, and Li 2018). Our findings provide evidence in support of this point, showing that even ideal group journalists seek personal benefit from aligning with the realistic group values.

Moreover, our findings show that journalists in the studied party newspaper do indeed take advantage of their limited agency by extracting specific resources from their newly gained role to expand their identity boundary. Most existing studies on role conceptions of Chinese journalists treat the notion of the profession as confined within media institutions (e.g., Hassid 2011; Ryfe 2017). We found, however, that when journalists step out of their traditionally defined domain of professional domain to assume roles in other institutions (e.g., acting as a police officer to sanction people instead of reporting on the police work), the boundaries of media expand almost naturally, to include other branches of state power. In the process, state-sponsored native advertising has made its way into the regular newsroom routines both as an order to be unquestioningly obeyed professionally and a promise of utilitarian benefits that are hard to resist personally, reducing journalists' identity branding to a process of paradox mitigation and reduction. The practice of repackaging secondhand government publicity materials is consistent with the notion of churnalism (Jackson and Moloney 2016) and forms part of the logic of earned media (Davies 2011) in the West. But the exchange between propaganda and profit is unique to China.

Theoretically, the fluidity in self-categorization is implied in SIT. As Tajfel (1978) originally proposed, individuals acquire the sense of social self through the cognitive process of categorizing themselves into the group that best fits their value. That is exactly what we found: individual journalists no longer stick to one group membership. The need for adaptation overrides the pursuit of professionalism.

All things considered, the process of sense making by individual journalists of the new structure and its embedded values may be slow and gradual, but a more likely scenario is that journalists would continue to perceive *TeKan* as an imposed responsibility and harbour the hope that it might be transient and replaceable at times of change. While striving for psychological balance compels journalists to legitimise the change for the sake of self-esteem and self-actualization internally, the new structure estranges and alienates them externally.

This is a qualitative study of one single new media center in one city-level newspaper. It is not representative of new media journalism in China, let alone journalism as a whole. We do not believe that other studies, using either qualitative or quantitative methods, will reproduce exactly the same findings. Rather, they are likely to demonstrate a much less polarized situation with a greater degree of integration between different groups of journalists, although western studies have demonstrated that, at least in the early days, there are clear distinctions of journalists' role conceptions, and the free choice of doing native advertising for self-gaining. We do not think, therefore, that all the findings of this study are likely to be generalizable. We do believe though that the emerging patterns in the fledging editorial-advertising relationship is informative of a new state-media relationship. In keeping with findings from recent studies on Chinese press (Wang and Sparks 2019a; Wang et al. 2020), results from our research demonstrate the resurgence of dominance of local party news organizations in contrast to the commercial press golden age during 2000s. Our depth analysis of the studied title yields compelling evidence about future development of Chinese media. Similar to previous studies on digital journalists in China (Zhou, Xu, and Li 2018), our participants showed declining enthusiasm in pursuing professionalism, let along sacrificing their personal interests for principles and ideals. Although whether this is solely caused by the prevalence of native advertising remains a contestable issue, the formalization of government sponsored content has indeed limited journalists' choices and perceptions in many ways. We believe that the problems we have identified, the theoretical apparatus we have used to address them, and patterns we have unveiled are representative of a general rather than specific phenomenon.

Acknowledgements

The authors wish to thank Professor Jonathan Hardy and the anonymous reviewers for their constructive comments and suggestions.

Disclosure Statement

No potential conflict of interest was reported by the author(s).

References

Abbott, A. 1988. *The System of Professions: An Essay on the Division of Expert Labor*. Chicago: The University of Chicago Press.

Artemas, K., P. T. Vos, and M. Duffy. 2018. "Journalism Hits a Wall." *Journalism Studies* 19 (7): 1004–1020.

Atal, M. 2018. "The Cultural and Economic Power of Advertisers in the Business Press." *Journalism* 19 (8): 1078–1095.

Cai, M. Z. 2016. "Shizhong luxing hao dangzhongyang houshe ermu zhize [Always Carrying out the Function of "Mouthpiece" and "Ear and Eye" for the Party]." State Council Information Office. March 15. http://www.scio.gov.cn/zhzc/10/Document/1472215/1472215.htm

Carlson, M. 2015. "When News Sites Go Native: Redefining the Advertising-Editorial Divide in Response to Native Advertising." *Journalism* 16 (7): 849–865.

Chen, Q., and Y. Hu. 2016. "Xuanchuan Luoji yu Shichang Luoji—Xin Meiti Shidai Zhongguo Xinwen Lunli de "Liangnan Kunju [The Logic of Propaganda and the Logic of Market: The Ethical Dilemma of News in China in the Age of New Media]." *Twenty First Century* 153: 4–17.

CNNIC. 2019. *Di 44 ci Zhongguo hulianwangluo fazhan zhuangkuang tongji baogao [The 44th China Statistical Report on Internet Development]*. http://www.cnnic.net.cn/hlwfzyj/hlwxzbg/hlwtjbg/201908/P020190830356787490958.pdf

Conill, R. F. 2016. "Camouflaging Church as State: An Exploratory Study of Journalism's Native Advertising." *Journalism Studies* 17 (7): 904–914.

Chinese Journalist Association. 2020. "Weishenme yao jianchi caibian he jingying liangfenkai liangjiaqiang? [Why Do We Have to Follow the Strict Separation of Editorial-Advertising?]." Chinese Journalist Association. April 08. http://www.zgjx.cn/2020-04/08/c_138956873.htm

Davies, N. 2011. *Flat Earth News: An Award-Winning Reporter Exposes Falsehood, Distortion and Propaganda in the Global Media*. London: Random House.

De Burgh, H. 2003. "What Chinese Journalists Believe about Journalism." In *Political Communications in Greater China: The Construction and Reflection of Identity*, edited by Gary D. Rawnsley, and Ming-Yeh T. Rawnsley, 83. London and New York: Routledge.

Deuze, M. 2005. "What is Journalism? Professional Identity and Ideology of Journalists Reconsidered." *Journalism* 6 (4): 442–464.

General Administration of Press and Publication. 2005. "Baozhi chuban guiding [Provisions on the Administration of Newspaper Publication]." General Administration of Press and Publication. September 30. http://www.gov.cn/gongbao/content/2006/content_375808.htm

General Administration of Press and Publication. 2017. "Guanyu kaizhan xinwen danwei caibian jingying liangfenkai qingkuang zhuanxiang ducha de tongzhi [Notice on the Special Supervision of the Separation of the Editing and Advertising of News Units]." State Administration of Press, Publication, Radio, Film and Television, June 19. http://press.gapp.gov.cn/reporter/contents/245/338567.html

Gioia, D. A., S. D. Patvardhan, A. L. Hamilton, and K. G. Corley. 2013. "Organizational Identity Formation and Change." *Academy of Management Annals* 7 (1): 123–193.

Grubenmann, S., and M. Meckel. 2017. "Journalists' Professional Identity: A Resource to Cope with Change in the Industry?" *Journalism Studies* 18 (6): 732–748.

Hanitzsch, T. 2017. "Professional Identity and Roles of Journalists." In *Oxford Research Encyclopedia of Communication*.

Hardy, J. 2017. "Marketers' Influence on Media: Renewing the Radical Tradition for the Digital Age." In *Critical Studies in Advertising: Critique and Reconstitution*, edited by J. Hamilton, R. Bodie, and E. Korin, 13–27. New York: Routledge.

Hassid, J. 2011. "Four Models of the Fourth Estate: A Typology of Contemporary Chinese Journalists." *The China Quarterly* 208: 813–832.

He, Z. 2000. "Working with a Dying Ideology: Dissonance and Its Reduction in Chinese Journalism." *Journalism Studies* 1 (4): 599–616.

Hotho, S. 2008. "Professional Identity—Product of Structure, Product of Choice." *Journal of Organizational Change Management* 21 (6): 721–742.

Iversen, M. H., and E. Knudsen. 2019. "When Politicians Go Native: The Consequences of Political Native Advertising for Citizens' Trust in News." *Journalism* 20 (7): 961–978.

Jackson, D., and K. Moloney. 2016. "Inside Churnalism: PR, Journalism and Power Relationships in Flux." *Journalism Studies* 17 (6): 763–780.

Jaros, K., and J. Pan. 2018. "China's Newsmakers: Official Media Coverage and Political Shifts in the Xi Jinping Era." *The China Quarterly* 233: 111–136.

Lee, C. C., Z. He, and Y. Huang. 2006. "Chinese Party Publicity Inc.' Conglomerated: The Case of the Shenzhen Press Group." *Media, Culture & Society* 28 (4): 581–602.

Lee, C.-C. 2000. *Power, Money, and Media: Communication Patterns and Bureaucratic Control in Cultural China*. Northwestern University Press.

Lewis, S. C. 2012. "The Tension between Professional Control and Open Participation: Journalism and Its Boundaries." *Information, Communication & Society* 15 (6): 836–866.

Li, R. 2013. "Media Corruption: A Chinese Characteristic." *Journal of Business Ethics* 116 (2): 297–310.

Li, Y. 2019. "Contest over Authority." *Journalism Studies* 20 (4): 523–541.

Lu, Y., and Z. Pan. 2002. "Chengming de xiangxiang: Zhongguo shehui zhuanxing guocheng zhong xinwen congye zhe de zhuanye zhuyi huayu jiangou [Imagining Professional Fame: Constructing Journalistic Professionalism in China's Social Transformation]." *Mass Communication Research* 71: 17–59.

Mayor XX. 2016. 2016 XX Zhengfu gongzuo baogao [2016 CityXX Government Work Report].

Molyneux, L., A. Holton, and S. C. Lewis. 2018. "How Journalists Engage in Branding on Twitter: Individual, Organizational, and Institutional Levels." *Information Communication and Society* 21 (10): 1386–1401.

Nesossi, E. 2016. "Interpreting the Rule of Law in China." August 3. http://www.chinoiresie.info/interpreting-the-rule-of-law-in-china/

Nielsen, R. K. 2016. "The Business of News." In *The Sage Handbook of Digital Journalism*, edited by T. Witschge, C. W. Anderson, D. Domingo, and A. Hermida, 128–143. London: Sage.

Ornebring, H., and R. Conill. 2016. "Outsourcing Newswork." In *The Sage Handbook of Digital Journalism*, edited by T. Witschge, C. W. Anderson, D. Domingo, and A. Hermida, 207–221. London: Sage.

Pan, Z. 2000. "Improvising Reform Activities: The Changing Reality of Journalistic Practice in China." In *Power, Money, and Media: Communication Patterns and Bureaucratic Control in Cultural China*, edited by C.-C. Lee, 68–105. Evanston, IL: Northwestern University Press.

Peng, H. 2017. "Shejiaomeiti zhong de zifashi "jizhe lianmeng": Shenfen huanjing lunli (The Spontaneous "Union of Journalists" in Social Meida: Function, Environment and Ethics)." *Guoji Xinwenjie (Chinese Journal of Journalism and Communication)* 39 (7): 149–168.

Repnikova, M., and K. Fang. 2018. "Authoritarian Participatory Persuasion 2.0: Netizens as Thought Work Collaborators in China." *Journal of Contemporary China* 27 (113): 763–779.

Ryfe, D. M. 2012. *Can Journalism Survive?: An Inside Look at Amercian Newsroom*. Cambridge: Polity.

Ryfe, D. M. 2017. *Journalism and the Public*. Cambridge, UK: Polity Press.

Scheurich, J. 1995. "A Postmodernist Critique of Research Interviewing." *International Journal of Qualitative Studies in Education* 8 (3): 239–252.

Shirk, S. L. 2011. *Changing Media, Changing China*. Oxford University Press.

Shoemaker, P. J., and S. D. Reese. 2014. *Mediating the Message in the 21st Century: A Media Sociology Perspective*. Routledge: New York.

Stockmann, D. 2013. *Media Commercialization and Authoritarian Rule in China*. New York: Cambridge University Press.

Sveningsson, S., and M. Alvesson. 2003. "Managing Managerial Identities: Organizational Fragmenta- Tion, Discourse and Identity Struggle." *Human Relations* 56 (10): 1163–1193.

Tajfel, H. 1978. "Social Categorization, Social Identity and Social Comparison." In *Differentiation between Social Groups: Studies in the Social Psychology of Intergroup Relations*, edited by H. Tajfel, 61–76. London: Academic Press.

Terry, D. J., and V. J. Callan. 1998. "Ingroup Bias in Response to an Organizational Merger." *Group Dynamics: Theory, Research and Practices* 2 (2): 67–81.

Tong, J. 2007. "Guerrilla Tactics of Investigative Journalists in China." *Journalism* 8 (5): 530–535.

Tong, J. 2018. "Journalistic Legitimacy Revisited." *Digital Journalism* 6 (2): 256–273.

Tong, J., and C. Sparks. 2009. "Investigative Journalism in China Today." *Journalism Studies* 10 (3): 337–352.

Tong, J. 2015. "Chinese Journalists' Views of User-Generated Content Producers and Journalism: A Case Study of the Boundary Work of Journalism." *Asian Journal of Communication* 25 (6): 600–616.

Tuchman, G. 1978. *Making News: A Study in the Construction of Reality*. New York, NY: Free Press.

Turner, J. C., M. A. Hogg, P. J. Oakes, S. D. Reicher, and M. S. Wetherell. 1987. *Rediscovering the Social Group: A Self-Categorization Theory*. Oxford, UK: Basil Blackwell.

Wang, H., and C. Sparks. 2019a. "Chinese Newspaper Groups in the Digital Era: The Resurgence of the Party Press." *Journal of Communication* 69 (1): 94–119.

Wang, H., and C. Sparks. 2019b. "Marketing Credibility: Chinese Newspapers' Responses to Revenue Losses from Failing Circulation and Advertising Decline." *Journalism Studies* 20 (9): 1301–1318.

Wang, D., and C. Sparks. 2020. "Smartphones, WeChat and Paid Content: Journalists and Sources in a Chinese Newspaper." *Journalism Studies* 21 (1): 37–53.

Wang, D., V. L. Huang, and S. Z. Guo. 2020. "Malleable Multiplicity and Power Reliance: Identity Presentation by Chinese Journalists on Social Media." *Digital Journalism* 8 (10): 1280–1297.

Willnat, L., D. H. Weaver, and G. C. Wilhoit. 2019. "The American Journalist in the Digital Age: How Journalists and the Public Think about Journalism in the United States." *Journalism Studies* 20 (3): 423–441.

Xi, J. 2014. "Guanyu tuidong chuantong meiti he xinmeiti ronghe fazhan de zhidao yijian [Directives on Boosting Integrated Development of Traditional Media and New Media]." *(The "8.18" talk)*, August 18. http://tv.people.com.cn/n/2014/0818/c141029-25489928.html

Xi, J. 2018. "Quanguo xuanchuan sixiang gongzuo huiyi [National Thoughtwork Conference]." August 22. http://media.people.com.cn/n1/2018/0828/c40606-30256090.html

Xiong, H., X. Liu, and Y. He. 2021. "Claiming Legitimacy: Journalists' Discursive Strategies for Rationalizing "Brand Propaganda" within Chinese Local Press." *Journalism Studies* 22 (4): 435–453.

Xiong, H., and J. Zhang. 2018. "How Local Journalists Interpret and Evaluate Media Convergence: An Empirical Study of Journalists from Four Press Groups in Fujian." *International Communication Gazette* 80 (1): 87–115.

Xu, D. 2016. "Red-Envelop Cash: Journalists on the Take in Contemporary China." *Journal of Media Ethics* 31 (4): 231–244.

XX News Organization. 2013. XX Baoshe 2013-2014 tekan shouru ji yugu. [Actual and estimated number of, and portion of revenue from, TeKan assignments for PaperX 2013-2014]. (for internal use; organization's name changed).

XX Press Group. 2017. X Baoye jituan 2017 niandu gongzuo zongjie [2017 Press Group X Annual Report] (for internal use; organization's name changed).

Yao, L., and W. Jin. 2017. "2016 Nian Zhongguo Baokan Chanye Fazhan Baogao [Development Report on China's Newspaper and Periodicals Industry 2016]." In *Report on Development of China's Media Industry (2017)*, edited by B. Cui. Beijing, China: Social Sciences Academic Press.

Zhang, S. I. 2009. "What's Wrong with Chinese Journalists? Addressing Journalistic Ethics in China through a Case Study of the Beijing Youth Daily." *Journal of Mass Media Ethics* 24 (2-3): 173–188.

Zhao, Y. 1998. *Media, Market, and Democracy in China: Between the Party Line and the Bottom Line*. Urbana: University of Illinois Press.

Zhao, Y. 2004. "Underdogs, Lapdogs and Watchdogs: Journalists and the Public Sphere Problematic in China." In *Chinese Intellectuals between State and Market*, edited by E. Gu and M. Goldman. Routledge Curzon.

Zhao, Y. 2008. *Communication in China: Political Economy, Power, and Conflict*. Lanham: Rowman & Littlefield Publishers.

Zhou, R., Y. Xu, and X. Li. 2018. "Yetai de lianjie: Lijie zhiye gongtongti dui baiyuwei zhongguo xinwen congyezhe de shendu fangtan [Liquid Connection: Understanding Occupational Community an in-Depth Interview with Journalists in China]." *Xinwen Yu Chuanbo Yanjiu [Journalism & Communication]* 126 (7): 27–48.

Sponsored Content in 2020: Back to the Future?

Lisa Lynch

ABSTRACT

This article revisits predictions I made in 2018 regarding the future of newsroom content studios in my book *Native Advertising: Advertorial Disruptions in the 21st Century News Feed*. As that book was going to press, the news industry was still optimistic that sponsored content —in particular, the native advertising produced by boutique 'content studios' at newsrooms around the globe — would serve as a robust alternative revenue stream for prestige publications. Over the past three years, these hopes have faded somewhat. Content studios are still around, but their limitations are becoming clear and news outlets (somewhat predictably) have set their sights on still other sources of revenue.

In mid-2018, I published a monograph focussing on the rise of sponsored content at news outlets in the US and EU, focussing on publisher's investment in content studios creating bespoke advertising for clients. These ads, designed to fit seamlessly into the publications that produced them, leveraged the reputation of news outlets to promote products, services, and (on occasion) political candidates. After considering the legal, ethical and logistical complexities of sponsored editorial content in newsrooms, I concluded by postulating a range of scenarios for its future. The fate of these studios, I argued, might not be as bright as their proponents suggested:

> The recent history of the news industry is marked by moments of misplaced hopefulness and the creation of failed partnerships or ventures intended to 'save' news media: why should native advertising be any different? [N]ative advertising's proponents in the news industry argue that native advertising studios are the industry's best hope to take back the control over advertising that they have ceded to the rest of the information ecosystem. But what are the tradeoffs in regaining that control? And what if regaining control is simply not possible? (Lynch 2018, 108)

Two years on, economic and geopolitical shifts have changed the context around native advertising in ways both predictable and unanticipated, and the idea that sponsored content might make news outlets financially viable has been put to the test. In this commentary, I revisit four of the six predictions that formed the concluding chapter to my book, assessing how changing circumstances may have negative

Prediction One: Native Advertising Becomes Dominant

The first hypothetical 'future' I described for native advertising in the concluding chapter of my book was in alignment with more optimistic predictions of the industry at the time: namely, that newsroom content studios would become a dominant revenue stream for many newsrooms. If this happened, I speculated, content studios could eventually integrate entirely into the newsroom, much as "online journalism" eventually integrated and then swallowed newsrooms between the mid-90s and late 2000s (Paterson and Domingo 2008). As studios expanded and demanded greater resources, the oft-noted 'Chinese Wall' between the business and editorial might begin to dissolve as editorial staffers and freelancers alike came to see content production as just another part of their workflow. Additionally, as sponsored content became an inextricable part of reading or watching the news, the public and professional stigma surrounding native advertising might subside.

As I write this, that earlier prediction seems like a distant possibility. Through the end of 2019, the news industry remained bullish on content studios, with advocates predicting aggressive expansion of the format (Sirrah 2019), and outlets ranging from business publications (Oliver 2019) to network news (NBC News Custom Studios, 2020) to news agencies (Australian Associated Press's AAP Studio, 2019) setting up new studios in an already crowded market. But in the first quarter of 2020, the emergence of the coronavirus pandemic shattered expectations for growth; instead, already-beleaguered newsrooms suddenly found themselves grappling with the near collapse of the advertising market. As quarantines and travel prohibitions spread internationally, advertisers moved to pause or cancel ad buys, in part due to a decline in consumer spending (particularly in the luxury and tourism sectors, both important to premium sponsored content), but also because of the long-standing reluctance of companies to associate their brands with bad news. Soon, news outlets confronted a paradox: their audiences grew at a rate that would have appealed to advertisers at any other moment, while the number of ads in their publications plummeted. In the US the situation became so dire that Digital Content Next, the trade organization representing major US news sites to advertisers, wrote an open letter to the advertising industry in March 2020 asking them to remove brand filters around coronavirus news (Graham 2020).

The effects of this advertising falloff were immediate and devastating for the news industry. Around 36,000 news workers were furloughed or laid off by early April (Tracy 2020a), and losses continued through the spring and summer of 2020. Editorial positions were cut, but so were an unusually large number of jobs on the business side of news publications, including newsroom content studios. At the Guardian, 110 of the 180 job losses were in marketing and advertising. Quartz announced that the majority of their layoffs would be in ad sales, as the company tried to shift to a subscription model. The New York Times took the same approach, making cuts at T Brand and deciding to shutter their in-house experiential advertising studio FakeLove (Sternberg

2020). And the Telegraph closed its award-wining sponsored content studio Spark, announcing that it would finish work with current clients and then shift to a subscription-first strategy (Tobitt 2020).

As the crisis deepened, newsroom content studios were forced to rethink their approach to potential advertisers, reducing fees and proposing shorter and less ambitious projects (Southern 2020a). A report in March by the Interactive Advertising Bureau showed significant declines in brand's 'direct buys' with prestige editorial publications, with similarly grim predictions for the next year (Interactive Advertising Bureau 2020). In this austerity-constrained environment, there are concerns that the cutbacks and lack of continued innovation may produce a "grim domino effect," limiting the appeal of these studios in the future (Southern 2020b) and making it harder to lure advertisers.

Prediction Two: Facebook Makes Newsroom Native Obsolete

Of course, even before the cutbacks of the past few months, newsroom content studios faced a series of other threats. Perhaps the most consequential has been the impact of the 'duopoly' of Facebook and Google, which has continued to siphon off an ever-greater share of advertising revenue and audience share from news publishers (Bell et al. 2017). In the conclusion to my book, a second scenario for the future of native content studios focussed on the duopoly's efforts to "swallow the Internet," while robbing news organizations not only of their revenue, but of their distinct identities as creators and publishers. I predicted that the homogenizing visual presentation of news on these two platforms would accelerate the separation between news content and news brands, to the point where newsrooms would struggle to assert that their brands were worthy of association. I also predicted that Facebook's algorithm would kneecap efforts to create content with broader reach.

For the most part, unfortunately, these predictions have proved accurate. The loss of advertising revenue to the duopoly remains a crisis across the entire advertising industry (Sinclair 2020; Napoli 2020). The consequences of this loss for news media in particular were starkly illustrated by a mid-2019 study showing that Google made almost as much money placing advertising against news content in 2018 – 4.6 billion dollars – as the entire US news industry made from advertising that year (Tracy 2019). Recently, the duopoly has faced a series of challenges – both companies suffered their own advertising losses as a result of the pandemic, and both are facing scrutiny from regulators in the US, the European Union, Australia and elsewhere (Helberger 2020) but this has not stopped them from capturing an even larger relative share of the market over the course of 2020 (Wakabayashi, Hsu, and Issac 2020).

Though both Facebook and Google have severely eroded news advertising revenue, the lion's share of news industry ire has been directed at Facebook, because that platform has done more damage to the industry's reputation and reach. Facebook's ever-evolving algorithm, as well as Zuckerberg's own capriciousness about the role of news content on his platform, have had a destabilizing effect beyond the loss of advertising revenue. In the wake of what one media observer described as the "algopocalypse" — Facebook's 2018 restructuring of its algorithms to prioritize posts emanating from a user's friends and family over posts from news publishers (Haik 2018) — news outlets have struggled to accommodate the changing demands of the platform. A 2019 study by the Tow Centre noted that major news publishers who had initially seen publishing on Facebook as an opportunity for increased digital reach had come to see the company as indifferent, if not antagonistic, to the news industry (Rashidian et al. 2020). This has led publishers to seek alternatives to the platform, though they acknowledge that Facebook still remains an important, if unpopular, part of the news ecosystem (Meese and Hurcombe 2020)

True to form, Facebook has remained resistant to the specific criticisms levied against it by the news industry. They have, however, acknowledged that their platform has created "disruption" for news publishers. And since 2017, they have offered to assist the industry with a series of interventions ranging from grants to hackathons to mentorships. In June of 2020, the platform unveiled what they described as a solution to issues faced by both news publishers and consumers – a distinct 'News' tab available in Facebook's mobile application (Isaac and Tracy 2019). This beta version of Facebook News is described in an FAQ as a journalist-curated experience prioritizing news that is "personalized" and "relevant to your community" (Facebook 2020), a statement which represents the company's effort to redefine 'news' as local (Owen 2020) in order to stay out of the political maelstrom.

Facebook's shift towards the local has meant that increasingly, the company has focussed attention on boosting local news revenue models, including the expansion of sponsored content in newsrooms. An initiative begun in 2019 by Facebook, the Branded Content Project, has attempted to push even more U.S. newsrooms towards content production, providing support and training for local and mid-sized newsrooms interested in developing campaigns or creating studios. Though it is possible to be cynical about the reasons Facebook is evangelizing the benefits of branded content to thousands of local newsrooms across the U.S. (perhaps less to 'save local news,' than to produce more content for Facebook), the initiative presumed that sponsored content is a key advertising strategy for news organizations (Localmedia.org 2019). It remains to be seen whether the recent downturn in the advertising market will cause Facebook to rethink the initiative or their commitment to an increasingly imperilled local news industry.

Prediction Three: Fake News Beats Native Advertising

Facebook's News tab is also a tacit acknowledgment of yet another way in which Facebook and other social platforms have undermined news organizations; namely, their lackadaisical attitude towards disinformation has played a role in media consumers' decreasing trust in any form of media, including news outlets (Ognyanova et al. 2020). This news credibility gap anchored the third scenario that my book considered for the future of newsroom content studios. I argued that such studios were dependent on the prestige behind their brand, predicting that they might suffer as the overall trust in media declined. More particularly, I pointed to the role of native advertising itself in contributing to this climate of distrust, noting the connection between native advertising and news distrust was at times articulated explicitly — for example, when the political right used the presence of sponsored content in mainstream media publications as an example of their "fake news" status (Lynch 2018) — and at times more subtly, tied to the ways in which news consumers feel deceived by what they initially mistake for editorial content.

Two years on, it is hard to weigh in definitively about this prediction. Undeniably, the integrity of the news media is under global assault, and in some countries, this has correlated with a sharp decline in trust (Prochazka and Schweiger 2020). In the US, there has been increasing concern about implications for the democratic functions of the media; for example, Serazio (2019, 14) has argued that "further erosion of public trust in news media" would have serious ramifications for the information credibility needed for democratic governance. Scholars focussed on native advertising have continued to raise concerns on the deceptive nature of native content and pushed for more labelling transparency (Windels and Porter 2020, Wojdynski & Evans 2020, Amazeen and Wojdynski 2019, Glaser et. al 2019, Krouwer, Poels, and Paulussen 2017), suggesting that advertising credibility remains a serious issue both for both scholars and practitioners. Others have argued that the rise of government-sponsored content in both the domestic and international press has also challenged both the autonomy of journalists as well as the ability of the press to accurately represent both the actions of public officials and the actions of states themselves (Balint 2021; Wang 2021).

Though such research is compelling, it is important to note that this is an emerging discussion: more work needs to be done to ascertain whether native advertising itself has been affected by, or has significantly facilitated, distrust in the news. Work on media delegitimization outside of the journalism and communications fields (for example, in political science) sees media distrust as a function of the rise of populism and issue polarization (Lischka 2019, Watson 2020, Egelhofer and Lecheler 2019) rather than on the role of deceptive advertising, so it is possible that interdisciplinary collaboration might produce a more nuanced account of the trust crisis.

In early 2020, an incident involving the US politics and culture site Teen Vogue illustrated the continued industry sensitivity around potential reputational damage from sponsored content. On January 8, the site ran an article with no byline or sponsorship label praising Facebook's 'election integrity' efforts and interviewing five female Facebook staffers that the article claimed were tasked with fighting misinformation. Readers complained about the laudatory tone of the article on Twitter, especially given that Facebook's stance around misinformation was the subject of public scrutiny at the moment the article was published. Rather than defending the publication, Teen Vogue's social media director reacted with similar scepticism, responding "literally IDK" when a reader tweeted "Teen Vogue, what is this?" (this response was later deleted from the Teen Vogue feed). What followed was a series of editorial missteps that baffled and angered observers: first, the article was incorrectly bylined; then the byline vanished and the article was given a sponsored content label; following that, the article was removed entirely from the website. Finally, shortly after the article's removal, Condé Nast issued a statement apologizing for a series of errors and insisting "we don't take our audience's trust for granted" (Abrams and Kang 2020).

The Teen Vogue debacle was something of a perfect storm. Not only was it a case of deceptive advertising (allegedly unintentionally so) that produced questions about the integrity of Teen Vogue; it also was an attempt by Facebook to leverage the integrity of Teen Vogue's brand in order to bolster its shaky reputation around integrity issues. The resulting fracas demonstrated that, even if research has not demonstrated that readers or advertisers are making choices based on anxieties around sponsored content, the public conversation around such content is negative and distrustful.

Prediction Four: News Platforms Lose Their Appeal

Thus far, I have updated three of my 2018 predictions about the future of native advertising in the newsroom, arguing that early confidence about the revenue boost from sponsored content is belied by 1.) the recent effects of market contraction, 2.) the inability to compete with the duopoly, and 3.) recent attacks on media credibility. To conclude, I want to consider one final scenario connected to all of these trends: that advertisers lose interest in news content studios because the changing media ecosystem offers them new, more tantalizing opportunities. In 2018, I noted that not only social media platforms, but music platforms such as Spotify had begun to aggressively court brands: more recently, video game consoles have emerged as a new advertising frontier (Patel 2020). All of these venues attract a younger, more diverse demographic than most news sites, and all of them are superior at tracking and targeting. Over the past several years, advertising investment has also increasingly shifted to mobile ads, which means a focus on simpler, display-based advertising instead of innovative or ambitious brand sponsored content projects.

New opportunities for advertisers are not only coming from outside of the news industry. Faced with the above challenges, news publishers are currently spending heavily on audio production, creating a new platform for ad sponsorship that might change how the industry conceives "sponsored content." A December 2019 study by The Reuters Digital News Project found that there were 60 different news podcasts gearing to launch internationally, many inspired by the success of The New York Times podcast The Daily. Like The Daily, these podcasts were tailored towards younger, diverse news audiences.

The investment in podcasts – signalled most recently by The New York Times's acquisition of Gimlet Media News — comes as podcasts around the globe have begun to attract the attention of the sort of "blue chip" advertisers commonly courted by newsroom content studios (Newman 2019; Ives 2020). A substantial part of their appeal to advertisers is their ability to contain native ads. Sponsorships blend seamlessly into the structure of podcast episodes, and exploit the trust relationship between host and listener, much as other forms of native exploit the trust between a publication and its readers. But this integration, thus far, does not seem to have altered the trust relationship between listener and host (Futuri Media and University of Florida 2019). Further, podcasts cannot be disaggregated in the same fashion as textual news: they must be downloaded in their entirety, ads and all.

Buoyed by market expansion, less susceptible to the duopoly, and more trusted than the mainstream press, podcasts might be the ideal medium for sponsored content. But whether their rise foretells the demise of the newsroom content studio is yet to be seen. Indeed, the hope that podcast advertising can help sustain newsrooms is predicated on the assumption that news outlets have will the resources to compete in the increasingly crowded podcast arena. In a moment when news organizations face unprecedented fiscal challenges (Napoli 2020), it is important to remain clear-eyed about the risks of placing too much faith in yet another 'pivot' in the revenue model for news.

Disclosure Statement

No potential conflict of interest was reported by the authors.

References

Abrams, Rachel, and Cecelia Kang. 2020. "The Mystery of Teen Vogue's Disappearing Facebook Article." *The New York Times*, January 8. https://www.nytimes.com/2020/01/08/business/media/teen-vogue-facebook.html

Amazeen, Michelle A., and Bartosz W. Wojdynski. 2019. "Reducing Native Advertising Deception: Revisiting the Antecedents and Consequences of Persuasion Knowledge in Digital News Contexts." *Mass Communication and Society* 22 (2): 222–247.

Balint, Anat. 2021. "It's in the air" — Sponsored Editorial Content as a Path for Stealth Government Propaganda: The Case of Israeli Media. Digital Journalism. doi:10.1080/21670811.2021.1899010.

Bell, Emily J., Taylor Owen, Peter D. Brown, Codi Hauka, and Nushin Rashidian. 2017. "The platform press: How Silicon Valley reengineered journalism." Tow Center Reports. https://www.cjr.org/tow_center_reports/platform-press-how-silicon-valley-reengineered-journalism.php

Egelhofer, Jana Laura, and Sophie Lecheler. 2019. "Fake News as a Two-Dimensional Phenomenon: A Framework and Research Agenda." *Annals of the International Communication Association* 43 (2): 97–116.

Facebook, 2020. *How Facebook News Works*. https://www.facebook.com/news/howitworks.

Futuri Media and University of Florida 2019. NAB Podcast Users National Survey Report. https://web.tresorit.com/l#KqPiA_b5Ruf3Zz2j-9f81Q

Graham, Megan. 2020. News Sites Ask Ad Industry to Get Comfortable Alongside Coronavirus Related Content. CNBC, March 29.

Haik, Corey Tolbert. 2018. The Algopocalypse. Global Editor's Network, February 8. https://medium.com/global-editors-network/the-algo-pocalypse-journalism-in-the-digital-dystopia-38c922bd7f05

Helberger, Natali. 2020. "The Political Power of Platforms: How Current Attempts to Regulate Misinformation Amplify Opinion Power." *Digital Journalism* 8 (6): 842–854.

Interactive Advertising Bureau 2020., Coronavirus Ad Spend Impact: Buy-Side. IAB, March 27. https://www.iab.com/insights/coronavirus-ad-spend-impact-buy-side/

Isaac, Marc, and Mike Tracy. 2019. "Facebook Calls Truce with Publishers as It Unveils Facebook News." New York Times, October 25. https://www.nytimes.com/2019/10/25/technology/facebook-publishers-news.html

Ives, Nat. 2020. Omnicom Plans $20 Million in Podcast Ads on Spotify. The Wall Street Journal, July 8. https://www.wsj.com/articles/omnicom-plans-20-million-in-podcast-ads-on-spotify-11594204200.

Krouwer, Simone, Karolien Poels, and Steve Paulussen. 2017. "To Disguise or to Disclose? The Influence of Disclosure Recognition and Brand Presence on Readers' Responses toward Native Advertisements in Online News Media." *Journal of Interactive Advertising* 17 (2): 124–137.

Lischka, Juliane A. 2019. "A Badge of Honor? How the New York Times Discredits President Trump's Fake News Accusations." *Journalism Studies* 20 (2): 287–304.

Lynch, Lisa. 2018. *Native Advertising: Advertorial Disruption in the 21st-Century News Feed.* Routledge.

Meese, James, and Edward Hurcombe. 2020. "Facebook, News Media and Platform Dependency: The Institutional Impacts of News Distribution on Social Platforms." *New Media & Society*. doi: 10.1177/1461444820926472.

Napoli, Philip. 2020. "Connecting Journalism and Public Policy: New Concerns and Continuing Challenges." *Digital Journalism* 8 (6): 691–703.

Newman, Nic. 2019. "Inspired by The Daily, Dozens of News Podcasts Are Punching Above Their Weight Worldwide." The Nieman Report, December 3. https://www.niemanlab.org/2019/12/inspired-by-the-daily-dozens-of-daily-news-podcasts-are-punching-above-their-weight-worldwide/

Ognyanova, K., D. Lazer, R. E. Robertson, and C. Wilson. 2020. Misinformation in action: Fake news exposure is linked to lower trust in media, higher trust in government when your side is in power. *Harvard Kennedy School Misinformation Review*. https://misinforeview.hks.harvard.edu/article/misinformation-in-action-fake-news-exposure-is-linked-to-lower-trust-in-media-higher-trust-in-government-when-your-side-is-in-power/

Oliver, Morely. 2019. Business News Publications are Investing in Brand Content Studios. Digiday, August 6. https://digiday.com/media/business-news-publishers-investing-brand-content-studios-attract-b2b-clients/.

Owen, Laura Hazard. 2020. The new Facebook News is filled with stories that are way too mainstream to do well on the rest of Facebook. Nieman Lab, June 10. https://www.niemanlab.org/2020/06/the-new-facebook-news-is-filled-with-stories-that-are-way-too-mainstream-to-do-well-on-the-rest-of-facebook/.

Patel, Sahel. 2020. Marketers Experiment with TV Ads in Console Videogames. The Wall Street Journal, July 26. https://www.wsj.com/articles/marketers-experiment-with-tv-ads-in-console-videogames-11595768400?mod=searchresults&page=1&pos=3

Paterson, Chris A., and David Domingo, eds. 2008. *Making Online News: The Ethnography of New Media Production.* Vol. 49. New York, NY: Peter Lang.

Prochazka, Fabian, and Wolfgang Schweiger. 2019. "How to Measure Generalized Trust in News Media? An Adaptation and Test of Scales." *Communication Methods and Measures* 13 (1): 26–42.

Rashidian, Nushin, Georgios Tsiveriotis, Peter D. Brown, Emily J. Bell, and Abigail Hartstone. 2020. "Platforms and publishers: The end of an era." Tow Center For Digital Journalism. https://www.cjr.org/tow_center_reports/platforms-and-publishers-end-of-an-era.php

Serazio, Michael. 2019. "The Other 'Fake'news: Professional Ideals and Objectivity Ambitions in Brand Journalism. *Journalism*. 1464884919829923." *Journalism* : 146488491982992.

Sinclair, John. 2020. "Cracking under Pressure: Current Trends in the Global Advertising Industry." *Media International Australia* 174 (1): 3–16.

Sirrah, Ava. 2019. Native Advertising May Jeopardize the Legitimacy of Newsrooms. Columbia Journalism Review, September 6. https://www.cjr.org/tow_center/native-ads-endanger-newsrooms.php.

Southern, Lucinda. 2020a. The Great Reset: How Sales Relationships and Structure Will Change on The Other Side of the Coronavirus. Digiday, July 13. https://digiday.com/media/the-great-reset-how-sales-relationships-and-structure-will-change-on-the-other-side-of-coronavirus/

Southern, Lucinda. 2020b. 'That innovation budget has gone': Publishers adapt to thwarted branded content studio growth. Digiday, August 4. https://digiday.com/media/that-innovation-budget-has-gone-publishers-adapt-to-thwarted-branded-content-studio-growth/.

Tobitt, Charlotte. 2020. "Telegraph Ditches Branded Content Putting Dozens of Jobs at Risk. 2020." *Press Gazette*, June 18. https://pressgazette.co.uk/telegraph-ditches-branded-content-putting-dozens-of-jobs-at-risk/

Tracy, Marc. 2019. Google Made $4.7 Billion From the News Industry in 2018, Study Says. The New York Times, June 9. https://www.nytimes.com/2019/06/09/business/media/google-news-industry-antitrust.html.

Tracy, Marc. 2020a. News Media Outlets Have Been Ravaged by the Pandemic. The New York Times, May 1. https://www.nytimes.com/2020/04/10/business/media/news-media-coronavirus-jobs.html

Wakabayashi, Daisuke, Tiffany Hsu, and Mike Issac. 2020. Even Google and Facebook May Face an Ad Slump. The New York Times, April 14. https://www.nytimes.com/2020/04/14/technology/coronavirus-google-facebook-advertising.html.

Wang, Dan. 2021. "Native Advertisement and Journalistic Identity in the Chinese Press: Two Paradoxes." *Digital Journalism*.

Windels, Kasey, and Lance Porter. 2020. "Examining Consumers' Recognition of Native and Banner Advertising on News Website Home Pages." *Journal of Interactive Advertising* 20 (1): 1–16.

Wojdynski, Bartosz W., and Nathaniel J. Evans. 2020. "The Covert Advertising Recognition and Effects (CARE) Model: Processes of Persuasion in Native Advertising and Other Masked Formats." *International Journal of Advertising* 39 (1): 4–31.

Journalism and the Voice Intelligence Industry

Joseph Turow

ABSTRACT

The voice intelligence industry is an emerging sector of society that involves smart speakers, car information systems, customer service calls to contact centers, and "connected-home" devices such as thermostats, home-security alarms and other tools. Linked to it are advanced machine learning and deep neural network programs that can discriminate prejudicially among individuals in ways that benefit the firms using their voice. This commentary explores the implications of these activities for journalism. For example, combining inferences about an individual's voice with a raft other information collected about that person might lead to a rearranging of the agendas of news articles, news videos, commercial messages, and even discounts differently for different people on the fly. The rise of voice will likely reshape programmatic advertising marketplaces as well as the more private ways journalism organizations work with a variety of branding engines to identify and persuade prospects. As these pieces of the new environment move into place, it is important for people who care about the future of journalism to consider how an era centering on voice-profiling might shape news agendas individuals receive, commercial messages that come with them, and interrelationships between journalism and commerce.

This essay aims to jumpstart discussions regarding profound implications the emerging "voice intelligence industry" can have for the creation and marketing of news. The voice intelligence industry is an emerging sector of society that involves smart speakers, car information systems, customer service calls to contact centers, and "connected-home" devices such as thermostats, home-security alarms and other tools. The best-known vehicles for such activities in the United States, UK, and European Union are Amazon's Alexa, Google Assistant, and Apple's Siri. Google Assistant, accessed mostly through smartphones and Google Home cylinders, is allegedly available in more than abillion devices. Amazon's Alexa personal assistant is by the company's count present in more than 100 million devices (Bohn 2019). At the same time, a different though related eco system of firms is creating major voice initiatives in customer contact centers.

Voice profiling is similar to facial profiling in using artificial intelligence for the bio-assessment of individuals. While both reflect new levels of social monitoring, voice profiling is currently more pervasive than facial in home-based and leisure parts of people's lives. When you phone a company's contact center for advice or help you are increasingly likely to be overheard by a computer that will make inferences about your emotions and sentiments. You may talk to the voice-driven devices to learn the weather, play music, get driving instructions, retrieve recipes, turn lights on, raise the thermostat temperature, answer a doorbell, or perform other activities of daily living. While you are doing that, "intelligent assistants" linked to the instruments can use algorithms generated by machine learning to draw inferences about you based on linguistic patterns as well as the physical sound of your voice (your voiceprint). Marketers who champion voice analytics tout its alleged ability to distinguish among individuals by using conclusions from how people speak to assess their feelings regarding a firm, its goods and services. Typically ignoring critics' caveats about algorithmic bias, voice industry discussions nowadays center on detecting individuals' emotions, sentiments, and personality characteristics to help persuade them, often in real time (Turow 2021). The goal in the not-so-distant future may be to home in on people's weight, height, age, ethnicity, menstrual situation, and more—all things scientists believe reflect through your voice (Singh 2019, 85–120).

The voice intelligence industry argues that the assistants are programmed simply to help people in a range of everyday activities at home, in cars, in stores, and on streets. But also tied to them are advanced machine learning and deep neural network programs that can discriminate prejudicially among individuals in ways that benefit the firms using their voice. Based on how individuals speak to the device and how they sound, companies can score individuals as more or less valuable, show them different products based on that valuation, give them different discounts, and treat them differently when they want help. Many customer contact centers, typically out of the public eye, are already applying these technologies to evaluate customers based on how they talk, take account of their purchase history with the firm, and tell a live agent what to say to mollify or upsell them. Amazon and Google reserve the right to use voice profiles for certain purposes but are not yet applying these tools for their maximum marketing potential because they are worried about inflaming current social worries around the collection of people's voices. Yet Amazon and Google have staked out numerous patents regarding voice profiling. (One asserts that Amazon's Echo could hear a sniffle in your voice, infer a cold, and offer to deliver aspirin to you within two hours—Huafeng and Wang, 2018). A few large advertising firms are also working on methods to infer customers' inclinations from how they speak. Their executives express confidence the approaches will eventually become part of marketing toolkits.

These developments reflect a dynamic I call *the unending spiral of personalization* that sits at the heart of 21st century marketing. Personalization is a process guided by marketers' belief that in order for their firms to remain competitive they must gather as much data as possible about current and prospective customers and send them individualized messages and product offerings. "Traditional" forms of personalization in the digital space have been based on demographics, location, internet behaviors, psychographics, and lifestyle. The never-ending spiral of personalization refers to a dilemma: because of intrinsic limitations in all audience research, marketers will eventually feel they are not doing enough to know their targets and reach them efficiently. They will consequently be open to technologies—voice profiling, for example—that promise new forms of information through progressively greater intrusions into people's lives. These practices will also turn out to be unsatisfying, though, and the drive for deeper ways to know the customer will continue—for instance, by linking voice intelligence to even more intrusive technologies.

My research on the voice intelligence industry aimed to explore how such considerations are justifying an emerging market for personalization based on people's speech patterns and voice prints. I interviewed 45 industry executives that averaged about close to an hour; conducted an in-depth exploration of trade magazine articles and general news sources on the topic; and analyzed dozens of voice-industry patents, among other methods. Behind the rise of voice has been worry of internet marketers—burst into the open during the 2010s—that traditional tracking, profiling, and targeting are fraught with challenges for the entire digital ecosystem. Data may not be up to date, profiles may be created based on multiple users of a computer or phone, names may be confused, and people may lie about their age, income, even gender in the hope of confusing digital marketers. Advertisers are also discontented with well-known problems of pervasive click fraud by websites (as high as 28% of all global web traffic, according to Adobe in 2018—Bruell, 2018) and ad blocking by web and app users. Increased government oversight such as the EU's General Data Protection Regulation (GDPR) and the California Consumer Privacy Act (CPPA) put even more pressure on the existing system. Confronting all these problems in a November 2019 report, the Gartner consultancy noted that firms also face difficulties in achieving success with personalization because of "the continuing decline in consumer trust" (Gartner Inc 2019).

Marketers I interviewed for this study as well as those quoted in the trade press don't discuss voice intelligence as a substitute for tracking known people on the Web, on apps, in stores, and everywhere in between. Voice is, in the words of consultant Pete Erickson, a "value-added" to the current personalization regime, not a replacement (Erickson 2019). "Reading human emotions [through voice] and then adapting consumer experiences to these emotions in real time" will "help to transform the face of marketing" exulted an executive from Affectiva, an MIT tech spinoff (Shapiro 2016). Executives in the customer contact center business also see the new technologies of voice-driven personalization as marking a new era with emotions analytics at its heart. The CEO of Clarabridge, a provider of phone response technology, predicted voice technologies will help identify "key indicators" of a particular caller's loyalty "such as effort, emotion, sentiment and intent" (Clarabridge, 2019).

The first stage toward a voice profiling era is the widespread use of dedicated voice devices at home, especially "smart speakers." It is already well under way in the US due to major price and public relations initiatives of the manufacturers (Google, Amazon, and others) and retailers (Walmart, Target, Best Buy). Their work is enhanced by a mainstream press that reports enthusiastically on extravagant sales events and presents voice-enabled devices as helping a logical, attractive style of living. I learned this through a wide-ranging analysis of digital news outlets' coverage of voice assistants as well as an in-depth examination of what the *New York Times*, *Wall Street Journal* and *Washington Post* told their readers about voice assistants and connected homes from August 2018 Prime Day to August 2019 (Turow 2021, chapter 5). I also found that the press presents as taken-for-granted the adoption of smart devices by its users even as it covers public concerns about the devices mistakenly recording home conversations and randomly auditing people's device commands. The occasional hand-wringing about surveillance through the devices is generally mixed with confusing assurances by the firms involved that it isn't as bad as some claim. Moreover, the mainstream press has encouraged Americans to believe that voice monitoring is an enduring fact of life. For example, a September 2018 *Washington Post* headline promoted an attitude the voice intelligence industry could feel comfortable with: "In today's homes, consumers are willing to sacrifice privacy for convenience" (Rao 2018).

In this early stage Amazon and Google are already allowing apps on their smart speakers to ask users to identify themselves and to track their habits as well as to link those data to other information about the individuals. Amazon and Google are also giving the app owners transcripts of exactly what individuals say to the apps, though they are not yet relaying the individuals' voiceprints. At the same time, executives worry that Google and Amazon, which do keep the voice prints, might use people's talk to other companies through smart speakers as a way to learn competitive information about customers. The concern has led Bank of America and other firms to create their own voice assistants for the Web or phones (Bank of America, no date). The proliferation of such branded voices may be a future wave that gives companies the assurance they alone control access to what and how they speak to customers, and (eventually) what they learn from their voices. For voice profiling to move further forward would involve firms routinely getting people's explicit (opt-in) permission to analyze their voices, undoubtedly in return for personalized benefits. That step would sync voice profiling with requirements by the EU's GDPR, California's CCPA, and the general direction of digital policies in the US.

Advertising-supported news from the New York Times, BBC, and other outlets is already a popular form of content via voice apps on smart speakers. As these pieces of the new environment move into place, it is important for people who care about the future of journalism to consider how an era centering on voice-profiling might shape news agendas individuals receive, commercial messages that come with them, and interrelationships between journalism and commerce. Combining inferences about an individual's voice with a raft other information collected about that person (a voice-plus profile) might even lead to a rearranging of the agendas of news articles, news videos, commercial messages, and even discounts differently for different people on the fly. The goal: to maximally enhance the chance of that individual's engagement with the branded journalistic package. That could mean viewing the "standard" news stories and the ads surrounding them, or it could mean interacting with sponsored editorial content as well as ads that the organization's computers have personalized for the individual based on the voice-plus profile.

Further analyses of factors affecting engagement could also lead to the alteration of a story about the same event to match an audience member's alleged real-time emotions as well as more enduring personality features inferred from demographic and lifestyle data. This dynamic creation process will diminish the journalist's role in making news, particularly if corporate research suggests people are more likely to click on, and spend time with, news stories and the ads surrounding them if the tales are personalized. Publishers will encourage editors to enlist computers for the creation of many versions of the same news event in ways that are tailored to differently profiled readers. If the app or site recites the story (an increasingly common occurrence), part of the tailoring will undoubtedly involve choosing a narration voice based on what research has found optimizes the engagement of individuals with certain profiles based on *their* voices and backgrounds.

The use of voice intelligence as a profitable vehicle for creating news and the commercial material surrounding it will likely raise new conflicts of interest regarding the news industry's coverage of the nature and future of surveillance. As the voice intelligence industry takes hold, our worlds will increasingly be filled by offers—not necessarily explicit ads— based on our putative emotions and sentiments. Discriminatory messages will be built into the process. We're already subject to differential offers and opportunities based on various facts about us–such as our income, where we live, our race and sex, and other attributes. Voice profiling adds an especially insidious means of doing this. What if an expensive restaurant decides it won't take your reservation because you sound low-class (read Black or a certain type of Hispanic, though the algorithm supposedly corrected for that), or too demanding, or somehow not cool enough for its image? What if voice profiling tells a prospective employer that your voice suggests you're a bad risk for a job that you covet–or desperately need? We could be denied loans, denied insurance or have to pay much more for it, or denied jobs on the basis of characteristics we can't change but whose existence is certified by a science that may not actually be that accurate at predicting behavior. Moreover, discrimination through voice profiling can be extremely subtle to detect–and therefore difficult to fight.

The prospect of tracking people and controlling them is as appealing to political marketers and government agencies as it is to commercial marketers. Facial recognition surveillance—a stock-in-trade of governments for public security—doesn't yet reach into the recesses of people's homes, but voice does. It shouldn't be surprising, then, when non-business institutions take notice of the bio-profiling technology. A political campaign may examine people's voice responses to political phone calls to decide on the fly how to describe a candidate's beliefs to them. A political marketer might stream certain commercials to particular individuals because their comments and voice characteristics suggest world views that can be reinforced by extreme arguments the marketer wouldn't want others to see.

Even if individuals are only dimly aware that these activities are widespread across several industries, they may start to worry about their position in the marketplace and to suspect the system of commerce (and perhaps politics) is arrayed against them. They may also begin to worry that opening their mouths anywhere in public may result in unwanted inferences about them, because microphones are everywhere. As Echo and Google Home were first gaining popularity, reviewers suggested that users push the off button when discussing topics they didn't want the voice assistant to know. Turning the device off, however, takes away the spontaneity of questioning that is at the heart of the assistants' seductiveness. So people leave it on, leaving themselves open to voice surveillance that statements and patents from Google, Amazon and others indicate will lead to discriminatory treatment in the American public sphere, where the self and shopping get defined together. Differential outcomes based on segmented or personalized data analysis already occur in a variety of media contexts (see, e.g. Turow 1996, Turow 2006, Turow 2011 and Turow 2017). Voice profiling crosses a new line, though. It represents the leading edge of emerging biometric technologies that have the potential to add emotions and sentiment as well as untold other inferences from unique bodies as elements driving personalized message creation and targeting.

The voice intelligence industry is at too early a stage to have attempt more than a few of these tactics (mostly around emotion and sentiment), and home-speaker companies currently seem to be wary about moving forward quickly with bio-profiling. But they have the technologies and the patents, and some have begun to use speech and voice analysis in ways that point to a future of treating people differently based on their physiologies. As these developments permeate society, will news outlets that are heavily invested in the voice intelligence industry for their basic news creation and sponsorship activities be likely to report on these very activities as social problems? If contemporary coverage of the voice intelligence industry by the mainstream press is currently so resigned to its development—when news practitioners so far have little skin in the game—why should that change when voice profiling becomes part of their daily news work?

The reader is invited to continue this speculation. The rise of voice will likely reshape programmatic advertising marketplaces as well as the more private ways journalism organizations work with a variety of branding engines to identify and persuade prospects. All this will ratchet up surveillance of huge populations with little attention to long-term social costs. These will include a decline in the very freedom of personal choice the industry contends it is gifting to people who go with its flow. There may still be time for academics and advocates to resist the consolidation of voice profiling in media, including journalistic outlets, before publics become resigned to the unending spiral of personalization that will inevitably affect the agendas of their lives.

References

Bank of America. no date. "Personalized, Proactive, Predictive: See What Erica Can Do." *Bank of America*. https://promo.bankofamerica.com/erica/

Bohn, Dieter. 2019. "Amazon Says More Than 100 Million Alexa Devices have been Sold—What's Next." *The Verge*, January 4. https://www.theverge.com/2019/1/4/18168565/amazon-alexa-devices-how-many-sold-number-100-million-dave-limp

Bruell, Alexandra. 2018. "Fraudulent Web Traffic Continues to Plague Advertisers, Other Businesses," March 28. https://www.wsj.com/articles/fraudulent-web-traffic-continues-to-plague-advertisers-other-businesses-1522234801

Clarabridge. 2019. "Clarabridge Unveils New Updates to the Clarabridge Banking Solution." *Clarabridge*, November 7. https://www.clarabridge.com/clarabridge-unveils-new-updates-to-the-clarabridge-banking-solution/

Erickson, Pete. 2019. Interview. June 21.

Gartner Inc. 2019. "Gartner Predicts 80% of Marketers Will Abandon Personalization Efforts by 2025." *Gartner Press Release*, December 2. Accessed March 11, 2020. https://www.gartner.com/en/newsroom/press-releases/2019-12-02-gartner-predicts-80–of-marketers-will-abandon-person

Huafeng, Jin, and Shu Wang, for Amazon Technologies, Inc. 2018. "Voice-based Determination of Physical and Emotional Characteristics of Users." *United States Patent Office*, October 9. http://patft.uspto.gov/netacgi/nph-Parser?Sect1=PTO2&Sect2=HITOFF&u=%2Fnetahtml%2FPTO%2Fsearch-adv.htm&r=2&f=G&l=50&d=PTXT&p=1&S1=(Amazon.AANM.+AND+voice-based.TI.)&OS=AANM/Amazon+and+TTL/voice-based&RS=(AANM/Amazon+AND+TTL/voice-based).

Rao, Sonia. 2018. "In Today's Homes, Consumers Are Willing to Sacrifice Privacy For Convenience." *Washington Post*, September 12, via Factiva.

Shapiro, Tom. 2016. "How Emotion-Detection Technology Will Change Marketing." *Hubspot.com*, October 17. https://blog.hubspot.com/marketing/emotion-detection-technology-marketing

Singh, Rita. 2019. *Profiling Humans from Their Voice*. Singapore: Springer.

Turow, Joseph. 1996. *Breaking up America*. Chicago: University of Chicago Press.

Turow, Joseph. 2006. *Niche Envy*. Cambridge: MIT Press.

Turow, Joseph. 2011. *The Daily You*. New Haven: Yale University Press.

Turow, Joseph. 2017. *The Aisles Have Eyes*. New Haven: Yale University Press.

Turow, Joseph. 2021. *The Voice Catchers*. New Haven: Yale University Press.

Index

Note: Figures are indicated by *italics*. Tables are indicated by **bold**. Endnotes are indicated by the page number followed by 'n' and the endnote number e.g., 20n1 refers to endnote 1 on page 20.

accountability 33
Adblocking software 4
Advertising Standards Authority (ASA) 6
advertorials 2–3, 5, 7–8, 11, 14, 34–7, 39, 47–9, 55, 93
AdVoice 3
agency model 12, 52, 58–9
aggregated/repurposed model 12
Alexa 71
Amazeen, M. A. 15, 35, 67, 113
Amazon's Alexa 136
American Press Institute Report 3
Anderson, C. E. 68
anti-BDS campaign 100
Apostol, Nicoleta-Elena 15
Apple's Siri 136
Area Metropolitana de Barcelona (AMB) 13
Artemas, Katie 12–13, 37
Asociacion de la Prensa de Madrid (APM) 28, 46, 58–9
Atlantic, The (magazine) 47
autonomous model 30, 38

Bachmann, P. 11
Balint, A. 14
Banjac, S. 34
banner blindness 4
Barban, Arnold 11
Barinagarrementeria, Iker 13, 17
Barnhurst, Kevin G. 70
Becker-Olsen, Karen L. 10
Big Brother 99
bio-profiling 140, 141
Boerman, S. C. 15
boundary erosion 116–17
Bourdieu's field theory 12
Boyles, Jan L. 12
branded content (BC) 4–8, **9**, 11, 23–7, 32, 38, 40n1, 41n2, 58; characteristic of 90; commercial sponsors 92–4; emerging development 89; features and disclosure 45–6; fluid nature of 89–90; government agencies 96–101;

interviewees, roles and main tasks **29**; labels **51**; labs **50**; Mouffe's Agnostic Pluralism theory 92; *vs.* propaganda 36; role performance, sectors involved and disclosure 49–52; sectors involved **51**; smaller publications 47
BrandsLab (BRL) 55
Braun, V. 28
business model innovation 4, 12, 13, 23–5, 27, 31, 37, 38, 40, 44, 47, 48, 111, 112, 116, 121
Buzzfeed 3

California Consumer Privacy Act (CPPA) 138, 139
Cannes marketing festival, 2013 3
Carlson, M. 13, 37–40
Carvajal, Miguel 13, 17
Chadha, Monica 12
China 112, 113, 121, 122; digital journalists in 123; digital native advertising 111; journalistic professionalism, advertisement and changes 114; native advertising 113–14
Chinese media 110, 114, 123
Chittum, Ryan 3
City News (Bendi xinwen) 117
Clarke, V. 28
Coddington, M. 12
coinciding/disclosing nature **73**
coinciding visual objects, full-page ad level *77*
Committee of Advertising Practice (CAP) 6
communicative action 91
comparative research 5, 8, 15
concealed strategic action 91
Condé Nast 131
conscious deception 91
consumer content marketing (CCM) 4
content analysis 11, 14, 16, 40, 48–9, 59, 66, 73, 81; datasheet **49**; sampling strategy and coding 48–9
content management system (CMS) 35
content marketing 4, 5, 56, 66–7
content placement (BRL) 56
content studios 3, 14, 16, 17, 36, 127–30, 132, 133

INDEX

convince audiences 67
Cornia, A. 13, 24, 36, 38, 40
Corporate Communication 30
Covid pandemic 2, 16
credibility 9, 10, 15, 24, 26, 34, 35, 40, 45, 46, 48, 57, **57**, 59, 66, 67, 82, 130–2

datasheet, content analysis **49**
De Maeyer, Juliette 68
Democratic Corporatist Model 71
Der Tagesspiegel (newspaper) 71–2
Deuze, M. 118
digital advertising 3, 25, 45
digital journalism 17
digital leaders 2
digital media 4, 45, 47, 52, 90, 98, 110, 111, 116
digital native media 48
directors 28
disclosing visual objects, full-page ad level *76*
disclosure's prominence 68
disclosure transparency 70
Domingo, D. 71
Drew, Kevin 12
Duffy, Margaret 12–13, 37

earned media 6, 7
ECBrands (ECB) 52, 55, 56
editorial content 65, 98; and advertising 91–2
editors 28
Einstein, M. 68
Eisend, Martin 15
El Confidencial (newspaper) 24, 28, 29, 48, 49
Eldiario.es (ED) 28, 48, 49
El Español (newspaper) 24, 28, 31, 48, 49
El Mundo (newspaper) 24, 28, 29, 31, 48, 49, 55
El País (newspaper) 24, 28, 29, 48, 49
embedded branding 90
emerging model 30, 38–9
European Advertising Standards Alliance (EASA) 68
European Union 136; GDPR 139
evangelization work 55
Evans, N. J. 14
ExxonMobile advertorials 47–8

Facebook 25, 129–30
FAPE 33
Ferrer-Conill, R. 5, 8, 11, 13–15, 81
Fighting the Boycott (Benzaquen) 98–9
Fulgoni, Gian 8, 11

GAA Bid Committee 98
General Data Protection Regulation (GDPR) 138
General Law 34/1988 of Publicity 46
General Law 7/2010 on Audiovisual Communication 46
Germany 15, 66, 71
Gimlet Media News 132

Gioia, D. A. 113
Google 25, 50, 129, 137, 139–41
Google Assistant 136
governance 2, 5–7, 10, 15–16, 67–8, 131
Government Advertising Agency (GAA) 93, 97, 99, 101
government-sponsored content (GSC) 88–90, 92–5, 98–103, 131; in Israel 92; in Israeli media market 89; organizational culture and professional conduct of digital journalism 89; primary exploration of 94
Grabe, Maria Elizabeth 70
Grey Content 95
grim domino effect 129
Grubenmann, S. 112–13
guanxi (social capital) 117
Guardian, The (newspaper) 3–4, 90
Guo, Steve Zhongshi 13, 14

Haaretz (newspaper) 100, 101
Habermas, J. 91
Hanusch, F. 17, 34
Hardy, J. 9
Hassid, J. 120
Hire, The (film) 46
Howe, Patrick 15
Huffington Post, The 3, **72**
Hugh, Nick 16
Hunziker, S. 11
hybrid editors 25
hyper-commercialism 10, 24

Ikonen, Pasi 81
4il 95
industry practices 11–13
integrated model 30, 38
intelligent assistants 137
Interactive Advertising Bureau (IAB) 5, 45, 49
intercoder reliability tests **74**
intrapreneurial units 12
investor uniformization 117–18
Irish Independent (newspaper) 14
Irish Times, The (newspaper) 14
Israel 15, 66, 71, **72**, **78**, **79**, 88, 92–7, 100, 101, 104n8
'Issues' and 'Role performance' 52, **54**
'Issues' and 'Sectors of activity' 52, **53**

Joint National Mission 96–7
journalistic profession 33, 37

Karlsson, Michael 81
Keshet 94–6, 98
Kim, Bong-Hyun 11
Knesset 100, 104n9
Krämer, Benjamin 70
Krippendorf's alpha 73, **74**
Krouwer, Simone 67
Kruskal-Wallis test 58

Latour, Almar 12
Lavanguardia.com (LV) 48, 49, 55
Law 3/1991 on Unfair Competition 46
Lewis, Seth C. 69
Lipsman, Andrew 8, 11
Li, Y. 26, 59
logistic regression models, countries and newspapers **79**
Lynch, Lisa 16, 26

Machin, David 66, 69, 73
Mako (film) 98
Manas-Viniegra, Luis 14
Marcas Ñ (MA Ñ) **50**, 55–6
market-driven journalism 10
mass-market organizations 82
material objects 16, 65, 81–2; ad recognition 68–9
material sensibility 68
Meckel, M. 112, 113
'Media' and 'Role performance' 51
'Media' and 'Sectors of activity' 51, **51**, 52
Mellado, Claudia 49
Ministry of Diaspora Affairs (MoDA) 95, 96, 99, 101
Ministry of Strategic Affairs and Public Diplomacy (MoSA) 95, 96, 98
Ministry of Transportation and Road Safety (MoTRS) 95, 97, 99
Mishpocheh 101
Mouffe, C. 92
Muller, Philipp 70

native advertising (NA) 1, 5, 8, 10, 25, 38, 45, 47, 89, 103n3; commercial nature of 74–6; by country and online news outlet **72**; definition 66–7, 72–3; fake news 130–2; interpretative signals 68–9; in journalistic contexts 66–8
Neff, Gina 69
neo-liberal economies 103
Nerone, John C. 70
Netanyahu, Benjamin 93
news platforms 132–3
newsroom content studios 129–30, 132–3
news websites, Spanish 48
New York Times (newspaper) 3, 90, 139
Nielsen, R. K. 13, 24, 36, 38, 40
non-advertising content 10
non-commercial content 9
nonpaid editorial content 5
norm entrepreneurs 39
Norway 15, 66, 71, 76
Núñez-Gómez, Patricia 14

object-oriented approach 66
online journalism 128
online-only outlets 82
Ordinary Least Square (OLS) regression model 74, 76, 77; countries and newspapers **78**
Oreskes, Naomi 14

paid advertising content 5
paid media 6, 7
Palau-Sampio, Dolors 13, 14
Pasadeos, Yorgo 11
Paulussen, Steve 67
Pettit, Raymond 8, 11
Piety, Tamara 9
platform model 12
podcasting 16
Poels, Karolien 67
Polarized Pluralist Model 71
Polzer, Lydia 66, 69, 73
Prensa Ibérica 29
Prisa Brand Solutions (PBS) 52–3
professional autonomy 26, 38, 58, 59
public sphere 91

Raeymaeckers, Karin 70
reputational effects 48
Reuters Digital News Project 132
role conceptions 122, 123
role performance 46, 49–52, **49**, **52**, **54**, 60, 115
R software 49
RuanWen 112
Ruedy, T. 11

Schindler, Johanna 70
Sehl, A. 13, 24, 36, 38, 40
self-categorization 112, 113, 118–22, *119*, 122
self-regulatory organization (SRO) 6, 32
Serazio, Michael 7, 12, 131
Sharethrough (n.d.) 5
shiny camouflage 67, 81
social identity theory (SIT) 112–13, 115, 118–19, 121
social media 3, 23–4
Sonderman, Jeff 8, 12, 47
Spain 3, 13, 15, 27, 28, 32, 33, 36, 38, 40n1, 46–8, 66, 71, 76
sponsored content 2, 3, 7, **9**, 17, 40n1, 132; journalism 8–9
sponsorship 6–7
SPSS 25.0 programme 50
SPSS Spreadsheet 49
stealth marketing 90
strategic action 91
Supran, Geoffrey 14
surveillance 139–41
sustainability and labs 46–7
Sveningsson, S. 113
Sweden 15, 66, 71

Tajfel, H. 113, 122
Teen Vogue (magazine) 131, 132
TeKan 112, 114, 115; group conflicts and fluid self-categorizations 118–21; news quality 120; power reliance 120–1; soliciting 119–20; work structure 116–18
Telegraph (newspaper) 16

Teufel, Brady 15
Theory of Communicative Action (Habermas) 91
Thomas, Ryan J. 12
Tran, Millie 8, 12, 47
transparency 14, 33, 34, 40, 46, 66, 67, 70, 71, 80–2, 94, 131
triangulation method 48, **48**
Trust Project 33
Turow, Joseph 16
Twitter 131

UE Studio (UES) 29, 52
UK 16, 136
undermine readers' trust 34
underwriting model 12
Unfair Commercial Practices Directive (UCPD) 6, 46, 68
United States (US) 6, 12, 127, 136, 138; digital policies 139
US Federal Trade Commission 46, 56
Usher, Nikki 69

Van Dalen, Arjen 49
Van Reijmersdal, E. A. 15

visual boundaries 14, 66–71, 81–3; journalism and advertising 70–1, 81–3
visual codes of journalism 80–2
visual objects 14, 65, 69–71, 80–3; coinciding or disclosing nature *73*; commercial nature of native ads 74–6; homepage level *75*
Vocento (Content Factory) 29
voice intelligence industry 136, 141
Vos, Tim P. 12–13, 37

Wall Street Journal, The (newspaper) 12–13, 90, 139
Wang, Dan 13–14
Wang, Y. 26
WAN-IFRA global study 3
Washington Post, The (newspaper) 90, 139
WeChat Moments 116, 120–1
Wojdynski, B. W. 5, 14, 67, 81

Yedioth Ahronoth 94, 95–6, 98, 100, 104n12
YNET **72**, 93, 100

Zamith, Fernando 14
Zhao, Y. 119